TOBACCO

Recent Titles in
Health and Medical Issues Today

Obesity
Evelyn B. Kelly

Stem Cells
Evelyn B. Kelly

Organ Transplant
David Petechuk

Alternative Medicine
Christine A. Larson

Gene Therapy
Evelyn B. Kelly

Sports Medicine
Jennifer L. Minigh

Nutrition
Sharon Zoumbaris

HIV/AIDS
Kathy S. Stolley and John E. Glass

TOBACCO

Arlene Hirschfelder

Health and Medical Issues Today

 GREENWOOD

AN IMPRINT OF ABC-CLIO, LLC
Santa Barbara, California • Denver, Colorado • Oxford, England

Library of Congress Cataloging-in-Publication Data
Hirschfelder, Arlene B.
 Tobacco / Arlene Hirschfelder.
      p. ; cm. — (Health and medical issues today)
   Includes bibliographical references and index.
   ISBN 978-0-313-35808-1 (hard copy : alk. paper)
ISBN 978-0-313-35809-8 (ebook)   1. Tobacco use.   I. Title.   II. Series: Health and medical issues today.
   [DNLM: 1. Tobacco—adverse effects—United States.   2. Health Policy—United States.   3. Smoking—adverse effects—United States.   4. Tobacco Industry—United States.   5. Tobacco Use Disorder—United States.   WM 290 H669t 2010]
   HV5733.H567   2010
   362.29'65610973—dc22   2010007135

ISBN: 978-0-313-35808-1
EISBN: 978-0-313-35809-8

14 13 12 11 10   1 2 3 4 5

This book is also available on the World Wide Web as an eBook.
Visit www.abc-clio.com for details.

Greenwood
An Imprint of ABC-CLIO, LLC

ABC-CLIO, LLC
130 Cremona Drive, P.O. Box 1911
Santa Barbara, California 93116-1911

This book is printed on acid-free paper ∞

Manufactured in the United States of America

Acknowledgments
Thanks to Rachel Ferat whose research enhanced the "Public Health and Tobacco" chapter.

Thanks to Karen D. Taylor whose indexing know-how will help readers access information in this book.

Contents

Series Foreword   vii

Part I: Overview

1   Demography of Tobacco Users   3

2   Tobacco Use, Health Risks, and Disease   19

3   Public Health and Tobacco   33

4   U.S. Surgeons General, Tobacco, and Public Health   51

5   Tobacco Advertising and Health   69

Part II: Controversies and Issues

6   Tobacco Excise Taxation and Health Policy   87

7   Filtered ("Low-Tar/Nicotine") Cigarettes,
     Advertising, and Health Risks   105

8   The Food and Drug Administration,
     Tobacco Regulation, and Health   117

9   Preventing/Reducing Tobacco Use by
     Children and Teens   131

10   Environmental Tobacco Smoke and Health Risks   145

Part III: References and Resources

A   Timeline of Tobacco Use and Health   161

B   Annotated Primary Source Documents   177

Notes   225
Further Reading   249
Index   257

SERIES FOREWORD

Every day, the public is bombarded with information on developments in medicine and health care. Whether it is on the latest techniques in treatments or research, or on concerns over public health threats, this information directly impacts the lives of people more than almost any other issue. Although there are many sources for understanding these topics—from Web sites and blogs to newspapers and magazines—students and ordinary citizens often need one resource that makes sense of the complex health and medical issues affecting their daily lives.

The *Health and Medical Issues Today* series provides just such a one-stop resource for obtaining a solid overview of the most controversial areas of health care today. Each volume addresses one topic and provides a balanced summary of what is known. These volumes provide an excellent first step for students and lay people interested in understanding how health care works in our society today.

Each volume is broken into several sections to provide readers and researchers with easy access to the information they need:

- Part I provides overview chapters on background information—including chapters on such areas as the historical, scientific, medical, social, and legal issues involved—that a citizen needs to intelligently understand the topic.
- Part II provides capsule examinations of the most heated contemporary issues and debates, and analyzes in a balanced manner the viewpoints held by various advocates in the debates.

- Part III provides a selection of reference material, such as annotated primary source documents, a timeline of important events, and a directory of organizations that serve as the best next step in learning about the topic at hand.

The *Health and Medical Issues Today* series strives to provide readers with all the information needed to begin making sense of some of the most important debates going on in the world today. The series includes volumes on such topics as stem-cell research, obesity, gene therapy, alternative medicine, organ transplantation, mental health, and more.

PART I

Overview

CHAPTER 1

Demography of Tobacco Users

For the past 50 years, statistics about tobacco usage by multiple demographic populations have been piling up. Federal and state public health officials, voluntary health agencies, statisticians, university health researchers, and others study tobacco use by age (adult and young people 18 and under), gender, ethnicity (Hispanic and non-Hispanic), and racial minority groups. They also study special populations, including educational and socioeconomic groups, regions of the country and individual states, pregnant women, and military personnel. Data have been collected by in-person or telephone interviews and by questionnaires mailed to people who could not be reached by phone. Sample sizes, types of surveys, interviewing procedures by trained collectors, low or high response rates, ages, and the types of sponsoring agencies are some of the variables that impact data analysis.

Once data on the prevalence of tobacco use have been collected, the figures communicate to policy makers and the public the nature, scope, and trends of tobacco use by different populations. Some prevalence data also show the progress in the increase or reduction of tobacco products over the past 45 years.

ADULT POPULATION

Since 1964, the year the U.S. surgeon general issued a landmark report about tobacco usage, a number of national and state-based agencies have conducted detailed surveys of representative samples of the U.S. adult population regarding the use of tobacco. Both telephone and in-person

---

TERMS RELATED TO RACE AND ETHNICITY
USED BY THE CENTERS FOR DISEASE CONTROL

African Americans. Individuals who trace their ancestry of origin to sub-Saharan Africa.

American Indian and Alaska Native. Persons who have origins in any of the original peoples of North America and who maintain that cultural identification through self-identification, tribal affiliation, or community recognition.

Asian American and Pacific Islander. Individuals who trace their background to the Far East, Southeast Asia, the Indian subcontinent, or the Pacific Islands.

Hispanic. Persons who trace their background to one of the Spanish-speaking countries in the Americas or to other Spanish cultures or origins.

White. Persons who have origins in any of the original peoples of Europe, North Africa, or the Middle East. The term may also correspond to non-Hispanic whites.

Source: U.S. Department of Health and Human Services. *Tobacco Use among U.S. Racial/Ethnic Minority Groups—African Americans, American Indians, Alaska Natives, Asian Americans and Pacific Islanders, and Hispanics: A Report of the Surgeon General*. Atlanta, Ga.: U.S. Department of Health and Human Services, Centers for Disease Control and Prevention, National Center for Chronic Disease Prevention and Health Promotion, Office on Smoking and Health, 1998.

---

interviews have showed that since 1965 the prevalence of cigarette smoking, the most common use of tobacco, has dropped steadily among American adults. Depending on the survey, *adult* has been defined as either 18 or 20 years of age and older. According to the National Health Interview Survey (NHIS), which has a large sample size and high response rate, approximately 40.4 percent of the population 20 years and older smoked cigarettes in 1965.[1] The overall smoking prevalence declined to 29.1 percent in 1987. Twenty years later, in November 2007, the Office on Smoking and Health of the Centers for Disease Control and Prevention (CDC) estimated that approximately 20.8 percent of U.S. adults 18 years and older smoked cigarettes. Although cigarette smoking, tobacco chewing, and snuff use have declined for all groups studied over the past 40 years, the declines during the past 10 years have been smaller than in previous decades.[2]

TOBACCO PRODUCTS

Tobacco products include cigarettes, smokeless tobacco produced in two general forms (chewing tobacco or snuff), cigars, and pipe tobacco.

There are three types of chewing tobacco: looseleaf, plug, and twist. Snuff has a much finer consistency than chewing tobacco and is held in place in the mouth without chewing.

Although smokeless tobacco is not subject to combustion and is usually used orally in the United States, products differ according to the tobaccos planted, parts of the plant that are used, the method of curing, moisture content, and additives. Looseleaf chewing tobacco is made from air-cured, cigar-type leaves from tobacco grown in Pennsylvania and Wisconsin. Dry snuff is made primarily from fire-cured dark tobacco grown in Kentucky and Tennessee.

TOBACCO USE BY MALES

Since Americans began using tobacco in a recreational context, it has been primarily a male phenomenon. In 1965 when the National Center for Health Statistics began collecting and analyzing data about tobacco use, it was estimated that 50.2 percent of male adults smoked cigarettes. The rate declined to 31.7 percent in 1987. Ten years later, in November of 2007, male smoking prevalence declined to 23.9 percent.[3]

In the 1970s smokeless tobacco, largely snuff and chewing tobacco, began to slowly shift from a product primarily used by older men to one used predominantly by young men and boys. Between 1970 (when telephone interviews were used to gather data about tobacco use) and 1986 (when household interviews were used), snuff use increased 15-fold, and chewing tobacco use more than 4-fold among males 17 to 19 years old. The prevalence of smokeless tobacco use among men 21 years and older showed a steady decline from 1964 to 1986. Smaller increases were observed for older men (age 50 and above).[4] The CDC's Youth Risk Behavioral Surveillance System for 2005 reported that 13.6 percent of U.S. high school boys used chewing tobacco and snuff, compared to 2.2 percent for high school females.[5] In some states, smokeless tobacco use among high school boys has been particularly high, especially in Kentucky (26.7%), Montana (20.3%), Oklahoma (24.8%), Tennessee (22.8%), West Virginia (27.0%), and Wyoming (21.3%).[6]

Cigar and/or pipe smoking occurs mainly among men. From 1964 to 1986, both cigar and pipe smoking declined among men. In 2007 the prevalence of cigar smoking declined from 29.7 percent to 6.2 percent; pipe smoking declined from 18.7 to 3.8 percent.[7] In 1986, the highest proportion of users were between the ages of 45 and 64 years.

Cigar smokers in the past have been mainly males between the ages of 35 and 64, with higher education and income, but recent studies suggest new trends. Most new cigar users today are teenagers and young adult males (ages 18 to 24) who smoke once in a while (less than daily).[8]

TOBACCO USE BY WOMEN

Cigarette smoking was rare among women in the early 1900s because of social conventions and legal restrictions. According to historian Robert N. Proctor, professor, History of Science at Stanford University, 5 percent of American women smoked in 1923, 12 percent in 1932, and 33 percent in 1965.[9] Female smoking prevalence remained stable at 31 to 32 percent from 1965 to 1977. Subsequently, prevalence began to decline slowly. In 1987 the surgeon general reported that 26.8 percent of American women smoked. Twenty years later, in November of 2007, the NHIS estimated that adult female smoking prevalence was 18.0 percent.[10] In the United States, men started cigarette smoking before women, and the prevalence of male smoking has always been higher than females. However, in 1964 the surgeon general's report noted that "the proportion of women smokers has increased faster than that of men in recent years."[11] The once-wide gender gap in smoking prevalence narrowed between 1965 and 1987. Since then, the decline has been comparable among women and men.

Although female use of smokeless tobacco is generally low, it prevails among women in certain geographic areas of the United States as well as within some cultures and populations. Some elderly women in the rural Southeast and some Native American females (for example: Eastern Band Cherokee women in western North Carolina, Lumbee women in eastern North Carolina, and Yupik women in southwestern Alaska) show a high rate of using smokeless tobacco.[12]

TOBACCO USE BY PREGNANT WOMEN

Smoking prevalence during pregnancy differs by race, ethnicity, age, and socioeconomic status. According to research findings from the Substance Abuse and Mental Health Services Administration's 2002–2005 National Surveys on Drug Use and Health (NSDUH), white women who were pregnant were more likely to have smoked cigarettes during each trimester than pregnant women who were black or Hispanic.[13] American Indian/Alaska

Native women had the highest rate of smoking during pregnancy (17.8%) compared to non-Hispanic white (13.9%) and non-Hispanic black women (8.5%). The smoking rate for Hispanic and Asian/Pacific Islander women who were pregnant was generally substantially lower (2.9% and 2.2%, respectively).[14] The NSDUH surveys also showed that younger pregnant women were more likely than their oldest counterparts to smoke cigarettes during their pregnancy: 24.3 percent of pregnant women aged 15 to 17 and 27.1 percent of pregnant women aged 18 to 25 compared with 10.6 percent of pregnant women aged 26 to 44 smoked cigarettes during their pregnancy in the past month of the survey.

The NSDUH surveys also showed that pregnant women with annual family incomes of less than $20,000 were more likely to smoke than those with higher family incomes. Among pregnant women 18 to 44 years old, those who had a college education were less likely to have smoked cigarettes during each trimester than pregnant women with less education.[15]

TOBACCO USE BY RACE AND ETHNICITY

In 1998 the surgeon general's report about tobacco use among U.S. racial/ethnic groups concluded that "no single factor determines patterns of tobacco use among racial/ethnic minority groups; these patterns are the result of complex interactions of multiple factors, such as socioeconomic status, cultural characteristics, acculturation, stress, biological elements, targeted advertising, price of tobacco products, and varying capacities of communities to mount effective tobacco control initiatives."[16] See Table 1.1 for an outline of tobacco use among racial/ethnic groups in the late 1980s and early 1990s. In 1998 tobacco use varied within and among racial/ethnic groups. Among adults, American Indians and Alaska Natives had the highest prevalence of tobacco use. African American and Southeast Asian men also had a high prevalence of smoking. Asian American and Hispanic women had the lowest use.[17] In 2006 broad disparities in tobacco use and cigarette smoking among racial groups still existed. The prevalence of cigarette smoking was highest among American Indians/Alaska Natives (32.4%), followed by African Americans (23.0%), whites (21.9%), Hispanics (15.2%), and Asians (excluding Native Hawaiians and other Pacific Islanders, 10.4%).[18]

TOBACCO USE BY AGE

According to the NSDUH, in 2007 an estimated 70.9 million Americans 12 years and older were current (past month) users of a tobacco product,

Table 1.1 Percentage of adults* who are current, former, and never smokers†, and percentage distribution of adult current smokers by number of cigarettes smoked per day, by race, ethnicity, and sex, from the National Health Interview Surveys, 1987, 1988, 1990, 1991 (combined)—United States.

| | Non-Hispanic | | | | | Hispanic | | | | | Total§ |
	White	Black	Asian/ Pacific Islander	American Indian/ Alaska Native	All	Mexican American	Puerto Rican American	Cuban American	Other	All	
Sex											
Male											
Smoking status											
Current	29.1	35.9	23.6	38.0	29.7	29.0	28.3	26.3	28.6	28.6	29.6
Former	32.1	19.6	19.6	26.0	30.3	22.1	19.4	24.1	20.8	21.6	29.6
Never	38.9	44.6	56.8	36.1	40.0	48.9	52.4	49.6	50.6	49.8	40.7
Cigarettes smoked per day¶											
<15	21.7	54.1	56.1	27.5	26.9	65.9	52.1	38.5	52.4	58.8	29.1
15–24	42.9	36.3	37.8	49.7	42.0	27.2	31.7	39.9	35.7	30.9	41.2
>25	35.4	9.6	6.1	22.8	31.2	6.9	16.2	21.6	11.9	10.3	29.7
Female											
Smoking status											
Current	25.7	25.4	7.8	36.2	25.3	15.5	22.7	16.4	17.2	17.0	24.6
Former	20.4	12.0	6.9	17.9	19.1	11.7	14.0	12.5	16.3	13.4	18.6
Never	53.9	62.6	85.3	46.0	55.7	72.7	63.3	71.1	66.5	69.5	56.8

Cigarettes smoked per day¶										
<15	32.1	65.8	64.6	52.3	36.6	72.8	52.3	49.2	65.9	65.2	38.1
15–24	46.9	27.9	27.6	30.9	44.3	23.2	41.1	40.4	26.6	28.8	43.5
>25	21.1	6.3	7.9	16.8	19.1	4.0	6.6	10.5	7.5	6.0	18.4
Total										
Smoking status										
Current	27.3	30.1	16.0	37.1	27.4	22.2	25.0	20.7	22.4	22.5	27.0
Former	26.0	15.4	13.4	21.9	24.4	16.8	16.3	17.5	18.4	17.2	23.8
Never	46.7	54.6	70.6	41.1	48.2	61.0	58.7	61.9	59.3	60.3	49.2
Cigarettes smoked per day¶										
<15	26.8	59.6	58.1	39.7	31.6	68.4	52.2	43.3	57.9	61.4	33.4
15–24	44.8	32.4	35.3	40.4	43.1	25.7	36.7	40.1	32.0	30.0	42.3
>25	28.3	8.0	6.5	19.9	25.3	5.9	11.1	16.6	10.1	8.6	24.3

*Persons ≥ 18 years of age.

†Current smokers reported smoking ≥ 100 and currently smoked. Former smokers reported smoking ≥ 100 cigarettes and did not currently smoke. Never smokers reported that they had smoked < 100 cigarettes.

§Includes other, unknown, multiple race, and unknown Hispanic origin.

¶Among current smokers.

Source: Centers for Disease Control and Prevention, "CDC Surveillance Summaries," November 18, 1994. *MMWR* 43, no. 55-3 (1991): 21.

which included cigarettes, chewing tobacco, snuff, cigars, and pipe tobacco. Young adults 18 to 25 had the highest rate of current use of any tobacco product (41.8%) compared with youths aged 12 to 17 and adults aged 26 or older. Young adult rates were 36.2 percent for cigarettes, 11.8 percent for cigars, 5.3 percent for smokeless tobacco, and 1.2 percent for pipe tobacco.[19] In 2007 the prevalence of current use of a tobacco product among youngsters 12 years or older was 15.4 percent for Asians, 22.7 percent for Hispanics, 26.8 percent for African Americans, 30.7 percent for whites, and 41.8 percent for American Indians or Alaska Natives. Current cigarette smoking among youths 12 to 17 and young adults 18 to 25 was more prevalent among whites than African Americans (12.2% versus 6.1% for youths and 40.8% versus 26.2% for young adults). African American and white adults 26 and older used cigarettes at about the same rate. The rates for Hispanic tobacco use were 6.7 percent among youths, 29.5 percent among young adults, and 21.0 percent among those 26 and older.[20]

The CDC examined changes in cigarette use among high school students in the United States from 1991 to 2007 by analyzing data from the national Youth Risk Behavior Survey. It reported that "the prevalence of lifetime cigarette use [i.e., ever tried cigarette smoking, even one or two puffs] was stable during 1991–1999 and then declined from 70.4 percent in 1999 to 50.3 percent in 2007. The prevalence of current cigarette use [i.e., smoked cigarettes on at least one day during the 30 days before the survey] increased from 27.5 percent in 1991 to 36.4 percent in 1997, declined to 21.9 percent in 2003, and remained stable from 2003 to 2007." Current frequent use [i.e., smoked cigarettes on 20 or more days during the 30 days before the survey] "increased from 12.7 percent in 1991 to 16.8 percent in 1999 and then declined to 8.1 percent in 2007."[21]

The Monitoring the Future (MTF) survey also showed declines in cigarette use among high school students since the early 1990s (see Table 1.2). In 2008, MTF reported the lowest levels of smoking by 8th, 10th, and 12th graders since 1991. Across the three grades combined, there was a significant decline in monthly smoking prevalence from 13.4 percent in 2007 to 12.6 percent in 2008. The greatest decline was among males and students who said they were college bound. All three grade levels showed a reduction in the use of smokeless tobacco since spit tobacco peaked in the mid-1990s. One in every 15 high school seniors was a current user of smokeless tobacco in 2008. Among 12th-grade boys, who account for almost all smokeless tobacco use, nearly 1 in 8 was a current user of smokeless tobacco.[22]

Smokeless tobacco use may be declining, but according to surveys from the CDC, the level of cigar use among teens in 2006–2007 was higher

Table 1.2 Prevalence of daily cigarette smoking* among high school seniors, by sex and race, from the Monitoring the Future Project—United States, 1976–1993.

Year	Total	Sex		Race	
		Male	**Female**	**White**	**Black**
1976	**28.8**	28.0	28.8	28.8	26.8
1977	**28.9**	27.2	30.1	29.0	23.7
1978	**27.5**	25.9	28.3	27.8	22.2
1979	**25.4**	22.3	27.9	25.8	19.3
1980	**21.4**	18.5	23.5	21.8	15.7
1981	**20.3**	18.1	21.7	20.9	13.6
1982	**21.0**	18.2	23.2	22.4	12.4
1983	**21.1**	19.2	22.1	21.9	12.6
1984	**18.7**	16.0	20.5	20.1	9.0
1985	**19.5**	17.8	20.6	20.7	10.8
1986	**18.7**	16.9	19.8	20.4	7.8
1987	**18.7**	16.4	20.6	20.6	8.1
1988	**18.1**	17.4	18.1	20.5	6.7
1989	**18.9**	17.9	19.4	21.7	6.0
1990	**19.1**	18.7	19.3	21.8	5.4
1991	**18.4**	18.8	17.9	21.1	4.9
1992	**17.2**	17.2	16.7	19.9	3.7
1993	**19.0**	19.4	18.2	22.9	4.4
Percentage point difference					
1976–1993	**−9.8**	−8.6	−10.6	−5.9	−22.4
1976–1984	**−10.1**	−12.0	−8.3	−8.7	−17.8
1984–1993	**+0.3**	+3.4	−2.3	+2.8	−4.6
Percentage change					
1976–1993	**−34.0**	−30.7	−36.8	−20.5	−83.6
1976–1984	**−35.1**	−42.9	−28.8	−30.2	−66.4
1984–1993	**+1.6**	+21.2	−11.2	+13.9	−51.1

* Daily cigarette smokers were persons who reported smoking >1 cigarettes per day during the 30 days before the survey.

Note: For any year, 95% confidence intervals do not exceed ±1.3% for the total population, ±1.6% for males, ±1.6% for females, ±1.4% for whites, and ±3.5% for blacks.

Source: Centers for Disease Control and Prevention, "CDC Surveillance Summaries," November 18, 1994. *MMWR* 43, no. 55-3 (1991): 34.

than that of spit tobacco use. In 2006, about 4 percent of teens in middle school (grades 6 to 8) had smoked a cigar in the past month. In a 2007 CDC survey of high school students, 8 percent of girls and 19 percent of boys polled had smoked a cigar within the previous month. Among the male students, the number of cigar smokers was twice as high among high school seniors as among freshmen—26 percent and 13 percent, respectively. Cigars continue to be the second most common form of tobacco used by teens in the United States overall, next to cigarettes. However, in a few states, cigars are now more commonly smoked by high school boys than are cigarettes. Much of this surge in cigar use is attributable to "little cigars," which resemble cigarettes.[23]

TOBACCO USE BY EDUCATION/COLLEGE STUDENTS

Education affects smoking rates. The more formal an education a male or female receives, the less likely he or she will smoke cigarettes. Trends in smoking among more- and less-educated groups have differed markedly since 1966, according to the 1989 surgeon general's report. College graduates decreased their smoking level from 37.7 percent in 1966 to 16.3 percent in 1987. High school graduates who did not attend college reduced their smoking from 41.1 percent in 1966 to 33.1 percent in 1987. Respondents without a high school diploma did not change appreciably from 1966 (36.5%) to 1987 (35.7%).[24]

Twenty years later, in 2007, the CDC's *Morbidity and Mortality Weekly Report (MMWR)* reported that smoking cigarettes was lowest among adults aged 25 years and older who had an undergraduate (11.4%) or graduate degree (6.2%). Smoking prevalence was higher among adults who had earned a general education development (GED) diploma (44.0%) and for people with 9 to 11 years of education (33.3%).[25] In 2007 the National Survey on Drug Use and Health showed that 3.5 percent of persons aged 18 and older who had not finished high school had used smokeless tobacco. The prevalence among college graduates was 2.1 percent.[26]

TOBACCO USE BY SOCIOECONOMIC STATUS/OCCUPATION

The first surgeon general's report in 1964 looked at socioeconomic status of people who smoked cigarettes, determining that smoking was more prevalent among "lower or working classes" but less prevalent among extremely poor (unemployed groups).[27] Periodic NHIS studies on smoking prevalence by occupation between 1970 and 1985 showed that there was a consistent pattern of higher smoking rates among blue-collar and service workers than among white-collar workers. In 1985 data showed that unemployed persons were more likely than employed persons to be current smokers.[28] In 2007 the NSDUH revealed a similar pattern: that current smoking was more common among unemployed adults aged 18 or older than among adults who were working full time or part time.[29] Also in 2007 the *MMWR* reported that smoking among adults whose incomes were below the federal poverty line was 28.8 percent compared to 20.3 percent for people whose incomes were at or above the poverty level.[30]

TOBACCO USE BY GEOGRAPHIC AREA (STATES AND REGIONS)

From 1982 to1984, the CDC's Behavioral Risk Factor Surveillance System (BRFSS) provided state-specific smoking prevalence estimates for adults 18 and older in about half of the United States. After 1984, the number of states participating in the system increased steadily. In 1987 the BRFSS showed that smoking prevalence ranged from 15 percent in Utah to 32 percent in Kentucky. Twenty years later, the BRFSS reported that Kentucky still led the 50 states with an estimated 28.6 percent of its adults between the ages of 18 and 35 years who currently smoked cigarettes every day or some days. Kentucky was followed by West Virginia (25.7%) and Mississippi and Oklahoma (both 25.1%). Utah still led the nation with a low prevalence rate of adults smoking cigarettes, 9.8 percent, but the U.S. Virgin Islands had the lowest rate, 9.1 percent.[31] In 1985 the Current Population Survey provided estimates of the prevalence of cigarette smoking according to regions of the country and states. Smoking was lowest in the Pacific region (26.3%) and Mountain (27.2%) census divisions, and highest in the East South central (31.8%) and South Atlantic (31.3%) divisions.[32]

Over twenty years later, the NSDUH reported that current cigarette smoking among persons 12 and older was lowest in the West (21.1%) and Northeast (22.1%), higher in the South (25.5%), and highest in the Midwest (27.2%). Smokeless tobacco use was higher in the Midwest (4.0%) and South (3.8%) than in the West (2.8%). The lowest rate was in the Northeast (1.8%). In the same report, cigarette smoking among persons 12 and older was highest in less-urbanized nonmetropolitan areas (29.5%) as opposed to 22.7 percent in large metropolitan regions. In completely rural counties, 23.6 percent of persons 12 and older were current cigarette smokers. Smokeless tobacco use among persons 12 and older was highest in completely rural nonmetropolitan counties (7.0%), and lowest in large metropolitan areas (2.0%).[33]

TOBACCO USE AMONG MILITARY PERSONNEL

There has been a historical connection between cigarettes and men in the armed forces. *Smokes* were included in K-rations and C-rations provided to troops. Cigarette advertisements on radio and in newspapers and magazines during World War II linked smoking and war. Camel cigarette ads pictured men in submarines, breaking through barbed wire, and lugging antitank guns. Chesterfield had its "Workers in the War Effort," and Raleigh offered cheap prices on gift cigarettes shipped to soldiers in the trenches.

In 1980, 1982, 1985, and 1988 the Department of Defense (DOD) surveyed cigarette smoking among military personnel in military installations around the world. Between 58 and 81 installations participated in the survey. The DOD found that "overall smoking prevalence among military personnel declined steadily from 53 percent in 1982 to 46 percent in 1985 to 42 percent in 1988." These figures, while declining, "were considerably higher than among all males or young males in the general population."[34] A 2007 study found that smoking rates in the military dropped from more than 50 percent in 1980, then increased markedly starting in the late 1990s. By 2005 about 33 percent of those in the military smoked.[35]

A 1997 study comparing veteran and nonveteran smoking found 35 percent of all veterans (male and female) were current smokers compared to 28 percent of the general population, and 77 percent had smoked during their lifetime compared to 49 percent of the general population.[36] A special report based on the 2005 NSDUH indicated that 18.8 percent of veterans smoked cigarettes daily compared to 14.3 percent of comparable nonveterans.[37] Another survey showed that cigars, pipes, and smokeless tobacco have been prevalent among male military personnel.[38]

In 2008 at the American College of Chest Physicians' Annual International Scientific Assembly Meeting, Dr. Michael A. Wilson presented the results of a preliminary study that American sailors and marines stationed in Iraq were more than twice as likely to use tobacco products as the average American. In a survey of 408 marines and sailors, Wilson found 64 percent used some form of tobacco: 52 percent smoked cigarettes, 36 percent used smokeless tobacco, and 24 percent used both. In contrast, the national average for tobacco use is 29.6 percent. Wilson found the rate of tobacco use is higher now among U.S. troops in Iraq than was found in a 2004 survey of troops returning from the war. He also said that "the U.S. seems to have a culture that fosters significantly higher use of tobacco products, particularly during combat deployments."[39]

SURVEYS

The National Health Interview Survey is "the principal source of information on the health of the civilian, noninstitutionalized population of the United States and is one of the major data collection programs of the National Center for Health Statistics (NCHS), which is part of the Centers for Disease Control and Prevention (CDC)." Since 1965, this source has had the best data for analyzing trends in tobacco usage by adults. Patients in long-term care facilities, troops on active duty, prisoners, and U.S. nationals living in foreign countries are excluded from taking the survey. (http://www.cdc.gov/nchs/nhis/about_nhis.htm)

The National Survey on Drug Use and Health (NSDUH), which provides "yearly national and state-level data" on the use of tobacco, alcohol, and illegal drugs, is sponsored by the Substance Abuse and Mental Health Services Administration, an agency of the U.S. Public Health Service and a part of the U.S. Department of Health and Human Services. It is "the primary source of information on the prevalence, patterns, and consequences of alcohol, tobacco, and illegal drug use and abuse in the general U.S. civilian non institutionalized population, age 12 and older." The NSDUH "includes a series of questions about the use of tobacco products, including cigarettes, chewing tobacco, snuff, cigars, and pipe tobacco." In-person interviewers collect confidential data through a computerized questionnaire administered in the participants' homes. (http://www.icpsr.umich.edu/cocoon/NACJD/SERIES/00064.xml; https://nsduhweb.rti.org)

The Behavioral Risk Factor Surveillance System (BRFSS), established in 1984 by the CDC, tracks "health conditions and risk behaviors" in the United States yearly. It collects data "monthly in all 50 states, the District of Columbia, Puerto Rico, the U.S. Virgin Islands, and Guam." More than 350,000 adults are interviewed each year, making the BRFSS "the world's largest ongoing telephone health survey system." The BRFSS Web site notes that "states use BRFSS data to identify emerging health problems, establish and track health objectives, and develop and evaluate public health policies and programs. Many states also use BRFSS data to support health-related legislative efforts." (http://www.cdc.gov/brfss/about.htm)

The Tobacco Use Supplement/Current Population Survey (TUS-CPS) is a "National Cancer Institute (NCI)-sponsored survey of tobacco use and policy information that has been administered as part of the Current Population Survey (CPS) since 1992." Conducted monthly for more than 50 years by the U.S. Census Bureau for the

U.S. Department of Labor, Bureau of Labor Statistics, the TUS-CPS "collects information on occupations, economic status, and demographic characteristics" and, from time to time, includes questions about the use of cigarettes, cigars, snuff, pipes, and chewing tobacco by the U.S. population. The TUS-CPS is also "a key source of national, state, and sub-state level data on smoking and tobacco use in U.S. households. It provides data on a nationally representative sample of about 240,000 civilian, non-institutionalized individuals ages 15 years and older." According to the TUS-CPS Web site, "about 70% of respondents complete the survey by telephone; the remainder complete it in person." (http://riskfactor.cancer.gov/studies/tus-cps/TUS-CPS_fact_sheet.pdf)

The Youth Risk Behavior Surveillance System (YRBSS) is a social epidemiologic surveillance system established by the CDC. It monitors tobacco use and five other "categories of priority health risk behaviors among youth." The YRBSS includes "a national school-based survey conducted by the CDC as well as state, territorial, and local school based surveys conducted by education and health agencies." The national Youth Risk Behavior Survey (YRBS) is conducted every two years since 1991 and provides data representative of high school students in public and private schools throughout the United States who complete self-administered questionnaires. (http://www.cdc.gov/mmwr/preview/mmwrhtml/rr5312a1.htm; http://www.answers.com/topic/youth-risk-behavior-surveillance-system)

According to the Monitoring the Future (MTF) Web site, its survey, launched in 1975 by the University of Michigan's Institute for Social Research, studies "the behaviors, attitudes, and values of American secondary school students, college students, and young adults. Each year, a total of approximately 50,000 8th, 10th, and 12th grade students" who attend "about 420 public and private secondary schools" are surveyed. Students complete self-administered, machine-readable questionnaires in their classrooms. "In addition, annual follow-up questionnaires are mailed to a sample of each graduating class for a number of years after their initial participation." The survey is supported by research grants from the National Institute on Drug Abuse. According to the MTF Web site, "the results of the study are useful to policymakers at all levels of government, for example, to monitor progress toward national health goals. Study results are also used to monitor trends in substance use and abuse among adolescents and young adults and are used routinely in the White House Strategy on Drug Abuse." (http://www.monitoringthefuture.org/purpose.html#Design)

Morbidity and Mortality Weekly Report

Morbidity and Mortality Weekly Report (*MMWR*) is a weekly epidemiological digest for the United States published by the CDC. According to the MMWR home page: "The *MMWR* weekly contains data on specific diseases as reported by state and territorial health departments and reports on infectious and chronic diseases, environmental hazards, natural or human-generated disasters, occupational diseases and injuries, and intentional and unintentional injuries. Also included are reports on topics of international interest and notices of events of interest to the public health community." (http://www.cdc.gov/mmwr/mmwr_wk.html)

CHAPTER 2

Tobacco Use, Health Risks, and Disease

The impact of tobacco use on health has been the subject of discussion for hundreds of years. So much has been written that "medical literature on tobacco alone [fills] shelves in medical libraries. ... Public health officials had explored the relationship between tobacco and disease, archiving large caches of additional documents for future researchers."[1] Centuries ago, many people, including some physicians, considered tobacco to have medicinal properties. In 1560 Jean Nicot de Villemain, France's ambassador to Portugal, wrote of tobacco's medicinal properties, describing it as a panacea. Besides sending rustica plants to the French court, Nicot sent snuff to Catherine de Medici, the Queen Mother of France, to treat her son Francis II's migraine headaches. In Germany in 1571, Dr. Michael Bernhard Valentini's *Polychresta Exotica* (Exotic Remedies) described numerous different types of clysters, or water enemas, to treat a variety of ailments. The tobacco smoke clyster was said to be good for treating colic, nephritis, hysteria, hernia, and dysentery. The same year in Spain, Nicholas Monardes, physician and botanist, wrote *De Hierba Panacea,* in which he listed 36 maladies that tobacco cured.

At the same time tobacco was being lauded, a growing number of people suspected that tobacco use could harm the body. Reports about the hazards of tobacco began accumulating in scientific and medical literature in the late 16th century, shortly after the plant was introduced to Europeans. In 1586 in Germany, "De plantis epitome utilissima" cautioned about the use of tobacco, calling it a "violent herb." In 1602 in England, publication of *Worke of Chimney Sweepers* (also called *Chimny-Sweepers or A Warning for Tabacconists* [sic]), by a doctor identified as Philaretes, stated that illness of chimney sweepers was caused by soot and that tobacco might have similar effects: "Tobacco works by evaporating man's 'unctuous and radical moistures'—as was demonstrated in the fact that it was employed to cure gonorrhea by drying up the discharge. But this process, if too long continued, could only end by drying up 'spermatical humidity,' too, rendering him incapable of propagation."[2] Philaretes discussed many of the health risks that were later proved to be true.[3] In 1603 English physicians, upset that tobacco was being used by people without a physician's prescription, complained to King James I. In 1604 "A Counterblaste to Tobacco" was published anonymously by King James in which he wrote the oft quoted: "Smoking is a custom loathsome to the eye, hateful to the nose, harmful to the brain, dangerous to the lungs, and in the black, stinking fume thereof nearest resembling the horrible Stygian smoke of the pit that is bottomless."[4] He also noted that autopsies found smokers' "inward parts" were "infected with an oily kind of soot." In 1653 Dr. Jacobus Tappius, professor of medicine at the University of Helmstedt, wrote that "blood and brain become heated and dried up—the whole head is turned into a noxious furnace—it is fatal to all genius [and acts] to dull the finest intellect."[5] The book included "anatomical illustrations showing the sad effects of tobacco on the smoker's brain."

In the United States, Benjamin Rush, the nation's most prominent American physician, issued an early warning in *Essays, Moral, Political, and Philosophical* published in 1798. Long before the arrival of manufactured cigarettes in the late 1800s, Rush cautioned that tobacco in any form, smoking, chewing, or snuff, caused certain diseases of the mouth, throat, stomach, and nervous system. He even warned against casual use, which he said could lead to impaired appetite, indigestion, tremors, and tooth loss. Besides asserting that tobacco was generally detrimental to health, he was also concerned that it created an "unnatural thirst" that led to drunkenness and moral decay, a belief widely held by antitobacco advocates 100 years later. Fifty years later, and 115 years before the famous 1964 surgeon general's report was published, Dr. Joel Shew attributed 87 different diseases or ill effects directly to tobacco, including tremors and indigestion, both identified by Rush, heart palpitations, breathing difficulty, and decayed teeth. Regarding gums, tongue, and lips, he wrote:

> For more than twenty years back, I have been in the habit of inquiring of patients, who came to me with cancers of these parts (the gums, tongue, and lips), whether they used tobacco, and if so, whether by chewing or smoking. If they have answered in the negative as to the first question, I can truly say, that, to the best of my belief, such cases of exemption are exceptions to a

general rule. When, as is usually the case, one side of the tongue is affected with ulcerated cancer, the tobacco has been habitually retained in contact with this part. The irritation of a cigar, or even from a tobacco pipe, frequently precedes cancers of the lip ... I believe cancers, severe ulcers, and tumors, in and about the mouth, will be found much more common among men than women. Since the former use tobacco much more generally than the latter, may not this be a cause.[6]

During the first quarter of the 20th century, as the custom of smoking spread in America and lung cancer became more common in men, physicians and public health educators broadcast the dangers of smoking. In 1909 Charles E. Slocum, M.D., Ph.D., summed up this point in his book *About Tobacco and Its Deleterious Effects:* "Many capable and conscientious physicians of all countries for generations, and in far increasing number and ability, have been careful observers of [tobacco's] evil effects in the systems of their patients, and friends."[7] In 1912 Dr. Isaac Adler published research in a monogram, "Primary Malignant Growths of the Lung a Bronchi," which, for the first time, argued strongly that smoking may cause lung cancer. Tobacco company executives raced to Adler's house and swore on a stack of Bibles that smoking did no such thing.

Dr. John Harvey Kellogg, medical director of the Battle Creek, Michigan Sanitarium, was among a handful of doctors who actively campaigned against cigarettes. In a 1917 article condemning the distribution of cigarettes to soldiers in World War I, he wrote that "more American soldiers will be damaged by the cigarette than by German bullets."[8] He felt they were dangerous because their smoke was inhaled and could damage internal organs, especially those of women. He believed smoking caused certain cancers and heart disease and predicted that science would eventually prove it. In 1922 Kellogg published *Tobaccoism, or, How Tobacco Kills,* in which he tried to prove that "there is perhaps no other drug which injures the body in so many ways and so universally as does tobacco."[9] Writing almost at the same time as Kellogg, Dr. Daniel H. Kress, another outspoken anticigarette physician, stated in 1921 that "the evils resulting from the almost universal use of cigarettes in America will, in time, be as apparent as were the evils in China from the smoking of opium."[10]

During the first quarter of the 20th century, physicians fused moral considerations about tobacco use with medical research on smoking, so much so that "moral considerations were practically indistinguishable from concerns about the health effects of cigarette smoking. Physicians tied cigarette use to hereditary degeneracy, decline of mental and physical development, and lives of decay. This conflation of the medical and moral

Tobacco is a Heart Poison

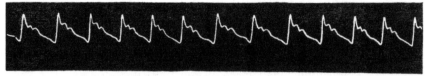

NORMAL PULSE—EACH VERTICAL LINE REPRESENTS A HEART BEAT

IRREGULAR PULSE OF TOBACCO HEART

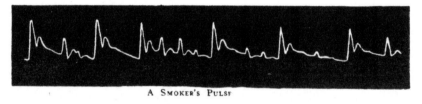

A SMOKER'S PULSE

Figure 2.1 John Harvey Kellogg (1852–1943), medical director of the Battle Creek, Michigan Sanitarium, regarded tobacco as a health threat. In his book, pamphlets, and a lantern slide show, one of his themes was that tobacco was a principal cause of heart disease. In 1922 he wrote that "the effect of tobacco upon the heart has been most carefully studied by many physiologists. All authorities agree that tobacco is a heart poison. A very small dose increases the work of the heart by contracting the arteries and raising the blood pressure."

Source: John Harvey Kellogg, *Tobaccoism, or, How Tobacco Kills* (Battle Creek, Mich.: The Modern Medicine Publishing Co., 1922), p. 59.

would serve as a significant obstacle (among many) to establishing the evidentiary basis of the harms of smoking."[11] During the early 20th century, physicians were divided over the health impact of cigarette smoking. But there was some consensus that smoking could harm children and adolescents. "It becomes plain that any insidious narcotic poison which exerts its chief effects upon the respiratory function and the motor nerve cells of the spinal cord and brain, can not fail to be disastrous to the young," explained one doctor in 1904.[12]

Once women took up smoking, some medical investigators pointed out the degenerative effects cigarettes had on their children. As Dr. Charles B. Towns summed it up in 1916: "No more pitiful sight on earth could possibly be imagined than the spectacle of some mother who is a cigarette smoker bringing into the world a poor, pitiful physically and mentally defective child."[13] Bertha Van Hoosen, a prominent Michigan physician argued that smoking had dire consequences for mothers-to-be: "Motherhood and to-bacco are as antagonistic as water and fire. ... Motherhood is too complex to tamper with tobacco or any other drug-forming habit."[14] Nevertheless, *Hygeia,* the American Medical Association's magazine for the general public, concluded in June of 1934 that "smoking by mothers is in all prob-ability, not an important factor" in infant mortality.[15]

Given the uncertainty of the data, many physicians recommended mod-eration over excessive smoking. In 1925 *American Mercury* magazine printed an editorial that opined: "A dispassionate review of the [scientific] findings compels the conclusion that the cigarette is tobacco in its mild-est form, and that tobacco, used moderately by people in normal health, does not appreciably impair either the mental efficiency or the physical condition."[16]

Through the first half of the 20th century, case studies, laboratory re-search, and animal experiments, which assessed the health risks of smok-ing, had not categorically proved that it *caused* serious diseases like cancer, heart disease, and stroke. After 1930, when physicians encountered cases of lung cancer with increased frequency, the issue of smoking received more significant attention. As early as 1932, Dr. William McNally of Rush Medical College suggested that cigarette smoking was an important factor in higher rates of lung cancer.[17]

Researchers took a more clinical approach to smoking and disease. They considered the possibility that chronic diseases could be attri-buted to genetic predispositions and environmental and behavioral exposures. According to Allan M. Brandt, "By the 1930s and 1940s, clinical anecdote carried considerable authority with physicians who carefully recorded their observations of the effects of tobacco upon their patients." Many investigations focused on the heart and circula-tion: "'Tobacco heart,' a well-known syndrome, included arrhythmias, angina, and sometimes cardiac arrest."[18] But these physicians and re-searchers did not move from clinical observations to more powerful studies that constituted *proof* in scientific and medical terms that ciga-rettes caused disease.

In 1938 Dr. Raymond Pearl, an eminent scientist and professor of biological statistics at Johns Hopkins University, did a pioneering study of the effects of smoking on life span that was published in the March 4, 1938, issue of *Science* under the title "Tobacco Smoking and Longevity." He reported to the New York Academy of Medicine that heavy smokers (who smoke more than 10 cigarettes a day) did not live as long as light smokers and that nonsmokers outlived both. He wrote: "Smoking of tobacco was statistically associated with the impairment of life duration ... This impairment is proportional to the habitual amount of tobacco usage by smoking, being great for heavy smokers and less for moderate smokers."[19] Of the 6,813 persons reported on, two-thirds of the nonsmokers had lived beyond 60, but only 46 percent of the heavy smokers reached age 60. *Time* magazine, which reported Pearl's findings, suggested that his results would frighten tobacco manufacturers to death and "make tobacco users' flesh creep."[20] Most major newspapers refused to publish the findings, and others buried the Pearl report in columns where people barely noticed it.

In 1936 Dr. Alton Ochsner, one of the foremost thoracic surgeons and medical teachers in U.S. history, made a connection between smoking and lung cancer, based on clinical observations rather than systematic studies that proved causation. He persisted in believing that cigarette smoking was the principal cause of the growing epidemic of lung cancer, a theory he publicized throughout the 1940s in the face of ridicule and attacks, even within the medical profession.

In 1939 Drs. Alton Ochsner and Michael DeBakey of New Orleans concluded that: "the increase in smoking with the universal custom of inhaling is probably a responsible factor" for an increase in cases of primary carcinoma of the lung.[21]

During the 1940s, medical investigators were aware that it could take many years, even decades, for smoking to cause disease, before "the full health implications of the mass consumption of cigarettes became statistically visible."[22]

Not all doctors agreed tobacco was hazardous. Many physicians and scientists were skeptical about the epidemiological evidence, because they felt a statistical connection between an increase in cigarette smoking and an increase in lung-cancer did not prove there was a causal connection. Dr. Evarts A. Graham, a prominent physician who had taught Ochsner, said: "Yes, there is a parallel between the sale of cigarettes and the incidence of cancer of the lung but there is also a parallel between the sale of nylon stockings and cancer of the lung." Years later, he became convinced there was a connection.[23]

Some physicians even defended smoking as an antidote to the stresses of modern life. As late as 1948, the *Journal of the American Medical Association (JAMA)* argued that "more can be said on behalf of smoking as a form of escape from tension than against it ... there does not seem to be any preponderance of evidence that would indicate the abolition of the use as a substance contrary to the public health."[24] Other physicians argued that an increasing atmospheric pollution from automobile exhausts might explain the rise in lung cancer.

The 1950s, however, ushered in bad news with reports of the studies done in the United States and England strongly incriminating cigarettes as a cause of diseases. Between 1950 and 1954, there were 14 studies informing the public that cigarette smoking was linked to lung cancer and other serious diseases. In May 1950, *JAMA* published Ernst L. Wynder and Evarts A. Graham's article about tobacco smoking as an etiological factor in bronchogenic carcinoma. Four months later, in September of 1950, the *British Medical Journal* carried Richard Doll and Austin Bradford Hill's first paper on smoking and lung cancer in which the men concluded that "smoking is an important factor in the cause of carcinoma of the lung."[25] Following the Wynder/Graham and Doll/Hill papers, studies with consistent findings added to a growing consensus about lung cancer and smoking. In 1952 Ochsner and his colleagues wrote in *JAMA* that there was a parallel between the sale of cigarettes and the incidence of bronchogenic carcinoma. Wynder, Graham, and other researchers at New York's Memorial Center for Cancer and Allied Diseases announced in the December 1953 issue of *Cancer Research* that they produced cancer in mice with tar condensed from cigarette smoke. In 1954 E. Cuyler Hammond and Daniel Horn, under the auspices of the American Cancer Society, reported conclusions of a large study that found men with a regular history of smoking cigarettes had a considerably higher death rate from lung cancer than men who never smoked or who smoked only cigars or pipes. By the mid-1950s, clinicians and researchers had collectively reached an important conclusion about the connection between smoking cigarettes and lung cancer, based on clinical observations, dozens of studies, and laboratory experiments with animals.

Nevertheless, some scientists attacked studies by Doll and Hill and others because they were committed to carefully designed experiments carried out in laboratories. They were skeptical about investigations that depended on data collected during patient interviews because they relied too heavily on the recollection of patients. They doubted the results of the production of cancer in animals, a model that could not perfectly replicate disease development in humans. Physicians who smoked heavily were also the most skeptical of research findings linking tobacco use to lung cancer.

The mainstream began to pay attention to the growing scientific literature and reports on the scientists' findings regarding the role of cigarettes as a cause of cancer, heart, other diseases, and death. *Readers Digest,* the most widely circulated publication at the time, published a series of articles titled "Cancer by the Carton," which relayed the findings of Wynder and Graham. Publicity in magazines such as *Time* and *Life* also triggered understandable public concern. Physicians and public health officials felt obliged to deal with smoking as a public health issue. In 1959, for the first time, the U.S. Public Health Service (PHS) took a position on the controversial subject of smoking and cancer. Surgeon General LeRoy Burney, one of the first federal officials to identify smoking as a cause of lung cancer, wrote in *JAMA* that the PHS believed it was justified in reporting that all the studies to date, 1959, implicated "smoking as the primary etiological factor in the increased incidence of lung cancer."[26] In response, Clarence Cook Little, scientific director of the Tobacco Industry Research Committee (TIRC), countered that "scientific evidence is accumulating that conflicts with, or fails to support, the tobacco-smoking theories of lung cancer." Other research reports about the effects of cigarette smoking elicited responses from the tobacco industry that the TIRC Scientific Advisory Board questioned "the existence of sufficient definitive evidence to establish a simple cause-and-effect explanation of the complex problem of lung cancer."[27]

Responding to pressure from voluntary health agencies that wanted the PHS to take action against smoking, in 1962 Surgeon General Luther L. Terry established a committee to assess health implications of smoking. On January 11, 1964, Surgeon General Terry released the landmark 387-page report concluding that "cigarette smoking is a health hazard of sufficient importance to warrant appropriate remedial action."[28] The committee of 11 experts that helped prepare the report said that smoking caused lung cancer in men, outweighing all other influencing factors including air pollution. Evidence pointed in the same direction for women even though data on smoking and lung cancer in females were unavailable. Women had begun smoking in substantial numbers only 20 years before. The report also stated that cigarette smoking represented a major cause of heart disease, chronic bronchitis, emphysema, and cancer of the larynx. The committee felt filter-tip cigarettes did little good in preventing disease. The only good news was that smokers could reduce health risks by quitting.

The surgeon general's report, which became a model for 29 subsequent reports on the harms of tobacco use published between 1967 and 2006, had an immediate but short-lived impact on cigarette sales. In 1963, the year before publication, 510 billion cigarettes were sold in America. In 1964, cigarette sales fell to 495 billion. A year later, cigarette sales picked up again.

After the release of the report, the Federal Trade Commission (FTC) proposed that a health warning be placed on cigarette packages and advertisements. Before the proposed rules went into effect, Congress passed the Federal Cigarette Labeling and Advertising Act of 1965. The text of the act began by declaring it was the intention of Congress to establish a federal program to inform the public of the possible health hazards of smoking. Besides requiring a package warning label "Caution: Cigarette Smoking May Be Hazardous to Your Health," the law required the Department of Health, Education, and Welfare to report annually to Congress on the health consequences of smoking. This initiated the series of surgeons general reports on tobacco and health. Congress also appropriated $2 million to collect data on smoking and health research.

Until the beginning of the 1970s, concern about tobacco was limited to how smoking harmed smokers. Little was known about the effects of secondhand smoke on nonsmokers, or innocent victims, which included nonsmoking women married to smokers and children with smoking parents. Scientists were not ready to say for certain that exposure to tobacco smoke caused serious illness in nonsmokers. Although the medical community and health groups had not yet focused on the passive smoking issue, in November of 1971, Surgeon General Jesse Steinfeld called for a national Bill of Rights for the Nonsmoker. His 1972 surgeon general's report included data on "the role of tobacco smoke as a source of air pollution for the nonsmoker."[29]

Fourteen years later, in 1986, two major reports focused on health risks associated with secondhand smoke. The National Academy of Sciences (NAS) reviewed scientific studies, finding that children of smokers were twice as likely to suffer from respiratory infections, bronchitis, and pneumonia than children whose parents did not smoke. Surgeon General C. Everett Koop's report, which confirmed the findings of the NAS, said "involuntary smoking is a cause of disease, including lung cancer in healthy nonsmokers."[30] It stressed the harmful effects of passive smoking on children. Koop's report dealt with the growth in restrictions on smoking in public places and workplaces but concluded that simple separation of smokers and nonsmokers within the same airspace reduced but did not eliminate exposure to environmental tobacco smoke. The surgeon general explained: "The right of the smoker to smoke stops at the point where his or her smoking increases the disease risk in those occupying the same environment." The NAS study estimated that environmental tobacco smoke caused between 2,500 and 8,400 lung cancer deaths per year in the United States. Koop placed the number at approximately 3,000.

During the 1980s, when Surgeon General Koop was in office, six other reports on the health hazards of smoking were released. In February 1982, the surgeon general's report dealt with cancer, and it was one of the strongest antismoking reports the PHS had written. Newspaper headlines around the country scared people with the news: "Cigarette Smoking Contributes to Bladder, Kidney, Pancreatic Cancer," "Report Finds Smoking Top Cancer-Death Cause," and "Cigarettes Blamed for 30 Percent of All Cancer Deaths." At the press conference where Koop released the report, he said for the first time what he repeated countless times afterward: "Cigarette smoking is the chief preventable cause of death in our society." He also said that 85 percent of lung cancer deaths would not have happened if the victims had never smoked. The report also called for more study of secondhand smoke, because it "may pose a carcinogenic risk to the nonsmoker." The next three years brought three more hard-hitting reports. Koop's 1983 surgeon general's report dealt with the connection between cigarette smoking and heart disease. The 1984 report connected cigarette smoking and chronic bronchitis and emphysema. In 1985 Koop's report pointed out that for American workers, cigarette smoking represents a greater cause of death and disability than their workplace environment.

In 1986 Koop also targeted smokeless tobacco, chewing (spit) tobacco, and snuff. The use of snuff, introduced in the United States in the early 1600s, and tobacco chewing, first mentioned in the early 18th century, was controversial. Some considered smokeless tobacco to have medicinal uses. Among Native American people, it alleviated toothaches, disinfected cuts, and relieved the effects of snake, spider, and insect bites. During the 19th and early 20th centuries, dental snuff was advertised to relieve toothache pain, to cure neuralgia and bleeding gums, and to prevent decay and scurvy.

The health effects of smokeless tobacco use were noted in 1761 by John Hill, a London physician and botanist. He reported five cases of polypuses, a "swelling in the nostril that was hard, black and adherent with the symptoms of an open cancer."[31] He concluded that nasal cancer would develop from the use of tobacco snuff. He published "Cautions against the Immoderate Use of Snuff," likely the first clinical study of tobacco effects. Hill warned snuff users that they were vulnerable to cancers of the nose. Thirty years later, he reported cases in which use of snuff caused nasal cancers. But it was not until many decades later, in 1858, that the renowned British medical journal, the *Lancet,* first raised fears about the health effects of smoking.

Evidence that suggested a possible association between smokeless tobacco and oral conditions in North America and Europe was not reported until 1915 when Dr. Robert Abbe described a series of oral cancer patients who were tobacco chewers, postulating tobacco use as a risk factor. In the United States, reports of oral cancer among users of snuff or chewing tobacco appeared in the early 1940s. The first epidemiologic study of smokeless tobacco was not conducted until the early 1950s.[32]

In 1979 Surgeon General Julius Richmond released his report on smoking and health, which contained a brief mention of smokeless tobacco. At the end of chapter 13, "Other Forms of Tobacco Use," the report concluded: "Tobacco chewing is associated with an increased risk of leukoplakia and oral cancer in Asian populations, but the risk for populations in the United States is not clear. An increased risk of oral leukoplakia associated with snuff use in the United States has not been demonstrated."[33]

Because smokeless tobacco products, especially snuff, had become popular again for the first time since the late 1800s and its use was rising among teens and young men, Surgeon General Koop became alarmed. Between 1970 and 1985, moist snuff use increased by 30 percent among all Americans, but eightfold in the 17- to 19-year-old groups. A large part of the rise was the result of heavy advertising by the United States Tobacco Company, maker of SKOAL and Copenhagen. Surgeon General Koop appointed an advisory committee to study the health hazards of smokeless tobacco. The 1986 report, which provided a comprehensive review of available epidemiological, experimental, and clinical data, concluded that the oral use of smokeless tobacco represented a significant health risk, that it could cause cancer and a number of noncancerous oral conditions. The report said that smokeless tobacco exposed users to nicotine, which plays a contributory or supportive role in the development of smoking-related diseases.

The culture of smokeless tobacco use in the United States has been centered on sports, particularly baseball. According to researchers, when impressionable youngsters see their heroes using smokeless tobacco on the playing field, there is a powerful incentive to try it. After the 1986 report was released, professional baseball responded with a program to help players quit and reduce their public use of smokeless tobacco. Major League Baseball worked with the National Cancer Institute to develop a guide to help major and minor league players quit smokeless tobacco. In April of 1991, Dr. Louis Sullivan, secretary of the Department of Health and Human Services, gave a keynote address to the First International Conference on

Smokeless Tobacco in Columbus, Ohio, cosponsored by the National Cancer Institute. He said that despite the fact that the baseball community responded with efforts to disassociate the sport from smokeless tobacco use, the downturn in sales of smokeless tobacco after the release of Koop's 1986 was not sustained. In 2003 more than one in three major league baseball players still used smokeless tobacco, mainly moist snuff.

According to studies on smokeless tobacco, today, major U.S. tobacco manufacturers are "putting more emphasis on smokeless products, such as snuff and snus," a moist powder tobacco product that is consumed by placing it under the lip for extended periods of time. They are eager "to gain market share and sales as the smoking rate among adults declines."[34] New products make it easier for tobacco users to consume tobacco without breaking laws or facing scornful looks. According to Matthew Myers, the executive director of the Campaign for Tobacco-Free Kids, "These new products pose serious threats to the nation's health. They are likely to appeal to children because they are flavored and packaged like candy, are easy to conceal even in a classroom."[35] Dr. Michael Thun, vice president of epidemiology and surveillance research at the American Cancer Society, "said that the debate about smokeless tobacco products has been complicated by the fact that some credible independent scientists have accepted the idea that because smokeless products are less lethal than smoking, they must therefore be useful in reducing the disease burden from smoking."[36]

Scientists, physicians, the public health community, government agencies, and health care organizations have emphasized the dire health consequences of tobacco use and dependence, the existence of effective treatments, and the importance of persuading more smokers to use such treatments. Progress has been made in tobacco control since 1964, when the first surgeon general's report was published. Thanks to formal cessation programs that are primarily behavioral and cognitive in nature, cessation clinics, commercial smoking cessation programs, self-help interventions, and nicotine replacement products, "the rate of quitting has so outstripped the rate of initiation that, today, there are more former smokers than current smokers."[37] But other strategies—publicity about health risks associated with using tobacco, high tobacco taxes, smoking restrictions in public places, and bans on tobacco advertising—have not helped reduce the difficulties of overcoming nicotine dependence.

In 2008 eight federal government agencies and nonprofit organizations collaborated on an update of recommended guidelines for clinicians, health care systems, insurers, and others dealing with tobacco use, dependence, and cessation. The updated guidelines "[reflect] the distillation of a literature base of more than 8,700 research articles," almost three times as many articles as appeared in the original 1996 guidelines on tobacco treatment. According to the 2008 update,

> tobacco dependence interventions, if delivered in a timely and effective manner, significantly reduce the smoker's risk of suffering from smoking-related disease. ... [Forty] years ago smoking was viewed as a habit rather than a chronic disease. No scientifically validated treatments were available for the treatment of tobacco use and dependence, and it had little place in health care delivery. Today, numerous effective treatments exist, and tobacco use assessment and intervention are considered to be requisite duties of clinicians and health care practitioners. Finally, every state now has a telephone quitline, increasing access to effective treatment.[38]

CHAPTER 3

Public Health and Tobacco

As early as 1836, opponents of tobacco organized to fight against its use because they thought tobacco in any form was dangerous. However, in those days, antitobacco people did not view tobacco as the main problem, but rather they believed smoking led to bad behaviors. The American Anti-Tobacco Society was formed primarily to prevent drunkenness. Its founder, Reverend George Trask, a former smoker, believed that "smoking only leads to drinking—drinking to intoxication—intoxication to bile— bile to indigestion—indigestion to consumption—consumption to death— nothing more! and therefore smoking should be stopped."[1]

By 1856 and 1857, in an ongoing debate about the dangers of smoking in *Lancet,* a prestigious medical journal, physicians argued about whether smoking cigarettes increased street crime among young boys.[2]

In the 1890s, Lucy Page Gaston, a temperance worker, became the leader of an antitobacco movement within her Women's Christian Temperance Union, which opposed smoking as well as drinking. Gaston, formerly a teacher in Illinois, had noticed that the most mischievous students in her classes were all smokers. In 1899 she founded the Chicago Anti-Cigarette League, which later became the Anti-Cigarette League, which aimed not only to prevent cigarette use by children but to completely prohibit cigarettes. By 1900 her followers, the Gastonites, had succeeded in gaining legislation outlawing the sale of cigarettes in Iowa, Tennessee, and North Dakota.[3]

During the early years of the 20th century, public health groups were more concerned with mental health and moral degeneration than physical health. Although medical reports and scientific inquiry about a relationship between tobacco use and cancer have had a long history, members of the scientific and medical communities were not immediately proactive

ANTI-TOBACCO JOURNAL.

Vol. I.   FEBRUARY AND MARCH, 1861.   No. 8.

CONTENTS.

An Appeal to a Poor Man to give up Tobacco. Six Reasons, ... 205
Dr. Twitchell's Theory of Sudden Deaths by Tobacco, ... 209
A Clergyman who Chews the Cud, . 211
Young Man, a Noble Girl wants you, 212
The Nature of Tobacco, ... 213
A Tobacco Dyspeptic, ... 217
A Street Nuisance, ... 219

Chewing Tobacco a Nuisance, . . . 220
The English are Awake, ... 221
English Facts, ... 222
A Word on Snuff-taking, ... 223
Affinities of Tobacco, ... 224
Correspondence of the Journal, . . 225
The Poet Lamb on Tobacco, ... 227
Appeal to a Conn. River Deacon, . . 228
Tobacco Statistics, ... 232

I publish this Journal quarterly, and as much *oftener as funds enable me to do it.* Subscribers can have twelve copies a year. Each copy can be divided and distributed as tracts. I ask the aid of all who think Tobacco an evil, and will do their part to stop its ravages. · The price is one dollar a year. I pay the postage. All Communications should be addressed to me, at FITCHBURG, MASS., where I reside.   GEO. TRASK.

BOSTON:
STEREOTYPED BY HOBART & ROBBINS, 66 CONGRESS STREET. — PRINTED BY WRIGHT & POTTER, 4 SPRING LANE.

Figure 3.1 Cover of the *Anti-Tobacco Journal,* edited by Reverend George Trask in Fitchburg, Massachusetts. Described as an entertaining and vigorous polemical publication, the poems, reports, articles, and quotations warned the public about the risks of tobacco. Reverend Trask contended that cancer and other tobacco-related illnesses killed 20,000 American annually.

Source: Anti-Tobacco Journal, 1, no. 8 (February / March 1861).

in public health matters. As early as 1665, the Paris School of Medicine suspected that tobacco consumption shortened lives, and in 1761 a London doctor reported 10 cases of cancer in snuff takers.[4] After an explosion of cigarette use in the early part of the 20th century, by the end of the 1920s, doctors noticed "more with curiosity than alarm" an increase in lung cancer, at the time a rare disease.[5] Between 1938 and 1948, lung cancer increased at five times the rate of other cancers.[6]

Some medical researchers began to suspect a relationship between smoking and lung cancer. But in the late 1940s, the medical profession did not think about smoking as a potential cause of major diseases. Physicians greeted the early findings of the smoking-cancer relationship with skepticism and derision, making it difficult to draw attention to scientific and public health issues regarding the relationship between smoking and lung cancer.

In 1947 Ernst Wynder, a third-year medical student at Washington University who earlier had been exposed to cancer research, and Dr. Evarts A. Graham, thoracic surgeon, who initially was unsure there was a need for a study, collaborated on a study of the relationship of smoking to lung cancer. Their paper, funded by the American Cancer Society (ACS), was published in the *Journal of the American Medical Association (JAMA)* in May of 1950, despite the fact that *JAMA*'s editors were not convinced that data on smoking and lung cancer deserved publication. The physicians concluded that "excessive and prolonged use of tobacco, especially cigarets [sic], seems to be an important factor in the induction of bronchiogenic carcinoma." The physicians were hesitant to use the word *cause* at that time, even though they found that 96.5 percent of patients with lung cancer were heavy smokers. The study called for more research, stating that "well controlled and large scale clinical studies are lacking" on the subject of whether smoking leads to cancer.[7] Wynder later wrote that it took him four more years before he used the word *cause* rather than the term *association* in spite of the strong evidence in its favor.[8]

Forty-seven years after the *JAMA* study appeared, at a time when the causative association of cigarette smoking and lung cancer had been well established, Wynder wrote: "In retrospect, the initial apathy of health professionals and their reasons for neither accepting nor promoting the evidence relating lung cancer to smoking some five decades ago make for an astounding lesson of public health history."[9] He wrote that public health policy depends on "vocal involvement of the medical and scientific leadership." Since these voices were silent in 1950, no significant public health policy against smoking could be implemented. Wynder concluded that a combination of factors led to a delay on the part of health authorities and those in the medical profession from recommending public health action against smoking: lack of appreciation of epidemiologic evidence, doubts about production of cancer in laboratory animals with tobacco tar, physicians who smoked themselves, and their concern over the economic and political power of the tobacco industry.[10]

When Dr. E. Cuyler Hammond, chief ACS statistician, reviewed the Wynder/Graham data, he "could not believe the strength of the correlation between smoking and lung cancer, and assumed that a statistical error had been committed."[11] He decided to study a large group of men over several years, because large-scale examinations were the best way to conduct epidemiological research, ensuring that statistics would be reliable. Because the study addressed causes of death, it was also important to have information about the men's behavior over time. The new study was huge, including men who did not have cancer, unlike the Wynder/Graham study, which only included patients with cancer.

Nobody had ever done a study like the one Hammond and Dr. Daniel Horn, his collaborator, envisioned. The research team was the size of an army: the ACS already had the Women's Field Army (WFA) in the field, "a legion of new volunteers whose sole purpose was to wage war on cancer." The ACS decided to use the women to achieve Hammond's research task.[12]

In 1952 the giant study began with 22,000 volunteers, located in 394 counties in 11 states, who were trained to conduct interviews and to recruit smokers and nonsmokers between the ages of 50 and 69. Each volunteer found 10 men, both nonsmokers and smokers without symptoms of disease in the desired age range, and kept up with major life changes on a regular basis over a long period of time. The study "found that the total death rate (from all causes combined) was much higher among men with a history of regular cigarette smoking than among men who had never smoked cigarettes regularly, and that the death rate increased with amount of cigarette smoking."[13] Hammond and Horn went further, stating that "there is no doubt in our minds as to the ... association found between cigarette smoking and cancer of the lung and ... cancer of other sites directly exposed to tobacco smoke products."[14] This study was also important because it demonstrated a clear link between cigarette smoking and heart disease. More of the deaths in the study (52.1% of unexpected deaths, as opposed to 13.5%) were from heart disease than lung cancer.[15] The study grew to include Oscar Auerbach, a pathologist, whose job was to dissect dead bodies to find out what killed them. Auerbach's research confirmed that biological changes were happening in the lungs of smokers.

A similar longitudinal study by British investigators also took place around the same time, although it was smaller in scope. Richard Doll, epidemiologist and physician, and Bradford Hill, lung cancer researcher, sent questionnaires to 60,000 doctors in Great Britain inquiring about their smoking habits, with follow-up periods on their health status. "The Mortality of Doctors in Relation to Their Smoking Habits," published in the *British Medical Journal in* 1954, included an analysis from over 40,000 British male physicians over 35 years of age who responded. The researchers concluded that "immoderate smokers are 24 times as likely to die of lung cancer as nonsmokers."[16]

In *Ashes to Ashes,* Kluger described the 1950s as a time when the tobacco industry attracted credentialed scientists, health professionals, and statisticians to the Tobacco Research Council, people not wholly convinced smoking caused lung cancer (based on what are now known to be unacceptable ideas). Because of the apparent diversity of opinion, physicians and other health professionals were not actively involved in antitobacco education or in a public antitobacco movement. As Wynder explained: "We can well understand why, in view of the climate of the late 1950s, the public at large and most physicians were still on the sidelines with regard to the smoking and lung cancer issue."[17]

Nevertheless, the issue of smoking and lung cancer came at a time when public health officials were adjusting their priorities. According to medical historian Allan M. Brandt, by midcentury, "systemic chronic diseases had overtaken infection as the major causes of death. ... The control of 'noncommunicable' diseases posed a new and entirely different set of problems. The identification of the tobacco as a cause of serious disease marked a critical turning point in the history of public health."[18] Public health officials questioned whether it was an appropriate role for them to counsel patients about how to avoid disease, the province of physicians. Many public health officials were wary about entering "the exclusive turf of clinical medicine by addressing matters of individual behavior."[19] But they soon realized that smoking was fast becoming a public health issue. Nevertheless, Brandt argues, that owing to public health anxieties about treading on the prerogatives of the medical profession and AMA, the public health community conceived "only a limited notion of its role in one of the biggest health issues of the country."[20]

In 1956 Surgeon General LeRoy Burney urged the ACS, American Heart Association (AHA), National Cancer Institute, and National Heart Institute to organize a study group on smoking and health. The group, which met regularly to assess scientific evidence, found that "sixteen studies has been conducted in five countries, all showing a statistical association between smoking and lung cancer." After many conferences, the group issued a statement that "the sum total of scientific evidence established beyond reasonable doubt that cigarette smoking is a causative factor in the increasing incidence of human epidermoid carcinoma of the lung."[21] The authors called for a public health response to their findings: "The evidence of a cause-effect relationship is adequate for considering the initiation of public health measures."[22]

In 1957 Dr. LeRoy Burney, surgeon general of the U.S. Public Health Service (PHS), issued a statement at a televised press conference that excessive cigarette smoking was one factor that caused lung cancer. It was the first time the PHS took a position on the controversial topic and, according to Burney, it was "the first official national recognition provided to the public through the media of the relationship between cigarette consumption and the increasing incidence of lung cancer."[23] Burney's statement was based on research conducted primarily by investigators in Great Britain and the United States over the years. The surgeon general's 1957 statement and supporting evidence was sent to all state medical societies and, with the assistance of the Office of Education, all state superintendents of education to inform and assist them in preparing materials and teaching content in health and physical education programs in local schools. According to Burney, the "reaction of organized medicine was muted—and for several years after 1957. The American Medical Association (AMA) had a rather detached, arms-length attitude."[24]

In 1959, as a result of additional evidence, Burney published a paper in *JAMA* in which he wrote: "the Public Health Service believes that the weight of the evidence at present implicates smoking as the principal etiologic factor in the increased incidence of lung cancer and that cigarette smoking particularly is associated with an increased chance of developing lung cancer."[25] A response to Burney's message by John Talbott, *JAMA*'s editor, said: "Neither the proponents nor the opponents of the smoking theory have sufficient evidence to warrant the assumption of an all-or-none authoritative position. Until definitive studies are forthcoming, the physician can fulfill his responsibility by watching the situation closely."[26]

By January of 1960, the ACS board declared that, based on clinical, epidemiological, experimental, chemical, and pathological evidence, it was now "beyond any reasonable doubt" that smoking was the major cause of lung cancer. ACS encouraged doctors to speak to their patients about avoiding cigarettes, emphasizing that prevention was the best way to control cancer. The ACS began distributing information to schools ("Is Smoking

Worth It?") and funded new studies on cancer prevention.[27] In 1960, the ACS began to take "a leading role in challenging and eliminating tobacco advertising."[28]

Finally pressure built up for the PHS to take action against smoking. In June of 1961, the American Lung Association (ALA) and the AHA asked President Kennedy to appoint a commission to study the effects of smoking, but he declined to respond (perhaps to avoid alienating Southern congressional delegations). Eventually Kennedy's surgeon general, Luther Terry, announced he would establish a committee to investigate the question of smoking and health. He convened a panel of well-known scientists, on both sides of the issue, and asked them to review the data and answer that question. The results, published in 1964, were clear: cigarettes were a cause of certain types of cancer, including cancer of the lung, chronic bronchitis, and a higher death rate from coronary artery disease. Surgeon General Terry also said, "The unnecessary disability, disease and death caused by cigarette smoking is our most urgent public health problem."[29] The publication received a great deal of media attention throughout the country.

According to Allan M. Brandt, "The identification of the cigarette as a cause of serious disease marked a critical turning point in the history of public health."[30] So, too, the "surgeon general's report was a pivotal document in the history of public health."[31] The surgeon general's report proved conclusively that cigarettes were the cause of two of the biggest killers of men in America: lung cancer and heart disease. Since a critical responsibility of the PHS, through its surgeon general, has been to educate the public on all matters relating to public health problems and issues, the report created a realm of action for the public health community.

The PHS tried to get the word out that cigarettes were dangerous by distributing 350,000 copies of the surgeon general's 1964 report, including one to every medical student in the country. It planned to post a summary of the report in 50,000 pharmacies by January 1965. Unfortunately, the surgeon general's office possessed few resources to establish significant public health programs.[32] But its report became the model for 29 subsequent reports on smoking and health risks and harms.

Terry's report and additional reports on the risks of smoking paved the way for the Federal Cigarette Labeling and Advertising Act of 1965, which required a warning label ("Caution: Cigarette Smoking May Be Hazardous to Your Health") on each package of cigarettes, and the Public Health Cigarette Smoking Act of 1969, which modified and strengthened the warning label to read: "WARNING: The Surgeon General Has Determined that Cigarette Smoking Is Dangerous to Your Health."

According to the Office of the Surgeon General Web site, "Luther Terry himself continued to play a leading role in the campaign against smoking after leaving the post of surgeon general, which he held through October 1, 1965. He chaired the National Interagency Council on Smoking and Health, a coalition of government agencies and nongovernment organizations, from 1967 to 1969, and served as a consultant to groups such as the American Cancer Society. Terry helped to obtain a ban on cigarette advertisements on radio and television in 1971. Late in his life, he led the effort to eliminate smoking from the workplace."[33]

Antitobacco activists called attention to cigarettes that were advertised to children as well as adults. Pressure from the ACS, the AHA, and other public health organizations led the tobacco industry to issue the 1965 Cigarette Advertising Code, an effort by the industry to regulate itself and avoid government regulation. The code's provisions stated that no one depicted in cigarette advertising would be or appear to be under 25 years old nor would advertising appear on television and radio programs aimed at children, in school newspapers, or in comic books.[34]

As more information came to light about the connections between smoking and heart disease, the AHA became involved in the fight against tobacco. Together with the PHS and the ACS, the agencies reviewed 18 years of studies and came out with a book, directed at the young, using nontechnical language to explain the complexities and health hazards of tobacco.[35] Three editions were published between 1969 and 1973 in Spanish and English.

Four years before the surgeon general's report, the National Association Board of Directors of the National Association for the Study and Prevention of Tuberculosis, renamed the American Lung Association in 1973, issued a warning on smoking as a policy statement: "Cigarette smoking is a major cause of lung cancer." In 1964, the board of directors "recommended that the organization conduct an aggressive campaign designed to educate the public—especially young people and those with chronic respiratory disease—about the hazards of cigarette smoking."[36]

Except for a brief dip in sales at the beginning of 1964, cigarette sales remained strong. It became obvious that getting the word about the dangers of smoking was not enough. In 1965 the National Clearinghouse for Smoking and Health, a unit added to the PHS, was formed to be a repository for all data, studies, and articles dealing with smoking. Besides functioning as a clearinghouse, directed by Daniel Horn who had worked with E. Cuyler Hammond on the groundbreaking ACS research in the 1950s, it educated the public about the possible health hazards of smoking. The clearinghouse produced pamphlets on quitting, posters distributed to public classrooms, as well as placards placed in New York subways and attached to the sides of U.S. mail trucks. In 1974 the clearinghouse was absorbed into the Centers for Disease Control and Prevention (CDC) and moved from Washington, D.C., to Atlanta, Georgia.

The 1967 and 1968 surgeon general's reports confirmed that people who quit smoking or smoked for a shorter time had lower death rates than people who smoked for a long time. At this time, the ALA began a program to educate children about the dangers of smoking and the "Kick the Habit" campaign to help people quit smoking.[37] Also in 1968, the ACS began to distribute "IQ" buttons, which stood for "I Quit Smoking."

The work of voluntary health agencies and the PHS began to pay off. A Gallup poll reported in 1968 that 71 percent of the country believed that smoking caused cancer; 10 years before, only 44 percent believed it. It was believed that 4 million people quit smoking.[38] And during the years the Federal Communications Commission (FCC) required all radio and television stations to air antismoking commercials, smoking rates dropped. Government statistics showed that as many as 10 million Americans quit smoking from 1967 to 1970.[39]

Beginning in the early 1970s, when civil rights and women's rights were being discussed everywhere, a shift in attitudes took place regarding public smoking and the rights of nonsmokers to clean air. For the first time, the 1972 *Surgeon General's Report on Smoking* identified the exposure of nonsmokers to cigarette smoke as a health hazard. Public health professionals and antismoking activists, drawing on suggestive evidence (scientific evidence came later) about the hazards, pushed for restrictions on smoking in a variety of public settings. They also used these restrictions on public smoking to undermine the social acceptability of smoking cigarettes, which led to a reduction in the prevalence of tobacco use. According to public health researchers, "By repositioning the bystander to center stage, public health advocates were able to press for changes, that if pursued directly, would have been politically unpalatable. Just as restrictions on advertising could most easily be justified in the name of protecting children from manipulation, restricting smoking could be justified by the claims of the bystander. It was possible to pursue the goal of a smokefree society without adopting the paternalistic posture that have been necessitated by expressly seeking to regulate the choices adults made on their own behalf."[40]

The Group Against Smokers' Pollution (GASP), Action on Smoking and Health, and other groups pressed for policies to restrict public smoking at a time when the public supported such measures. Up until this point, smokers were allowed to smoke on buses, airplanes, and trains, and in movie theaters and waiting rooms. This had always annoyed some nonsmokers, and some antitobacco advocates had complained about it earlier in the century. In 1973 the Civil Aeronautics Board ordered domestic airlines to provide separate seating for smokers and nonsmokers. (In 1989 a law was passed banning smoking on 99% percent of domestic flights.) In 1974 the Interstate Commerce Commission ruled that smoking be restricted to the rear 20 percent of seats in interstate buses.

States and local governments began to impose restrictions in a "context of scientific uncertainty and some skepticism about the precise nature of the physical harms, if any, incurred by secondhand exposure to tobacco smoke."[41] In 1973 Betty Carnes successfully lobbied the Arizona legislature to ban smoking in elevators, libraries, theaters, museums, concert halls, and on buses. Arizona became the first state to limit smoking in some public spaces as a measure to protect the health of nonsmokers. In 1974 Connecticut became the first state to restrict smoking in restaurants. In 1975 Minnesota passed a comprehensive statewide law to protect public health by prohibiting smoking in public spaces and at public meetings. In 1977 Berkeley, California, became the first local community to limit smoking in restaurants and other public settings. In 1983 San Francisco became the first municipality to pass an ordinance requiring workplaces to establish nonsmoking sections for employees. Activists learned that local, focused laws were easier to get passed than broad, national legislation.

During the 1980s, President Ronald Reagan advocated against regulation in all areas of the federal government. However, Surgeon General C. Everett Koop became a new force in public health and nonsmokers' rights within the Reagan administration itself. In his 1982 surgeon general's report, he said, "Although the currently available evidence is not sufficient to conclude that passive or involuntary smoking causes lung cancer in nonsmokers, the evidence does raise concern about a possible serious public health problem."[42] In his 1986 surgeon general's report, Koop said that environmental tobacco smoke (ETS) caused cancer. His report changed everything in the battle for nonsmokers' rights. If secondhand smoke caused cancer, then restrictions on smoking in public places became not a matter discomfort, but rather a matter of health.

During the 1980s, the publication of scientific articles about health risks of ETS on nonsmokers impacted public perceptions and concerns. Antismoking activists used the emerging scientific evidence to mobilize public opinion for even greater restrictions despite the opposition of the tobacco industry. A 1983 Gallop poll found that 82 percent of nonsmokers believed that smokers should not smoke in their presence.[43] By 1986 a total of 41 states, the District of Columbia, and 89 cities and counties had enacted statutes that imposed restrictions on smoking. That year both the National Academy of Science and Surgeon General Koop issued reports that documented the dangers of tobacco smoke exposure to non-smokers.

While the tobacco industry tried to focus on the limitations of the data, public health advocates accepted the findings as reason for action. In the years that followed the two reports, smoking restrictions increased. By 1988 some 400 local ordinances had been enacted.[44] In 1998 more than 800 were on the books. In January 2009 the Americans for Nonsmokers' Rights Foundation stated that "2,982 municipalities in the U.S. have local laws that restrict where smoking is allowed."[45]

In 1992 the Environmental Protection Agency designated ETS as a "known human carcinogen." From that time on, it became impossible to stop the passage of regulations that limited smoking in places where people congregated. Advocates for smoking bans built upon the evidence in Surgeon General Koop's reports to support their arguments, and they succeeded in passing ordinances that banned cigarettes on all flights, in restaurants, in bars, in offices, and near the doors of offices.

According to public health researchers Ronald Bayer and James Colgrove, "the changing social class composition of smoking" has made the campaign against ETS less difficult. Since people of lower socioeconomic status have higher rates of tobacco consumption, it has become easier to stigmatize their behavior as undesirable. "In this way," according to Bayer and Colgrove, "efforts by public health activists to reduce smoking mirror campaigns by Progressive Era reformers to impose hygienic behavior on the 'lower orders' in the name of public health." But they point out that unlike these earlier efforts, "contemporary antismoking strategies have not been overly paternalistic."[46] Nevertheless, some antismoking activists are concerned that the ETS movement has taken on "the taint of moralism and authoritarianism" in imposing bans on outdoor smoking, which can be justified in terms of "annoyance abatement," not of disease prevention.[47] Some communities, however, have outdoor smoking bans because of concerns about fire risks and reducing litter.

By the 1990s, although adult smokers remained a target of the tobacco control community, the public health community turned its attention to children and teens under 18 years of age. Because tobacco use often begins in adolescence and because it's difficult to stop once regular use is established, David Kessler, who headed the Food and Drug Administration (FDA) at the time, called smoking a "pediatric disease." The FDA stated, "Reducing tobacco use by children is the key to reducing the toll of tobacco."[48] Studies showed that teens did not understand the risks of smoking and a third of those interviewed didn't know that cigarettes could make a person become seriously ill. Underage sales of tobacco, the availability of tobacco samples at rock concerts and other venues, and ubiquitous advertising in magazines, on billboards, and in sports stadiums, "encouraged teenagers to think that smoking [was] a nearly universal phenomenon."[49]

Tobacco control advocates advocated aggressive intervention and education campaigns. In California, Proposition 99 raised the state's cigarette tax, and revenues from the increase were devoted to an antismoking educational campaign to educate the public about the risks of smoking and to help them quit. According to historian Richard Kluger, "Three hundred public health workers went on the payroll statewide to train and oversee local health workers in tobacco controls set up in each of California's fifty-eight counties and 1,000 school districts. A fourteen-month advertising campaign budgeted at almost $30 million ... was launched in 1990; conducted in eight languages, it involved 69 television stations, 147 radio stations, 130 newspapers, and 775 billboards." The antismoking campaign had a big impact: "California smokers began quitting at twice the national rate, and by 1991, the percentage of smokers in the state had dropped from 25 to 21, one of the lowest figures in the nation."[50]

In 1993 the state of Massachusetts implemented the Massachusetts Tobacco Control Program (MTCP), one of the most prominent public health initiatives in the United States. Supported by the state's tobacco excise tax, the program has funded a media campaign, school health services, smoking intervention programs, research and demonstration projects, and funding of local boards of health to raise public awareness of the need for tobacco control policies. The MTCP has resulted in the decrease of the state's smoking rate to 16.4 percent, the fourth lowest in the nation, cutting in half the illegal sale of tobacco in 2007, and protecting state residents from secondhand smoke, a 98 percent compliance rate.[51]

In 1998 in Florida, the public health community launched a comprehensive, multipronged program "to prevent and reduce youth tobacco use by implementing an innovative and effective education, marketing, prevention, and enforcement campaign that empowered youth to live tobacco-free." A unique aspect of the program was its youth-led tobacco use prevention program, which included a youth-directed media campaign marketing the "truth" brand and slogan ("Our brand is truth, their brand is lies") as well as school-based education, and enforcement of laws restricting sales to minors.[52] Surveys by students of the Florida Pilot Program on Tobacco Control (FPPTC) showed that tobacco use decreased in 1999 and 2000, following implementation of the FPPTC.[53]

During the 1990s, partnerships developed among U.S. philanthropies, voluntary health groups, medical societies, women's and minority health advocates, and others to deal with tobacco control and public health. In 1993 the ACS partnered with the National Cancer Institute on a five-year 30-state project called ASSIST (American Stop Smoking Intervention Study for Cancer Prevention). The goal was to attack smoking in homes, schools, health care centers, community groups, work sites, and the mass media. Statewide efforts relied on the cooperation of community groups and ACS volunteers to reach 91 million people, or a third of the U.S. population, including about 20 million smokers.

The SmokeLess States Program, a national tobacco prevention and control program, was established as a partnership between the Robert Wood Johnson Foundation and the AMA. (Although the AMA had historically been opposed to antitobacco legislation and slow to denounce smoking, a change in leadership in the 1980s brought the AMA to an active antitobacco position.)[54] The program became the largest nongovernmental funded national effort. The foundation invested more than $99 million in SmokeLess States during the 10 years (1994–2004) the program was active. It funded statewide tobacco control coalitions in 19 states, which addressed tobacco use in different ways. Some focused on educating the public about tobacco-related harm with powerful media campaigns, others involved young people, still others focused on public policy initiatives, and many coalitions worked on a combination of approaches simultaneously. Alaska's coalition worked in partnership with organizers of the Iditarod dogsled race and sponsored a dogsled musher to educate Alaskans about harms of tobacco use. New Jersey's coalition concentrated on increasing public support for raising tobacco excise taxes.

In 2000 the foundation shifted the direction of the program to focus solely on advocacy regarding tobacco. States were required to concentrate exclusively on advancing policies to reduce tobacco use, including increasing excise taxes, comprehensive clean indoor air policies, and expanded public and private insurance coverage of tobacco dependence treatment. The foundation made 42 grants to states and the District of Columbia.

In the foundation's assessment of the program, it stated that advocacy was an effective way to improve the health of the public, although it found advocacy work "messy" and "time-intensive." According to the foundation, the program was successful, and most of the SmokeLess state coalitions intended to continue to work on tobacco policy advocacy after the demonstration program ended.[55]

In the mid-1990s, to secure compensation for health care expenditures for ailments arising from tobacco use, 46 states and two jurisdictions filed lawsuits in their state courts against the tobacco industry. The cases were settled on June 20, 1997, when Mississippi state attorney general Michael Moore announced "the most historic public health achievement in history"[56] and the largest proposed industry payout in history. While the massive tobacco deal, called the Global Settlement, drew some praise, it also drew vitriolic criticism from former surgeon general C. Everett Koop, public health groups, and trial lawyers across the country who argued that the settlement was flawed, the payout too small, and the provisions too soft on the tobacco industry, especially regarding advertising, restrictions on FDA regulation of nicotine levels in cigarettes, elimination of punitive damages and class actions, and other provisions. To make the settlement binding on all 50 states, congressional action was necessary. A number of bills were introduced but failed to pass.

Meanwhile, four states (Florida, Minnesota, Mississippi, and Texas) had previously reached individual settlements with the tobacco industry, amounting to $40 billion over the next 25 years. On November 16, 1998, an agreement—known as the Master Settlement Agreement (MSA)—between 46 states, five U.S. territories, and the tobacco industry resulted in a deal to settle pending state cases and defuse potential claims in the remaining states. The industry agreed to pay the states "$206 billion over the next 25 years. In addition, $5 billion will be made to 14 states to compensate them for potential harm to their tobacco-producing communities."[57] The MSA also set up a foundation for public health and smoking cessation.

According to the Michigan Nonprofit Association and the Council of Michigan Foundations: "The new deal did not require congressional approval because it did not include provisions pertaining to federal jurisdiction over the nicotine contained in tobacco products. It also did not grant the industry's major wish: a limit on future lawsuits. The agreement did not specify how the states would spend the money they received in the tobacco settlement, but it generally was seen as a unique opportunity for the states to reduce the financial and health burden that tobacco use imposes on American families and government."[58]

Many states have used their tobacco settlement dollars to fill budget shortfalls; build schools; pave roads; fund economic development initiatives, senior prescription drugs, early childhood programs, higher education; and improve tourism rather than use the payments to support tobacco prevention and control. Some states, such as Arizona, Michigan, South Carolina, and West Virginia, have not used settlement funds for tobacco prevention. A few that have invested more heavily in antismoking programs have lowered their smoking rates.

Almost 10 years after the 1998 MSA, the Campaign for Tobacco-Free Kids reported that "recent research also shows that tobacco company marketing and promotions in the retail environment (point of purchase marketing/POP) have increased dramatically and impact kids."[59] The American Legacy Foundation (ALF), a national, independent public health foundation located in Washington, D.C., was created in 1999 out of the landmark MSA. Its programs include truth®, a national youth smoking prevention campaign launched in 2000 and aimed at 12- to 17-year-olds. It has been cited as contributing to significant declines in youth smoking. ALF's model is "that 'truth' will change youths' attitudes toward smoking, and that attitudinal changes, in turn, will change their smoking behavior, prevent them from initiating smoking, or both." ALF findings "suggest[ed] that an aggressive national tobacco countermarketing campaign can have a dramatic influence within a short period of time on attitudes toward tobacco and the tobacco industry, These attitudinal changes were also associated with reduced intentions to smoke among those at risk."[60] The results paralleled those of the Florida "truth" campaign, in which shifts of attitude preceded changes in behavior.

The ALF Web site spells out its programs, which include EX®, an innovative public health program designed to speak to smokers in their own language and change the way they approach quitting; research initiatives exploring the causes, consequences, and approaches to reducing tobacco use; and tobacco prevention and cessation in priority populations—youth, low-income Americans, the less educated, and racial, ethnic, and cultural minorities.[61]

The ALF (http://www.americanlegacy.org) works through television, film, Internet, research, advocacy, and grant making. Its motto is "Building a world where young people reject tobacco and anyone can quit." In line with that mission, ALF has created campaigns like "infect truth," which is targeted at teens; "don't pass gas," which encourages adults not to smoke around others; and "Great Start," which helps pregnant women to quit smoking.

In 2000 the ALF launched the first comprehensive national antismoking campaign since the Fairness Doctrine era of 1967, when the FCC ruled that all radio and television stations broadcasting cigarette commercials donate significant free airtime for antismoking messages. Modeled after a successful program in Florida, the ALF campaign features teenagers in "truth" ads. The campaign "kept 450,000 young people from smoking just in its first four years and saved as much as $5.4 billion in medical care costs in it first two years"[62]

The landmark 1998 MSA, recognizing the enormous impact film has on our culture, banned paid tobacco product placement in movies. In November 2005, *Pediatrics* published a study that said more than one-third of youth smoking can be traced to exposure to smoking in films.[63] To follow up, the ALF has joined a host of prominent health and parent organizations around the country—including the World Health Organization, American Medical Association and AMA Alliance, American Academy of Pediatrics, AHA, ALA, and more—to urge the Motion Picture Association of America and major movie studios to adopt policies that would help counter the impact of smoking in movies on youth starting to smoke.

Parents, adults, and researchers all agree that movie smoking can influence kids to smoke. Both the President's Cancer Panel and the Institute of Medicine (IOM) recommend that meaningful efforts be made to eliminate or counter exposure to the billions of smoking impressions that Hollywood leaves with young moviegoers.

In 2007 the ALF asked the IOM to conduct a major study of tobacco use in the United States. In the report *Ending the Tobacco Problem: A Blueprint for the Nation,* the IOM committee found evidence that comprehensive state tobacco control programs can achieve substantial reductions in tobacco use. But states must maintain over the long term comprehensive integrated tobacco prevention and cessation programs at levels recommended by the CDC. In 2007 only three states (Delaware, Colorado, and Maine) met that standard. Twenty-eight states and the District of Columbia spent less than half of the CDC minimum, and five states (Michigan, Mississippi, Missouri, New Hampshire, and Tennessee) provided no significant state funding. Large budget cutbacks in many states' tobacco control programs have jeopardized success. The committee also found that MSA payments have not been a reliable source of funds in most states.

Over the past 100 years, the attitude toward smoking has changed dramatically in the public health community and in the country as a whole. A century ago, public health advocates were concerned that smoking would lead to moral depravation. Today, it is assumed that everyone knows smoking is dangerous to one's health, and that the safety of children depends on their ability to reject tobacco use in all its forms.

A great deal of medical information has come to light in the past century about health risks and illnesses attributable to tobacco use, especially during the 1950s. Since 1964, when the first surgeon general's report on smoking and health was issued, the public health community has recognized that "the unnecessary disability, disease and death caused by cigarette smoking is our most urgent public health problem."[64]

CHAPTER 4

U.S. Surgeons General, Tobacco, and Public Health

According to the National Library of Medicine Web site, since 1968, the main duties of the surgeons general, all of whom have medical degrees, "has been to advise the Secretary of Health and Human Services and the Assistant Secretary of Health on affairs of preventive health, medicine, and health policy" as well as to take "a more proactive role in informing the American public on health matters." Because of their political independence, "they make themselves into the most visible and, in the public's mind, impartial and therefore trusted government spokespersons on health issues affecting the nation as a whole." Surgeons general are appointed by the president with Senate approval for a four-year term of office.[1]

The first surgeon general, appointed in 1871, headed the Marine Hospital Service, which was established in 1798 to take care of sick and injured merchant seamen; the Marine Hospital Service was reorganized as the U.S. Public Health Service (PHS) in 1912.

Over the past 40 years, the surgeons general have become respected voices on public health issues, preventive medicine, and health promotion through their public appearances, speeches, interviews, organizing conferences, and influential reports, all of which are available online: http://www.cdc.gov/tobacco/data_statistics/sgr/index.htm.

As the National Library of Medicine points out, the surgeon general "has often been called upon to deal with difficult and controversial issues, such as smoking and sexual health. In some cases, the public health message has generated controversy, when it ran counter to the political beliefs of the time. But the Surgeon General's public statements often served to generate debate where there had been silence, to the benefit of the nation's health."[2]

Before 1964 PHS officers published pathbreaking reports on a range of issues regarding public health including sanitation, typhoid fever, and radiation hazards. Despite their importance to the public, these reports received little attention.

The first time that a surgeon general discussed the health hazards of tobacco took place in 1929, when Surgeon General Hugh Cumming "claimed that cigarettes tended to cause nervousness, insomnia and other ill effects in women. He warned that smoking could lower the 'physical tone' of the nation." Surgeon General Cumming's antismoking message was aimed only at women smokers, who were puffing cigarettes in greater numbers. Like many other physicians of his time, Cumming believed that "women were more susceptible than men to certain injuries, especially of the nervous system. While he was not convinced that smoking by women was harmful in all cases, he was concerned about the damage that excessive smoking might do to young women."[3] Cumming, a smoker who distanced himself from antitobacco reformers of the day, spoke up principally because of aggressive advertising aimed at women and young people. Like other physicians of his time, he did not view smoking as a significant health threat for most people.

During the 1930s, 1940s, and 1950s, research studies by U.S. and British epidemiologists, pathologists, and laboratory scientists mounted, providing evidence for the case against smoking. In 1956 members of the American Cancer Society (ACS), American Heart Association (AHA), National Heart Institute (NHI), and the National Cancer Institute (NCI), an agency of the PHS, met regularly to assess the growing body of scientific evidence, concluding that the "sum total of scientific evidence establishes beyond a reasonable doubt that cigarette smoking is a causative factor in the rapidly increasing incidence of human epidermoid carcinoma of the lung." While the group stated that more research would be beneficial, it also agreed that the evidence was "adequate" for considering the initiation of public health measures by official and voluntary agencies.[4]

Dr. Michael Shimkin, the NCI representative, brought the overwhelming evidence implicating cigarette smoking to the attention of Surgeon General LeRoy Burney (1956–1961), his friend and colleague. The mounting evidence compelled the PHS to make a firm statement about the hazards of cigarette smoking. After gathering other opinions from trusted people, Burney asked Shimkin to draft a statement for him about the smoking issue. On July 12, 1957, Surgeon General Burney, a smoker himself, issued a statement at a televised press conference, "the first official position on the question to be taken by any U.S. administration."[5] He said that "while there are naturally differences of opinion in interpreting the data on lung cancer and cigarette smoking, the Public Health Service feels the weight of the evidence is increasingly pointing in one direction: that excessive smoking is one of the causative factors in lung cancer." At the time, this was a controversial statement because many physicians and scientists believed that other factors, such as increasing atmospheric pollution from automobile exhausts, might explain the rise in the incidence of the disease. Other than sending out the statement to public health officers of every state and to the American Medical Association, no national educational campaign was planned.[6]

In 1959, as the result of additional scientific evidence, Surgeon General Burney expanded on his 1957 statement in an article about smoking and lung cancer published in the *Journal of the American Medical Association (JAMA)*. He wrote that the "weight of evidence at present implicates smoking as the principal etiological factor" in the increased incidence of lung cancer. Burney elevated smoking from being "one" of the causative factors to being "the principal" causative factor in the increased incidence. He felt "stopping cigarette smoking even after long exposure is beneficial."[7] But the statement was not a policy position or call to action by the federal government. Nevertheless, Burney's statements paved the way for Luther L. Terry, surgeon general under President Lyndon B. Johnson, to issue a landmark report on smoking and health in 1964.

In June 1961, four voluntary health organizations urged President John F. Kennedy to set up a commission to study the health hazards of cigarette smoking and seek a "solution to this health problem that would interfere least with the freedom of industry or the happiness of individuals."[8] After four months, the coalition threatened to tell the press about the administration's inaction, which resulted in a meeting between the four voluntaries and the new top health officer, Surgeon General Terry (1961–1965). From the beginning, Terry made sure the tobacco industry had input into the formation of the Surgeon General's Advisory Committee of experts so it could not discredit the findings. Terry sent the tobacco industry a list of 150 outstanding medical scientists in the United States and asked it to delete any unacceptable names.

Eventually, 11 scientists were chosen whose names were acceptable to everyone. Terry acted as chairman, and Dr. James M. Hundley, assistant surgeon general, as vice chairman. The other members of the committee were announced on October 27, 1962: Dr. Stanhope Bayne-Jones, former dean, Yale School of Medicine; Dr. Walter J. Burdette, head of the Department of Surgery, University of Utah School of Medicine; William G. Cochran, professor of statistics, Harvard University; Dr. Emmanuel Farber, chairman,

Department of Pathology, University of Pittsburgh; Louis F. Fieser, professor of organic chemistry, Harvard University; Dr. Jacob Furth, professor of pathology, Columbia University; Dr. John B. Hickam, chairman, Department of Internal Medicine, Indiana University; Dr. Charles LeMaistre, professor of internal medicine, University of Texas Southwestern Medical School; Dr. Leonard M. Schuman, professor of epidemiology, University of Minnesota School of Public Health; and Dr. Maurice H. Seevers, chairman, Department of Pharmacology, University of Michigan. One was dismissed shortly after his appointment for telling a reporter that evidence "definitely suggests that tobacco is a health hazard."[9]

The committee worked over a year in absolute secrecy in a windowless basement office of the new National Library of Medicine in Bethesda, Maryland. Besides pouring over key information provided by the tobacco industry and some 6,000 articles in 1,200 publications, the committee questioned hundreds of witnesses. Despite efforts by journalists to break the secrecy of the committee's deliberations, security was maintained to the end. At the government printers, the report was treated with a security classification similar to military and state secrets.

The report was released in a dramatic manner. The press was invited to a Saturday morning press conference in a State Department auditorium affixed with signs announcing "no smoking." At 9:00 A.M., as 200 reporters walked in, they were given a copy of the 387-page report and time to review it. Locked in the room so they could not leave till the news conference was over, Terry and his experts marched them through the document. The captive reporters were given 90 minutes to ask questions and were then released. The committee of experts had concluded that smoking was causally related to lung cancer in men, outweighing all other factors including air pollution. Evidence pointed in the same direction for women, even though information on smoking and lung cancer in women was not available because women had begun smoking in substantial numbers only 20 years before. The report also stated that cigarette smoking was a major cause of heart disease, chronic bronchitis, emphysema, and cancer of the larynx. The committee found insufficient evidence that filter-tipped cigarettes did any good. The only good news reported was that smokers could reduce health risks by quitting. Surgeon General Terry halted the free distribution of cigarettes to 16 public hospitals and 50 Indian hospitals under the direction of the PHS.

According to Terry, the "report hit the country like a bombshell. It was front page news and a lead story on every radio and television station in the United States and many abroad." *Newsweek* called the report "monumental," and the ACS said it was "a landmark in the history of man's fight against disease."[10]

The 1964 report is generally credited with establishing cigarette smoking as the cause of lung cancer, although one might question why Surgeon General LeRoy's 1957 and 1959 statements were not given their due. According to historian Mark Parascandola, Burney's statements were presented as "opinions" of the surgeon general and PHS, and "there was no claim that they represented an objective scientific assessment of the evidence. ... In contrast, Surgeon General Terry had no involvement in the deliberations or conclusions of the advisory committee." The report was designed to be the result of a scientific review by neutral experts, free of political influence.[11]

The 1964 report on smoking and health marked the beginning of a series of authoritative scientific statements by the surgeons general. These reports have commanded public attention and have helped shape the debate on the responsibility of government, physicians, scientists, the public health community, voluntary health organizations, and individual citizens for the nation's health. In 1964, the PHS established a small unit called the National Clearinghouse for Smoking and Health. Through the years, the clearinghouse and its successor organization, the Office on Smoking and Health (OSH), have been responsible for reporting on the health consequences of tobacco use.

OSH has been a focal point for smoking and health activities in the United States. Located in Atlanta, Georgia, it is a division of the National Center for Chronic Disease Prevention and Health Promotion, Centers for Disease Control and Prevention (CDC), PHS, U.S. Department of Health and Human Services. Since 1986, when OSH became part of the CDC, it has targeted tobacco-related diseases.

OSH develops and distributes the surgeon general's report on the health consequences of smoking, coordinates a national public information and education program on tobacco use and health, and coordinates tobacco research efforts. It distributes information about health risks of smoking in brochures, pamphlets, posters, scientific reports, and public service announcements. Every year OSH distributes millions of dollars to support tobacco control initiatives. Its Global Tobacco Control Unit collaborates with the World Health Organization (WHO) and WHO regional offices on a global tobacco surveillance system (GTSS) monitoring tobacco use among youth and selected adult populations. The GTSS provides significant data to inform comprehensive global health promotion approaches to tobacco use prevention and control.

In response to Surgeon General Terry's report, Congress passed the Cigarette Labeling and Advertising Act in 1965, which required all cigarette packages sold in the United States to carry a nine-word health warning: "Caution: Cigarette Smoking May Be Hazardous to Your Health." The act did not require labels on advertising for three years. Soon after, the Federal Trade Commission (FTC) recommended that the 1965 law be amended so that the warnings were made in the name of the surgeon general. Congress passed the Public Health Cigarette Smoking Act of 1969, signed into law by President Richard Nixon in April of 1970. Besides banning cigarette ads from television and radio, the act required that health warnings on cigarette packs (but not on smokeless tobacco) carry the statement: "WARNING: The Surgeon General Has Determined that Cigarette Smoking Is Dangerous to Your Health." The law temporarily preempted the FTC requirement of health labels on advertisements. The law also required the surgeon general to produce an annual report reviewing the latest scientific findings on the health consequences of smoking. As a result, since 1964 more than half of all surgeons general reports have dealt with the health hazards of tobacco use.

A historical overview of the role of the surgeons general reports that "in 1968, an organizational reform greatly reduced the surgeon general's administrative role, abolishing the Office of the Surgeon General (though not the position of Surgeon General itself) and transferring line authority for the administration of PHS to the Assistant Secretary for Health within the Department of Health, Education, and Welfare (since 1980, the Department of Health and Human Services)." Since 1968, the official duty of the surgeons general has been to "advise the secretary and assistant secretary of Health and Human Services on affairs of preventive health, medicine, and health policy." Since the 1960s, the surgeons general, all of whom are physicians, politically independent, and impartial, have undertaken a visible role in informing the American public on health matters. In the public's mind, they have become trusted government spokespersons on health issues affecting the nation as a whole.[12]

Between 1977 and 1981, the surgeon general's position was consolidated with that of the assistant secretary for health, but since 1981 it has been a separate position. The surgeon general's position was vacant for four years, from 1973 to 1977, when the office itself said that the acting surgeon general, Dr. S. Paul Ehrlich Jr., was active only in ceremonial functions. A surgeon general's role is now determined almost entirely by the force of his or her personality and how he or she chooses causes and uses the bully pulpit to advance them.

SURGEONS GENERAL REPORTS, 1964–2006: MAJOR CONCLUSIONS

1964: *Smoking and Health: Report of the Advisory Committee to the Surgeon General of the Public Health Service*, Surgeon General Luther Terry, 1961–1965

The first official report of the federal government on smoking and health concluded that "cigarette smoking is a health hazard of sufficient importance in the United States to warrant appropriate remedial action."

> *The Effects of Smoking: Principal Findings:* In view of the continuing and mounting evidence from many sources, it is the judgement of the Committee that cigarette smoking contributes substantially to mortality from certain specific diseases and to the overall death rate.
>
> *Lung Cancer:* Cigarette smoking is causally related to lung cancer in men; the magnitude of the effect of cigarette smoking far outweighs all other factors. The data for women, though less extensive, point in the same direction.
>
> *Chronic Bronchitis and Emphysema:* Cigarette smoking is the most important of the causes of chronic bronchitis in the United States, and increases the risk of dying from chronic bronchitis and emphysema. ... Studies demonstrate that fatalities from this illness are infrequent among non-smokers.
>
> *Cardiovascular Diseases:* It is established that male cigarette smokers have a higher death rate from coronary artery disease than non-smoking males. ... Although a causal relationship has not been established, higher mortality of cigarette smoking is associated with many other cardiovascular diseases, including miscellaneous circulatory diseases, other heart diseases, hypertensive heart disease, and general arteriosclerosis.
>
> *Other Cancer Sites:* Pipe smoking appears to be causally related to lip cancer. Cigarette smoking is a significant factor in the causation of cancer of the larynx. The evidence supports the belief that an association exists between tobacco use and cancer of the esophagus.[13]

1967: *The Health Consequences of Smoking: A Public Health Service Review*, Surgeon General William H. Stewart, 1965–1969

This report confirmed and strengthened the conclusions of the 1964 report. It stated: "The case for cigarette smoking as the principal cause of lung cancer is overwhelming." While the 1964 report described the relationship between smoking and coronary heart disease as an "association," the 1967 report found that evidence "strongly suggests that cigarette smoking can cause death from coronary heart disease." The report also concluded that "cigarette smoking is the most important of the causes of chronic non-neoplastic bronchiopulmonary diseases in the United States."[14]

1968: *The Health Consequences of Smoking*, Surgeon General William H. Stewart

This report was a 1968 supplement to the 1967 Public Health Service review. This report updated information presented in the 1967 report. It estimated that smoking-related loss of life expectancy among young men as eight years for "heavy smokers" (over two packs per day) and four years for "light" smokers (less than half a pack per day).[15]

1969: *The Health Consequences of Smoking*, Surgeon General William H. Stewart

This 1969 supplement to the 1967 Public Health Service review also supplemented the 1967 report. It confirmed the association between maternal smoking and infant low birth weight. It identified evidence of increased incidence of prematurity, spontaneous abortion, stillbirth, and neonatal death.[16]

1971: *The Health Consequences of Smoking: A Report of the Surgeon General*, Surgeon General Jesse L. Steinfeld, 1969–1973

This report reviewed the entire field of smoking and health, emphasizing the most recent literature. It discussed new data including associations between smoking and peripheral vascular disease, atherosclerosis of the aorta and coronary arteries, increased incidence and severity of respiratory infections, and increased mortality from cerebrovascular disease and nonsyphilitic aortic aneurysm. It concluded that smoking is associated with cancers of the oral cavity and esophagus. It found that "maternal smoking during pregnancy exerts a retarding influence on fetal growth."[17]

1972: *The Health Consequences of Smoking: A Report of the Surgeon General*, Surgeon General Jesse L. Steinfeld

The report examined evidence on immunological effects of tobacco and tobacco smoke, harmful constituents of tobacco smoke, and "public exposure to air pollution from tobacco smoke." The report stated that tobacco may impair protective mechanisms of the immune system, nonsmokers' exposure to tobacco smoke may exacerbate allergic symptoms, and carbon monoxide in smoke-filled rooms may harm health of persons with chronic lung or heart disease. The report found that tobacco smoke contains hundreds of compounds, several of which have been shown to act as carcinogens, tumor initiators, and tumor promoters. Finally, carbon monoxide, nicotine, and tar are identified as smoke constituents most likely to produce health hazards of smoking.[18]

1973: *The Health Consequences of Smoking*, Surgeon General Jesse L. Steinfeld

The report presented evidence on the health effects of smoking pipes, cigars, and little cigars. It found that the mortality rates of pipe and cigar smokers was higher than those of nonsmokers but lower than those of cigarette smokers. It found that cigarette smoking impairs exercise performance in healthy young men. The report presented additional evidence on smoking as a risk factor in peripheral vascular disease and problems of pregnancy.[19]

1974: *The Health Consequences of Smoking*, Acting Surgeon General Paul Ehrlich, Jr., 1973–1977

The tenth anniversary report reviewed and strengthened evidence on the major hazards of smoking. It reviewed evidence on the association between smoking and atherosclerotic brain infarction and on the synergistic effect of smoking and asbestos exposure in causing lung cancer.[20]

1975: *The Health Consequences of Smoking*, Acting Surgeon General Paul Ehrlich, Jr.

This report updated information on the health effects of involuntary (passive) smoking. It noted evidence linking parental smoking to bronchitis and pneumonia in children during the first year of life.[21]

1976: *The Health Consequences of Smoking: A Reference Edition*, Acting Surgeon General Paul Ehrlich, Jr.

The National Library of Medicine Profiles in Science Web site provides a description of the 1976 surgeon general's report: "This reference report contains selected chapters of previous reports to Congress of summations of known health hazards from smoking, i.e., cardiovascular disease, cancer, and respiratory disease. An overview of the 1975 report is followed by chapters on cardiovascular disease; chronic obstructive bronchopulmonary disease; cancer; pregnancy; peptic ulcer disease; involuntary smoking; allergy; tobacco amblyopia; pipes and cigars; exercise performance; and harmful constituents of cigarette smoke. The consensus of scientific evidence is that risk of disease is dose-related and reduction of tars and nicotine intake reduces harmful effects."[22]

1978: *The Health Consequences of Smoking, 1977–1978*, Surgeon General Julius B. Richmond, 1977–1981

This combined two-year report focused on smoking-related health problems unique to women. It cited studies showing that use of oral contraceptives potentiates harmful effects of smoking on the cardiovascular system.[23]

1979: *Smoking and Health: A Report of the Surgeon General,* Surgeon General Julius B. Richmond

The fifteenth anniversary report presented the most comprehensive review of the health effects of smoking ever published. It was the first surgeon general's report to carefully examine the behavioral, pharmacological, and social factors influencing smoking. It also was the first report to consider the role of adult and youth education in promoting nonsmoking as well as the first report to review the health consequences of smokeless tobacco. One new section identified smoking as "one of the primary causes of drug interactions in humans."[24]

1980: *The Health Consequences of Smoking for Women: A Report of the Surgeon General,* Surgeon General Julius B. Richmond

This report devoted to the health consequences of smoking for women reviewed evidence that strengthened previous findings and permitted new ones. It noted projections that lung cancer would surpass breast cancer as the leading cause of cancer mortality in women. It identified the trend toward increased smoking by adolescent females.[25]

1981: *The Health Consequences of Smoking—The Changing Cigarette: A Report of the Surgeon General,* Surgeon General Julius B. Richmond

This report examined the health consequences of "the changing cigarette" (i.e., lower tar and nicotine cigarettes). It concluded that lower-yield cigarettes reduced the risk of lung cancer but found no conclusive evidence that they reduced the risk of cardiovascular disease, chronic obstructive pulmonary disease, and fetal damage. The report noted the possible risks from additives and their products of combustion. It discussed compensatory smoking behaviors that might reduce potential risk reductions of lower-yield cigarettes. It emphasized that there is no safe cigarette and that any risk reduction associated with lower-yield cigarettes would be small compared with the benefits of quitting smoking.[26]

1982: *The Health Consequences of Smoking—Cancer: A Report of the Surgeon General,* Surgeon General C. Everett Koop

The report reviewed and extended an understanding of the health consequences of smoking as a cause or contributing factor of numerous cancers. The report included the consideration from the first surgeon general's report of emerging epidemiological evidence of increased lung cancer risk in nonsmoking wives of smoking husbands. It did not find evidence at that time sufficient to conclude that relationship was causal but labeled it "a possible serious public health problem." The report discussed the potential for low-cost smoking cessation interventions.[27]

1983: *The Health Consequences of Smoking—Cardiovascular Disease: A Report of the Surgeon General*, Surgeon General C. Everett Koop

The report examined the health consequences of smoking for cardiovascular disease. It concluded that cigarette smoking was one of three major independent causes of coronary heart disease (CHD) and, given its prevalence, "should be considered the most important of the known modifiable risk factors for CHD." It discussed relationships between smoking and other forms of cardiovascular disease.[28]

1984: *The Health Consequences of Smoking—Chronic Obstructive Lung Disease: A Report of the Surgeon General*, Surgeon General C. Everett Koop

The report reviewed evidence on smoking and chronic obstructive lung disease (COLD). It concluded that smoking was the major cause of COLD, accounting for 80 to 90 percent of COLD deaths in the United States. It noted that COLD morbidity has greater social impact than COLD mortality because of extended disability periods of COLD victims.[29]

1985: *The Health Consequences of Smoking—Cancer and Chronic Lung Disease in the Workplace: A Report of the Surgeon General*, Surgeon General C. Everett Koop

The report examined the relationship between smoking and hazardous substances in the workplace. It found that for the majority of smokers, smoking is a greater cause of death and disability than their workplace environment. The report characterized the risk of lung cancer from asbestos exposure as multiplicative with smoking exposure. It observed the special importance of smoking prevention among blue-collar workers because of their greater exposure to workplace hazards and their higher prevalence of smoking.[30]

1986: *The Health Consequences of Involuntary Smoking: A Report of the Surgeon General*, Surgeon General C. Everett Koop

The report concluded that "involuntary smoking is a cause of disease, including lung cancer, in healthy nonsmokers." It also found that, compared with children of nonsmokers, children of smokers have higher incidence of respiratory infections and symptoms and reduced rates of increase in lung function. It presented a detailed examination of growth in restrictions on smoking in public places and workplaces. It concluded that simple separation of smokers and nonsmokers within the same airspace reduces but does not eliminate exposure to environmental tobacco smoke.[31]

1988: *The Health Consequences of Smoking—Nicotine Addiction: A Report of the Surgeon General,* Surgeon General C. Everett Koop

The report established nicotine as a highly addictive substance, comparable in its physiological and psychological properties to heroin and cocaine and other addictive substances of abuse.[32]

1989: *Reducing the Health Consequences of Smoking—25 Years of Progress: A Report of the Surgeon General,* Surgeon General C. Everett Koop

This report examined the fundamental developments over the past quarter century in smoking prevalence and in mortality caused by smoking. It highlighted important gains in preventing smoking and smoking-related diseases, reviewed changes in programs and policies designed to reduce smoking, and emphasized sources of continuing concern and remaining challenges.[33]

1990: *The Health Benefits of Smoking Cessation: A Report of the Surgeon General,* Surgeon General Antonio C. Novello, 1990–1993

The report concluded that smoking cessation has major and immediate health benefits for men and women of all ages. Benefits apply to persons with and without smoking-related disease. It noted that former smokers live longer than continuing smokers. For example, persons who quit smoking before age 50 have one-half the risk of dying in the next 15 years compared with continuing smokers. The report explained that smoking cessation decreases the risk of lung cancer, other cancers, heart attack, stroke, and chronic lung disease. Women who stop smoking before pregnancy or during the first three or four months of pregnancy reduce their risk of having a low-birth-weight baby to that of women who never smoked. Finally, the report concluded that the health benefits of smoking cessation far exceed any risks from the average five-pound weight gain or any adverse psychological effects that may follow quitting.[34]

Figure 4.1 Since 1964, 30 reports of the surgeon general have dealt with the issue of smoking and health.

1992: *Smoking in the Americas: A Report of the Surgeon General,*
Surgeon General Antonio C. Novello

Developed in collaboration with the Pan American Health Organization,
the report examined epidemiological, economic, historical, and legal aspects of tobacco use in the Americas. The report concluded that the
prevalence of smoking in Latin America and the Caribbean varies but is
50 percent or more among young people in some urban areas. It noted
that substantial numbers of women have begun smoking in recent years.
The report explained that in Latin America and the Caribbean, the tobacco
industry restricts smoking-control efforts and that economic arguments
for support of tobacco production are offset by the long-term economic
effects of smoking-related diseases. Finally, the report concluded that
a commitment to surveillance of tobacco-related factors (prevalence of
smoking; morbidity and mortality; knowledge, attitudes, and practices; tobacco consumption and production; and taxation and legislation) is crucial
to the development of a systematic program for prevention and control of
tobacco use.[35]

1994: *Preventing Tobacco Use among Young People: A Report of*
the Surgeon General, **Surgeon General Joycelyn Elders, 1993–1994**

This report focused on the adolescent ages of 10 through 18 when most
users start smoking, chewing, or dipping and become addicted to tobacco.
It examined the health effects of early smoking and smokeless tobacco use,
the reasons that young men and women begin using tobacco, the extent to
which they use it, and efforts to prevent tobacco use by young people.[36]

1998: *Tobacco Use among U.S. Racial/Ethnic Minority Groups—*
African Americans, American Indians and Alaska Natives, Asian
Americans and Pacific Islanders, and Hispanics: A Report of the
Surgeon General, **Surgeon General David Satcher, 1998–2002**

This report concluded that cigarette smoking is a "major cause of disease and death in each of the four population groups studied," with African
Americans bearing the greatest health burden. It reported that "tobacco
use varies within and among racial/ethnic groups; among adults, American
Indians and Alaska Natives have the highest prevalence of tobacco use,
and African American and Southeast Asian men also have a high prevalence of smoking. Asian American and Hispanic women have the lowest
prevalence. Among adolescents, cigarette smoking prevalence increased
in the 1990s among African Americans and Hispanics after several years
of substantial decline among adolescents of all four racial/ethnic groups."
The report concluded that tobacco use is the result of "multiple factors

such as socioeconomic status, cultural characteristics, acculturation, stress, biological elements, targeted advertising, price of tobacco products, and varying capabilities of communities to mount effective tobacco control initiatives."[37]

African Americans

In the 1970s and 1980s, death rates from respiratory cancers (mainly lung cancer) increased among African American men and women. From 1990 to 1995, these rates declined substantially among African American men and leveled off in African American women. Middle-aged and older African Americans are far more likely than their counterparts in the other major racial/ethnic groups to die from coronary heart disease, stroke, or lung cancer.

Smoking declined dramatically among African American youths during the 1970s and 1980s but has increased substantially during the 1990s. Declines in smoking have been greater among African American men with at least a high school education than among those with less education.

American Indians and Alaska Natives

Nearly 40 percent of American Indian and Alaska Native adults smoke cigarettes, compared with 25 percent of adults in the overall U.S. population. They are more likely than any other racial/ethnic minority group to smoke tobacco or use smokeless tobacco.

Since 1983, very little progress has been made in reducing tobacco use among American Indian and Alaska Native adults. The prevalence of smoking among American Indian and Alaska Native women of reproductive age has remained strikingly high since 1978.

American Indians and Alaska Natives were the only one of the four major U.S. racial/ethnic groups to experience an increase in respiratory cancer death rates in 1990–1995.

Asian Americans and Pacific Islanders

Estimates of the smoking prevalence among Southeast Asian American men range from 34 percent to 43 percent—much higher than among other Asian American and Pacific Islander groups. Smoking rates are much higher among Asian American and Pacific Islander men than among women, regardless of country of origin.

Asian American and Pacific Islander women have the lowest rates of death from coronary heart disease among men or women in the four major U.S. racial/ethnic minority groups.

Factors associated with smoking among Asian Americans and Pacific Islanders include having recently moved to the United States, living in poverty, having limited English proficiency, and knowing little about the health effects of tobacco use.

Hispanics

After increasing in the 1970s and 1980s, death rates from respiratory cancers decreased slightly among Hispanic men and women from 1990 to 1995.

In general, smoking rates among Mexican American adults increase as they learn and adopt the values, beliefs, and norms of American culture.

Declines in the prevalence of smoking have been greater among Hispanic men with at least a high school education than among those with less education.

Factors that are associated with smoking among Hispanics include drinking alcohol, working and living with other smokers, having poor health, and being depressed.[38]

2000: *Reducing Tobacco Use: A Report of the Surgeon General,* Surgeon General David Satcher

This report is the first to offer a composite review of the various methods used to reduce and prevent tobacco use. This report evaluates each of five major approaches to reducing tobacco use: educational, clinical, regulatory, economic, and comprehensive. Further, the report attempts to place the approaches in the larger context of tobacco control, providing a vision for the future of tobacco use prevention and control based on these available tools. Approaches with the largest span of impact (economic, regulatory, and comprehensive) are likely to have the greatest long-term, population impact. Those with a smaller span of impact (educational and clinical) are of greater importance in helping individuals resist or abandon the use of tobacco.[39]

2001: *Women and Smoking: A Report of the Surgeon General,* Surgeon General David Satcher

This report summarizes what is now known about smoking among women, including patterns and trends in smoking habits, factors associated with starting to smoke and continuing to smoke, the consequences of smoking on women's health, and interventions for cessation and prevention. What the report also makes apparent is how the tobacco industry has historically and contemporarily created marketing specifically targeted at women. Smoking is the leading known cause of preventable death and disease among women. In 2000 far more women died of lung cancer than of breast cancer. Smoking is a major cause of coronary heart disease among women. They also face unique health effects from smoking such as problems related to pregnancy. In the 1990s the decline in smoking rates among adult women stalled, and at the same time, rates were rising steeply among teenaged girls, blunting earlier progress. Smoking rates among women with less than a high school education are three times higher than for college graduates. Nearly all women who smoke started as teenagers—and 30 percent of high school senior girls are still current smokers.[40]

2004: *The Health Consequences of Smoking: A Report of the Surgeon General,* Surgeon General Richard Carmona, 2002–2006

The report concludes that smoking harms nearly every organ of the body, causing many diseases and reducing the health of smokers in general; quitting smoking has immediate as well as long-term benefits, reducing risks for diseases caused by smoking and improving health in general; smoking cigarettes with lower machine-measured yields of tar and nicotine provides no clear benefit to health; and the list of diseases caused by smoking has been expanded to include abdominal aortic aneurysm, acute myeloid leukemia, cataract, cervical cancer, kidney cancer, pancreatic cancer, pneumonia, periodontitis, and stomach cancer. These are in addition to diseases previously known to be caused by smoking, including bladder, esophageal, laryngeal, lung, oral, and throat cancers, chronic lung diseases, coronary heart and cardiovascular diseases, as well as reproductive effects and sudden infant death syndrome.[41]

2006: *The Health Consequences of Involuntary Exposure to Tobacco Smoke: A Report of the Surgeon General,* Surgeon General Richard Carmona

The report concludes that many millions of Americans, both children and adults, are still exposed to secondhand smoke in their homes and workplaces despite substantial progress in tobacco control. Secondhand smoke exposure causes disease and premature death in children and adults who do not smoke. Children exposed to secondhand smoke are at an increased risk for sudden infant death syndrome (SIDS), acute respiratory infections, ear problems, and more severe asthma. Smoking by parents causes respiratory symptoms and slows lung growth in their children. Exposure of adults to secondhand smoke has immediate adverse effects on the cardiovascular system and causes coronary heart disease and lung cancer. The scientific evidence indicates that there is no risk-free level of exposure to secondhand smoke. Eliminating smoking in indoor spaces fully protects nonsmokers from exposure to secondhand smoke. Separating smokers from nonsmokers, cleaning the air, and ventilating buildings cannot eliminate exposures of nonsmokers to secondhand smoke.[42]

CHAPTER 5

Tobacco Advertising and Health

Since the creation of mass-produced cigarettes on the Bonsack machine in 1884, as well as innovations in distributing and marketing tobacco on a national scale, cigarettes, snuff, chew, and cigars have been among the most advertised products in the United States. Tobacco companies have spent billions of dollars annually to advertise and promote tobacco products, claiming that the purpose of marketing has been to provide information to and influence brand selection among people who smoke cigarettes or use other kinds of tobacco products, although an estimated 10 percent of smokers switch brands in any one year. Tobacco companies argue that smoking is an adult habit and that adult smokers choose to smoke. However, many medical and public health researchers assert that most of the adults who smoke started as children who were targeted by tobacco companies through advertising, marketing, and promotions.

National tobacco advertising began in 1889 when James Buchanan Duke, who had installed Bonsack machines in his factory, hired the services of advertising agencies to help him create a market for the 834 million cigarettes his company manufactured. Duke's advertisements in newspapers and magazines, and on billboards, posters tacked to storefronts, and his colorful packaging with attention-grabbing, brightly colored paper labels, catchy names, and images attracted male smokers.

Between 1885 and 1892, Duke and dozens of other tobacco manufacturers attracted customers to their brands by putting small lithographed picture cards in each cigarette pack. The small cards, arranged in series, pictured a variety of images from birds, dogs, flags, and flowers to actresses, great American Indian chiefs, presidents, and baseball players,

Tobacco & Snuff of the beſt quality & flavor,
At the Manufactory, No. 4, Chatham ſtreet, near the Gaol
By Peter and George Lorillard,
Whete may be had as follows :

Cut tobacco,	Prig or carrot do.
Common kitefoot do.	Maccuba fnuff,
Common fmoaking do.	Rappee do.
Segars do.	Straſburgh do.
Ladies twiſt do.	Common rappee do.
Pigtail do. in fmall rolls,	Scented rappee do. of dif-
Plug do.	ferent kinds,
Hogtail do.	Scotch do.

The above Tobacco and Snuff will be fold reaſonable,
and warranted as good as any on the continent. If not
found to prove good, any part of it may be returned, if
not damaged.

N. B. Proper allowance will be made to thoſe that
purchaſe a quantity. May 27—1m.

Figure 5.1 In 1789 Peter and George Lorillard, who set up P. Lorillard Co., the
first tobacco company in the American colonies, published this advertisement for
tobacco and snuff. It is considered the earliest ad for a tobacco company.

the new national heroes. Duke used other promotions to attract smokers including coupons in Sovereign cigarettes that could be redeemed for half a cent. In Mecca cigarettes, there were postcards (without stamps) that were suitable for the U.S. mail. Some Duke cigarette brands offered buyers coupons redeemable for miniature college pennants. Coupon programs lasted until after the First World War, when most tobacco companies stopped them.

Around 1912 tobacco companies inserted *silks* in cigarette boxes. These colorful silk rectangles were aimed at women smokers (then a small minority) who bought the cigarettes, collected the silks, and stitched them onto pillows and bedspreads. Small silk rugs were also the perfect size for dollhouses. Some companies packaged miniature silk rugs in envelopes and slipped them into cigarette boxes or inserted leather patches printed with college seals.[1] Like Duke, Richard Joshua Reynolds believed in marketing and advertising his cigarettes. On October 21, 1913, his ad agency launched the first multimillion-dollar national cigarette advertising campaign for Camels, the first "modern" blended cigarette, containing Turkish and domestic tobaccos. The ads explained that the cost of the tobaccos used in the Camel blend was too great to permit anything except the product itself. People bought the message, and by 1919 Camels was the number-one seller among cigarette brands.

By the 1920s, women were smoking in greater numbers, and advertising firms created ads that made smoking appear attractive to men and women. Once people got used to seeing women smoke in public, ad agencies devised ways to convince them to smoke their brands. By the second half of the 1920s, tobacco advertisers began to push their products directly at women. A 1926 Chesterfield ad showed a woman asking her date who is smoking to "Blow some my way." A storm of protest greeted the ad, but other tobacco companies soon followed suit. In 1927 Marlboro ads showed a woman's hand in silhouette holding a lit cigarette. The same year, Camel put women into their ads, but didn't show them actually smoking until 1933. The 1930s saw even more ads aimed at women. Major middle-class women's magazines pictured wealthy-looking American women, opera stars, and athletic-looking women promoting cigarette brands.

The distribution of free cigarettes during World War I and World War II contributed to the massive growth of the smoking habit, but so did advertising campaigns. Tobacco advertisers placed ad campaigns that linked smoking, war, and patriotism directly into radio programs. Camels ran a "Thanks to Yanks" radio campaign. Contestants who correctly answered game show questions could send 2,000 Camels to the serviceman of their choice. If game contestants could not answer a question correctly, 2,000 cigarettes went into the "Thanks to Yanks" duffle bag. By January of 1943, some 29,250 packs of Camels had been shipped to service men free of charge.[2]

Cigarette ads in magazines especially linked smoking and war. Camel ads showed men in torpedo rooms of submarines, breaking through barbed wire, and lugging antitank guns. Chesterfields had its "Workers in the War Effort" campaign. Pall Mall used military themes, and Raleighs offered cheap prices on gift cigarettes sent to soldiers overseas. Tobacco companies showed women hard at work in the national effort as well. Camel ran a series of ads picturing and naming women who worked in war industries. Chesterfields went after feminine war workers in their "Workers in the War Effort" campaign. By the second half of the 1940s, tobacco companies portrayed wives and sweethearts waiting for returning husbands and boyfriends while they smoked.

During the 1920s, cigarette manufacturers were among the most enthusiastic pioneers in using radio for coast-to-coast advertising. After magazines, it was the second-greatest national advertising medium. George Washington Hill's American Tobacco Company was one of the first tobacco companies to charge into radio. Two months after Lucky Strikes commercials had their debut on 39 radio stations in September 1928, sales skyrocketed by 47 percent. Soon other cigarette companies shifted their ad budgets from outdoor signs to the powerful new medium.[3]

In the late 1940s, tobacco advertisers were quick to recognize the potential of another powerful advertising medium—television. In 1947 Lucky Strikes began sponsoring college football games, and in 1948 the Lucky Strike "Barn Dance." In 1948 Camel sponsored the "Camel News Caravan."

In the late 1920s, the Federal Trade Commission (FTC) began monitoring the business practices of tobacco companies. In1929 the FTC commissioners summoned American Tobacco Company lawyers to its offices and advised them to discontinue the company's implicit claim that Lucky Strike cigarettes were weight-reducing devices. In 1938 Congress passed the Wheeler-Lea Act, which widened the commission's powers giving the FTC authority to regulate "unfair or deceptive acts or practices in commerce."[4] The agency had the authority to subpoena documents, lay down fair-practice guidelines, and seek civil penalties in the federal courts of up to $10,000 per day per violation. Congress, however, denied the FTC power to enjoin the suspect practice throughout the proceedings against wrongdoers. A typical action took four years.

In August of 1942, for example, the FTC told tobacco manufacturers to stop making false and misleading claims: Pall Mall cigarettes did not protect throats from irritation, Lucky Strike cigarettes were not *toasted,* as that term was commonly understood by the public, nor did they contain less nicotine than other brands. Camels did not aid digestion, and Kools did not give extra protection against colds. In 1950 when the FTC investigated Old Gold cigarette's claim that it contained less nicotine than the other brands, it was discovered that the difference was only 0.4 percent, a margin that was found to be physiologically without significance. The FTC ordered the manufacturer to stop making its claim. In 1955 the FTC barred from ads all phony testimonials and any medical approval of cigarette smoking. Between 1950 and 1954, more than a dozen studies informed the public that cigarette smoking was linked to lung cancer and other serious diseases.

Although the FTC tried to halt the tobacco industry's explicit health and other kinds of claims, it never did so aggressively or on its own initiative. It moved against a tobacco company when an aggrieved customer or competitor brought cases to it. In 1957 U.S. Rep. John A. Blatnik (D-MN) showed that the FTC had not done its job when it investigated deceptive filter-tip cigarette advertising. Blatnik, chairman of the Legal and Monetary Subcommittee of the Government Operations Committee, conducted hearings to define the responsibility of the FTC regarding advertising claims for cigarettes. The Blatnik subcommittee concluded the following: "The Federal Trade Commission has failed in its statutory duty to 'prevent deceptive acts or practices' in filter-cigarette advertising. The activities of the Commission to prevent this deception were weak and tardy. As a result, the connection between filter-tip cigarettes and "protection" has become deeply embedded in the public mind."[5]

After trying to work out a standard testing procedure for tar and nicotine content, the FTC decided that no reliable test existed. Weary of deciding the legal merits of individual tobacco company claims, the FTC decided to knock the tar and nicotine claims out of cigarette advertising altogether. On December 17, 1959, it sent a letter to manufacturers advising them that "all representations of low or reduced tar or nicotine, whether by filtration or otherwise, will be construed as health claims ... Our purpose is to eliminate from cigarette advertising representations which in any way imply health benefit."[6]

It was not until the early 1960s, however, that major regulatory moves against tobacco began in earnest. Shortly after the release of the U.S. surgeon general's report for 1964, which declared cigarette smoking a major hazard, the FTC proposed a strong health warning regarding the risk of death from disease caused by tobacco use. Congress agreed that a warning was needed but in 1965 passed the Federal Cigarette Labeling and

Advertising Act, a law with a weaker warning than the kind the FTC wanted. As of January 1, 1966, cigarette packs had to carry a nine-word warning: "Caution: Cigarette Smoking May Be Hazardous to Your Health." The law temporarily prohibited the FTC and states from requiring health warnings in cigarette advertising. It also required that "not later than January 1971, and annually thereafter," the FTC report annually to Congress about the effectiveness of the warning label and the practices of cigarette advertising and promotions, with "recommendations for legislation that are deemed appropriate."[7]

The same year Congress acted to regulate the tobacco industry, it wrote the Cigarette Advertising Code of 1965, which promised to stop pitching ads to young people under the age of 21 in comic books, newspaper sections with comics, and college publications. The industry code also promised to use models who were at least 25 years old.

After the passage of the 1965 advertising and labeling act, the FTC developed a machine system for measuring tar and nicotine yield of cigarettes and provided, in its annual report to Congress, the yields of tar and nicotine of the most popular brands. The system was modified in 1981 to include carbon monoxide. Cigarette manufacturers were required to disclose tar and nicotine yields of their brands in advertisements.

In its first report to Congress, the FTC recommended extending the health warning to cigarette advertising and strengthening the wording. The subsequent Public Health Cigarette Smoking Act of 1969 strengthened the package warning label to read: "The Surgeon General Has Determined That Cigarette Smoking Is Hazardous to Your Health." Again, the FTC was temporarily restricted from issuing regulations that would require a health warning in cigarette advertising.

During the 1960s, tobacco companies gave financial support to professional sports teams. In 1963 R. J. Reynolds Tobacco Company sponsored eight different baseball teams, and the American Tobacco Company sponsored six more. Philip Morris sponsored National Football League games on CBS, Brown & Williamson Tobacco Corporation sponsored football bowl games, and Lorillard was a sponsor of the 1964 Olympics. Angry that the airwaves were saturated with an endless barrage of commercials telling children and teens that cigarette smoking was a glamorous and pleasant habit with no health risks, the Federal Communications Commission (FCC) recommended and Congress acted to ban all cigarette advertising from television and radio effective January 2, 1971.

After the broadcast ban, tobacco companies poured hundreds of millions of advertising dollars into billboards that associated smoking with success, athletics, social acceptance, youth, glamour, thinness, and healthy outdoor fun. Tobacco companies also poured money into the print media. In 1970, before the TV/radio ban, tobacco companies spent $50 million on magazine advertising; in 1979 the figure rose to more than $257 million.[8]

In 1968 Philip Morris introduced Virginia Slims, the first cigarette brand created specifically for women, and launched the "You've come a long way, baby" marketing campaign. The slogan appealed to many women who were moving into more assertive, independent roles. Magazine ads contrasted the old social order with the new by belittling dated restrictions on women. After cigarette ads were banned from the broadcast media effective January 2, 1971, tobacco companies shifted their advertising to women's magazines. Virginia Slims and other cigarette advertising flooded women's magazines, newspapers, and Sunday supplements. By 1979 cigarettes were the most advertised product in some women's magazines, with as many as 20 ads in a single issue. Virginia Slims prompted an explosion of feminine cigarettes, with brand names like Eve, Capri, Misty, and others. Tobacco companies manufactured cigarettes that were long and thin; brand names like Superslims, Newport Stripes, and Misty 120's (120 pounds was considered by some to be an ideal weight for women) associated cigarettes with slimness. In 2009 the Campaign for Tobacco-Free Kids released a report, *Deadly in Pink: Big Tobacco Steps Up Its Targeting of Women and Girls*. It stated: "During the 1970s, tobacco companies responded to women's growing concerns about the health risks of smoking by targeting them with ads implying that 'light' and 'low-tar' cigarettes were safer, despite knowing this was not the case."[9]

Cigarette makers also poured money into new promotions. In 1971 Philip Morris launched a series of tennis matches called the Virginia Slims Invitational. Also in 1971 RJR Nabisco's Winston Cup auto racing began. Philip Morris sponsored the Marlboro Grand Prix, Marlboro 500, Marlboro Challenge, and Laguna Seca Marlboro Motorcycle Grand Prix. Television cameras picked up cigarette logos on stock cars, stadium billboards, and clothing carrying tobacco ads.[10]

In late 1971 the FTC announced its plan to file complaints against cigarette companies because they failed to warn consumers in their advertising that smoking was dangerous to their health. To head off government regulation, the tobacco industry volunteered to disclose the results of FTC testing in their ads. The consent order of 1972 between tobacco companies and the FTC required that all cigarette advertising in newspapers and magazines and on billboards "clearly and conspicuously" display the same health warning required by Congress for cigarette packages.[11]

In 1981 the FTC sent a staff report to Congress that concluded that the warning appearing on cigarette packages and in advertisements had become overexposed, "worn out," too abstract, and was no longer effective. The report recommended changing the shape of the warning and increasing its size as well as replacing the existing single warning with a rotational system of warnings.[12]

The 1981 FTC staff report eventually helped pass the Comprehensive Smoking Education Act of 1984 signed by President Ronald Regan. It replaced the previous health warning on cigarette packages and ads with four rotating strongly worded health warnings that took effect October 12, 1985:

> SURGEON GENERAL'S WARNING: Smoking Causes Lung Cancer, Heart Disease, Emphysema, and May Complicate Pregnancy
> SURGEON GENERAL'S WARNING: Quitting Smoking Now Greatly Reduces Serious Risks to Your Health
> SURGEON GENERAL'S WARNING: Smoking by Pregnant Women May Result in Fetal Injury, Premature Birth, and Low Birth Weight
> SURGEON GENERAL'S WARNING: Cigarette Smoke Contains Carbon Monoxide

Two years later, in 1986, Congress passed the Comprehensive Smokeless Tobacco Health Education Act. Tobacco-sponsored sporting events put smokeless tobacco on television despite the broadcast ban, so one provision called for banning radio and television advertising, effective August 27, 1986. Another provision mandated health warning labels on all smokeless tobacco products and advertisements, except for outdoor billboards, effective February 27, 1987:

> WARNING: This Product May Cause Mouth Cancer
> WARNING: This Product May Cause Gum Disease and Result in Tooth Loss
> WARNING: This Product Is Not a Safe Alternative to Cigarette Smoking

In 1991 the FTC took action against the Pinkerton Tobacco Company, makers of Red Man chewing tobacco. The FTC charged the tobacco company with violating the 1986 Smokeless Tobacco Act, which prohibited television advertising of smokeless tobacco. Pinkerton, which sponsored televised truck and tractor-pull events known as the Red Man Series, agreed to stop the display of the Red Man brand name on banners, billboards, clothing, and vehicles and only use the Red Man as part of the event's title if it did not resemble the Red Man logo.

Besides billboard advertising and sports events sponsorship, cigarette makers poured millions into point-of-purchase ads and displays in drugstores, supermarkets, gas stations, and bowling alleys. Other promotions included free cigarette samples or smokeless tobacco products and gifts (T-shirts, coffee mugs, lighters, ash trays, key chains) and catalog merchandise in exchange for coupons from cigarette packs. Cigarette advertising expenditures for catalog promotions quadrupled from $184 to $756 million between 1991 and 1993.[13]

In the early 1990s, one of the most controversial issues came before the FTC. Surgeon General Antonia Novello, the American Medical Association, and several health groups requested that the FTC take action against the R. J. Reynolds cartoon character Old Joe Camel and order Reynolds to stop using it in its cigarette advertising, promotion, and marketing. They argued that Camel cigarette sales to children spiked after the introduction of Joe Camel in 1988, increasing more dramatically than sales to adults.

In 1993 the FTC staff recommended that the agency seek an outright ban on the Joe Camel advertising campaign. In 1994 after reviewing tens of thousands of pages of Reynolds' documents, the agency found no grounds for action and voted not to pursue the complaint that the company's advertising was aimed at children. In 1996, however, the agency reopened its investigation of Reynolds' advertising practices after receiving a bipartisan petition from 67 members of the House of Representatives and one from 7 senators arguing that the Joe Camel campaign was in part responsible for an alarming increase in smoking among teenagers.

On May 28, 1997, the FTC filed an unfair advertising complaint against the R. J. Reynolds Tobacco Company alleging that its Joe Camel advertising campaign was illegally aimed at minors and tried to entice youngsters to smoke Camels. This was the first time the FTC accused the tobacco industry of aiming its products at minors. The Commission voted 3–2 in favor of filing the complaint, largely on the strength of new evidence that was not available in 1994 when the FTC decided not to act. The Food and Drug Administration (FDA) supplied the FTC with many of the documents it acquired through its own investigation of tobacco companies. Not all the commissioners were on board. Roscoe B. Starek III, one of the two dissenting commissioners, wrote in the May 28 FTC press release that "intuition and concern for children's health are not the equivalent of—and should not be substituted for—evidence sufficient to find reason to believe that there is a likely causal connection between the Joe Camel advertising campaign and smoking by children."

In the complaint filed with an administrative judge within the FTC, the agency said the campaign violated federal law that prohibited marketing of cigarettes to children. The campaign, the complaint said, was so successful that Camel's market share among kids exceeded its share among adults.

Before the Joe Camel campaign began in 1987, Camel's share of the youth smoking market was less than 3 percent. In two years, its share jumped to almost 9 percent, and by 1993 the brand was used by 13.2 percent of minors.[14]

R. J. Reynolds Tobacco denounced the FTC complaint. In a written statement, the tobacco company denied that it focused on underage smokers and said that it had a First Amendment right to advertise its products in an appealing way. On July 10, 1997, without any mention of the FTC, Reynolds announced it would phase out the cartoon camel character in domestic advertising and replace it with a stylized version of Camel cigarettes' original camel trademark that has appeared on Camel cigarette packs since the brand's introduction as the first nationally advertised cigarette in 1913. The company insisted dropping the cartoon camel was a marketing decision. Joe Camel and his camel buddies disappeared from billboards, print advertisements, display signs, and door store stickers, although they continued to appear in advertising overseas.

A combination of factors in the 1990s affected the advertising and marketing practices of tobacco companies. These included the impact of advertising campaigns like R. J. Reynolds Tobacco Company's Old Joe Camel on children and teens, the increase in tobacco use by children and teens, and the emergence of secret tobacco documents that showed how the tobacco companies studied the smoking habits of teens and looked for ways to attract young smokers. Furthermore, the 1994 series of nationally landmark televised congressional hearings on tobacco industry practices examined the possibility of providing the FDA with regulatory authority over tobacco products, including a proposal to classify nicotine in tobacco as a drug. David Kessler, FDA commissioner, proposed policies centering on preventing children from becoming addicted to cigarettes because 80 percent of smokers begin regular use before the age of 18. Referring to tobacco use by children as a "pediatric disease," Kessler proposed regulations to restrict smoking ads that appealed to minors, restrictions on billboards near schools and playgrounds, restrictions on promotional items aimed at children, and a ban on free samples and "kiddie packs" of small numbers of cigarettes.

As soon as the FDA issued its rules on tobacco, the industry sued in a North Carolina district court, arguing that only Congress had authority to regulate tobacco. In 1997 Judge William L. Osteen, Sr., ruled that the FDA could "impose access restrictions and labeling requirements but that the agency did not have authority to limit advertising to youth."[15] The decision was appealed by both sides to the U.S. Circuit Court of Appeals for the Fourth Circuit, which struck down the FDA rules in June 1998.

Several months later, 46 states and the tobacco industry settled tobac-co-related lawsuits for $246 billion to recover tobacco-related health care costs, joining 4 states—Mississippi, Texas, Florida, and Minnesota—that had reached earlier, individual settlements. In the Master Settlement Act (MSA) of 1998, the cigarette manufacturers agreed to new limits for the advertising, marketing, and promotion of cigarettes. The MSA prohib-ited tobacco advertising that targets people younger than 18; eliminated cartoons in cigarette advertising and outdoor, billboard, and public tran-sit advertising of cigarettes; and banned cigarette brand names on cloth-ing. In the late 1990s, tobacco companies, adapting to restrictions, lined up new ways to advertise and market their products from Internet sites to new packaging to direct mail and publishing magazines like *Marlboro Unlimited*. Annual tobacco marketing expenditures grew from $6.9 billion in 1998 to $13.4 billion in 2005, the most recent year for which the FTC has reported such data.[16] The five major U.S. smokeless tobacco manu-facturers spent $250.8 million of the expenditures on smokeless tobacco advertising and promotion in 2005. The smokeless tobacco industry spent $15.75 million on sports and sporting events in 2005.[17]

According to the *2007 National Survey on Drug Use and Health,* each day in the United States, approximately 3,600 young people between the ages of 12 and 17 years initiate cigarette smoking, and an estimated 1,100 young people become daily cigarette smokers.[18] Nationally, an estimated 4 percent of all middle school students were current smokeless tobacco users in 2006, with estimates slightly higher for males (5%) than for fe-males (3%).[19] An estimated 13 percent of males in high school were current smokeless tobacco users in 2007.[20] Forty-eight percent of smokers aged 12 to 17 prefer Marlboro, followed by Newport (23%) and Camel (10%). These are the brands most heavily advertised in the United States.[21]

If current youth tobacco use trends continue, the Campaign for Tobacco-Free Kids calculates that one-third of the youngsters will die prematurely from tobacco-related diseases. Since nearly all first-time tobacco use oc-curs before high school graduation, if youngsters are kept smoke free, they will not risk their health as adults.[22]

According to the Campaign for Tobacco-Free Kids, tobacco companies pursue activities designed to attract youths to begin and continue smok-ing. These activities include the following: advertising in youth-oriented publications; using imagery and messages that appeal to teenagers; mar-keting in convenience stores and other places that teens frequent; pricing products to attract youths; increasing marketing at point-of-sale locations with promotions, self-service displays, and other materials; and sponsor-ing sporting and entertainment events, many of which are televised or otherwise broadcast and draw large youth audiences.[23] A poll of teens and adults conducted for Kick Butts Day 2008 revealed that teens were almost twice as likely as adults to remember tobacco advertising in the last two weeks, that they felt targeted by tobacco companies, and that it remained easy for them to buy tobacco products.[24]

The issue of marketing tobacco in retail outlets is important because point-of-purchase advertising attracts the attention of teens, three out of four of whom visit convenience stores at least once a week. A study in the May 2007 issue of *Archives of Pediatrics and Adolescent Medicine* found that retail cigarette advertising and promotions increased the likelihood that youth would start smoking and move from experimenting to regular smoking.[25] Again, once teens start smoking and chewing, the greater their risks of developing life-threatening diseases as adults.

Women have also been targeted in tobacco marketing, and tobacco companies still produce brands specifically for women. In 2007 and 2008 the nation's two largest tobacco companies—Philip Morris USA and R. J. Reynolds—launched new marketing campaigns that depict cigarette smoking as feminine and fashionable, rather than the harmful. In *Deadly in Pink: Big Tobacco Steps Up Its Targeting of Women and Girls,* a report by the Campaign for Tobacco-Free Kids, the American Heart Association, the American Lung Association, the Robert Wood Johnson Foundation, and the American Cancer Society Cancer Action Network, the organizations stated that in October of 2008 "Philip Morris USA announced a makeover of its Virginia Slims brand into 'purse packs,' small, rectangular cigarette packs that contain 'superslim' cigarettes. Available in mauve and teal and half the size of regular cigarette packs, the sleek 'purse packs' resemble packages of cosmetics" and fit in small purses. Philip Morris manufactured the cigarettes in "'Superslims Lights' and 'Superslims Ultra Lights' versions, continuing the tobacco industry's history of associating smoking with slimness and weight control and of appealing to women's health concerns with misleading claims such as 'light' and 'low-tar.'" In January 2007 the same report noted that R. J. Reynolds manufactured Camel No. 9, "packaged in shiny black boxes with hot pink and teal borders. The name evokes famous Chanel perfumes, and magazine advertising featured flowery imagery and vintage fashion. The ads carried slogans including 'Light and luscious' and 'Now available in stiletto,' the latter for a thin version of the cigarette pitched to 'the most fashion forward woman.'" Ads for Camel No. 9 ran in *Vogue, Glamour, Cosmopolitan, Marie Claire, InStyle,* and other magazines popular with women and teen girls. Promotional giveaways included "flavored lip balm, cell phone jewelry, tiny purses and wristbands, all in hot pink."[26]

The report further stated that the new marketing campaigns targeting women and girls can have a "devastating impact on women's health." The latest U.S. cancer statistics, released in December 2008, showed that lung cancer death rates are decreasing for men, the overall cancer death rates are decreasing for both men and women, but lung cancer death rates have not declined for women. Lung cancer is the leading cancer killer of women, surpassing breast cancer in 1987. Smoking puts women and teen girls at greater risk of getting a wide range of deadly diseases, including heart attacks, strokes, emphysema, and numerous cancers. According to the Campaign for Tobacco-Free Kids, smoking is the leading cause of preventable death among women, killing more than 170,000 women in the United States each year. In addition to the well-known risk of lung cancer, women who smoke increase their risk of coronary heart disease, which is "the overall leading cause of death among both women and men." More women than men now die from chronic obstructive pulmonary disease (bronchitis and emphysema), which is caused primarily by smoking and has become "the fourth leading cause of death in the U.S."[27]

Besides marketing to women, tobacco companies have marketed cigarettes to African Americans, Asian Americans, and Hispanic/Latino communities. Marketing toward Hispanics and American Indians/Alaska Natives has included advertising and promotion of cigarette brands with names such as Rio, Dorado, and American Spirit, and the tobacco industry has sponsored Tet festivals and activities related to Asian American Heritage Month. Research in 1998 showed that three African American publications, *Ebony, Jet,* and *Essence,* received proportionately higher revenues from tobacco companies than mainstream publications did.[28]

Besides cigarette smoking and chew, cigar use (which includes cigarillos, little cigars the size of cigarettes) began to rise in the United States around 1992. Cigar and other magazines, shops, bars, clubs, and accessories increased the visibility of cigar consumption and normalized its use.

According to John Slade's 1998 piece about the marketing and promotion of cigars, most advertising for cigars appears in magazines. In some advertisements, cigars are presented as "lavish, yet affordable luxuries," while others depict the history and tradition of cigar making. Dr. Slade wrote: "Many ads create a personal link with the company owners, founders, or the artisans and the farmers who create the product and its raw material. Some ads show movie, TV stars, supermodels, famous athletes, and other prominent people, who have been paid to pose, smoking cigars."[29]

Cigars have been aimed at the public through promotional activities. The Slade study pointed out that "the cigar resurgence in the United States has been closely associated with the lifestyle magazine *Cigar Aficionado,* published by Marvin R. Shanken" in the fall of 1992. The magazine's success led to *Smoke,* another tobacco lifestyle magazine, launched in 1996 by Lockwood, a tobacco trade publisher. Also available as an online magazine, *Smoke* keeps in touch with cigar and pipe smokers through Twitter, a social network. *CigarLife—The Internet Cigar Magazine* also promote cigar culture to readers through its Web site. Smoking clubs, bars, and trendy restaurants that provide areas for cigar-smoking patrons sprang up in many metropolitan communities in the mid-1990s. Social clubs organized around cigars began to appear on a number of college campuses.[30]

Cigars have been featured in upscale catalogs and on the World Wide Web. The manufacturer-operated sites provide information and images about specific brands and link customers with retailers who carry their products. Discussion groups, news groups, and blogs revolve around cigars. The cigar craze has fueled the manufacture of cigar accessories including lighters, cutters, ashtrays, and humidors; books; videos; cigar label lithographs and paintings; and clothing. Cigars are also common props in fashion photography.

In the 1990s cigar smokers were mainly male, between the ages of 35 and 64, white, middle class, and well educated. Studies in 2006 showed that new cigar users were teenagers and young adult males (18 to 24). According to a 2006 CDC survey, the level of cigar use among teens was higher than that of spit tobacco use. About 4 percent of teens in middle school grades six through eight had smoked a cigar in the past month. A 2007 CDC survey showed that more than 13 percent of high school students became current cigar smokers in 2007, with estimates higher for males (19%) than for females (8%). After cigarette smoking, cigar smoking became the second most popular form of tobacco used by teens in the United States overall. But in some states, more boys smoked cigars than cigarettes. Much of the surge was due to little cigars.[31]

Cigar use among college students is rapidly increasing. The 1999 College Alcohol Survey conducted by the Harvard School of Public Health revealed that of the among 14,000 randomly selected students, 37 percent smoked cigars. The College Alcohol Survey was the first to consider both cigarette and noncigarette tobacco use by college students. Nancy Rigotti, the lead author of the College Alcohol Survey and an associate professor at the Harvard Medical School, said college students were risking a lifetime of nicotine addiction. According to Dr. Rigotti, "Young people who are smoking cigars may not think that they are at risk of getting hooked, but they are. Repeated exposure to any tobacco product puts students at increased danger of becoming addicted to nicotine."[32]

Part of the resurgence of cigars in the 1990s was due to the widespread but mistaken belief that cigars were less dangerous or addicting than cigarettes. At the time, cigars were not required to carry labels with health warnings on advertising, except in California and Massachusetts. That changed in late June 2000 when a consent decree was signed by seven of the largest makers of premium cigars and cigarillos. The consent degree required warnings to appear on displays, and they had to be placed on various types of advertising, such as magazines, point-of-purchase displays, T-shirts, hats, humidors, and catalogs.

Under the agreement, which took effect in February of 2001, virtually every cigar package, advertisement, promotion, and piece of merchandise was required to clearly display one of the following warnings on a rotating basis:

SURGEON GENERAL WARNING: Cigar Smoking Can Cause Cancers of the Mouth and Throat, Even if You Do Not Inhale
SURGEON GENERAL WARNING: Cigar Smoking Can Cause Lung Cancer and Heart Disease
SURGEON GENERAL WARNING: Tobacco Use Increases the Risk of Infertility, Stillbirth and Low Birth Weight
SURGEON GENERAL WARNING: Cigars Are Not a Safe Alternative to Cigarettes
SURGEON GENERAL WARNING: Tobacco Smoke Increases the Risk of Lung Cancer and Heart Disease, Even in Nonsmokers

The landmark agreement followed the release of a report in 1998 by the National Cancer Institute detailing the health risks of cigar smoking. The report analyzed years of medical and survey data, arguing that people who smoke just cigars have a significantly higher risk of smoking-related death than those who never smoked. Cigars, while not deeply inhaled like cigarettes, can cause cancer of the lung, oral cavity, larynx, and esophagus.

The impact of tobacco advertising on health was addressed by Judge Gladys Kessler of the Federal District Court. On August 17, 2006, Judge Kessler found the companies violated civil racketeering laws and defrauded the American people by lying for decades about the health risks of smoking. In her 1,683-page final opinion, Judge Kessler detailed the tobacco companies' unlawful activity and the consequences for our nation's health over more than 50 years, saying that the defendants marketed and sold their lethal products with zeal, with deception, with a single-minded focus on their financial success, and without regard for the human tragedy or social costs that success exacted.[33]

PART II

Controversies and Issues

CHAPTER 6

Tobacco Excise Taxation and Health Policy

Historically, the United States and other governments have taxed tobacco to generate revenues. Over the past few decades, however, taxing tobacco products has been used as a strategy to prevent initiation of using tobacco by teens, reduce cigarette consumption, increase the number of smokers who quit, and improve public health.

In the United States, tobacco is taxed by federal, state, and local governments. In a 1993 report by the Institute of Medicine, a chapter devoted to taxation of tobacco in the United States explained that "tobacco products are taxed in two ways: the unit tax, which is based on a constant nominal rate per unit (that is, per pack of cigarettes), and the ad valorem tax, which is based on a constant fraction of either wholesale or retail price." At the time, federal taxes on cigarettes, small cigars, and smokeless tobacco products were unit taxes; federal taxes on large cigars were ad valorem taxes.[1]

In 2009 cigarettes and other tobacco products continue to be taxed by federal, state, and local governments, including excise taxes, which are levied per unit (per pack of 20 cigarettes). A May 2009 *MMWR Weekly* explained that "federal and state excise tax rates are set by legislation, are contained in federal and state statutes, and typically are collected before the point of sale (i.e., from manufacturers, wholesalers, or distributors), as denoted by a tax stamp."[2] In 2008 the Tax Foundation reported that 12 states (Alabama, Arizona, Connecticut, Delaware, Iowa, Kentucky, Montana, New Jersey, North Dakota, Utah, Vermont, and Wisconsin) chose to tax smokeless tobacco products with the unit tax, which taxes them based on weight, rather than as a percent of their wholesale price.[3]

TOBACCO TAXATION AT THE FEDERAL LEVEL

To the federal government, tobacco has been a financial asset. It was one of the first consumer goods to be taxed in North America. The federal government began to tax tobacco products in 1794, when Alexander Hamilton's proposed to Congress a bill with the first federal excise tax on refined sugar, tobacco, and snuff, much to the dismay of snuff manufacturers. The proposal engendered one of the first tax debates in the U.S. Congress over taxing manufactured tobacco and snuff, not leaf tobacco. Congress took the position that since snuff was a fad for the vain, it should be taxed, while ordinary people who smoked a pipe or chewed should not be burdened. During the debate on this bill, James Madison delivered the opinion opposing a tax on tobacco:

> As to the subject before the House, it was proper to choose taxes the least unequal. Tobacco excise was a burden the most unequal. It fell upon the poor, upon sailors, day laborers, and other people of these classes, while the rich will often escape it. Much has been said about the taxing of luxury. The pleasures of life consisted in a series of innocent gratifications, and he felt no satisfaction in the prospect of their being squeezed. Sumptuary laws had never, he believed, answered any good purpose.[4]

In 1794 Congress compromised with a tax on snuff and did not tax chew and pipe tobacco. In 1796 the tax was repealed.

Following the War of 1812, a war-cost tax was imposed on all manufactured tobacco, but that, too, was repealed after only 10 months. Tobacco was taxed during the Civil War. The federal government needed revenue. On July 1, 1862, a tax was imposed on cigars for the first time. In 1864 it levied the first federal tax on cigarettes as well as other tobacco products as a means of raising revenue for the Union war effort. In its first year of enforcement the tax netted only $15,000. Taxes were increased and then, when producers and consumers opposed the taxes, they were repealed. Even the Confederacy wanted to levy a tax-in-kind on tobacco crops but was precluded from doing so by the inspection system, which required the inspector to deliver the full amount of tobacco specified in the warehouse receipt.

Taxes were raised again in 1865, 1866, and 1875. A temporary reduction followed, until the end of the 19th century when the Spanish-American War necessitated a steep increase on cigarettes as a way of financing the war. Taxes jumped from 50¢ to $1 per thousand cigarettes in 1897 and to $1.50 in 1898.

During the first half of the 20th century, federal taxes were increased to help finance U.S. military involvement in various wars. Another increase took place on November 1, 1951, during the Korean War. The tax was increased from 7¢ to 8¢ per pack and remained at that level for the next 30 years. In 1983 the federal tax on cigarettes doubled to 16¢ per pack. Taxes were raised to deal with the increasing federal budget deficit. In 1991 the federal taxes on cigarettes were increased to 20¢ per pack; in 1993 these taxes rose to 24¢; in 2000 to 34¢; and in 2002 to 39¢, mandated by the Balanced Budget Act of 1997. Table 6.1 shows increases in the federal tax rate from 1976 to 2002

Table 6.1 National cigarette tax trends.

Year	Federal tax rate per pack (cents)	Federal revenues (millions)[1]	Consumption (millions of packs)	Percent change in consumption
1976	8.0	$2,434.8	30,955.9	NA
1977	8.0	$2,279.2	29,812.8	−3.7
1978	8.0	$2,374.1	30,477.3	2.2
1979	8.0	$2,356.1	30,755.9	0.9
1980	8.0	$2,604.4	30,288.3	−1.5
1981	8.0	$2,488.2	31,666.4	4.6
1982	8.0	$2,496.1	31,611.8	−0.2
1983	8.0/16.0[2]	$3,424.4	29,991.1	−5.1
1984	16.0	$4,749.2	29,837.0	−0.5
1985	16.0	$4,442.5	29,770.9	−0.2
1986	16.0	$4,430.8	29,051.2	−2.4
1987	16.0	$4,752.3	28,965.5	−0.3
1988	16.0	$4,466.5	27,790.8	−4.1
1989	16.0	$4,237.8	26,487.5	−4.7
1990	16.0	$4,069.8	25,436.5	−4.0
1991	16.0/20.0[2]	$4,754.6	25,376.5	−0.2
1992	20.0	$5,043.0	25,215.7	−0.6
1993	20.0/24.0[2]	$5,528.0	24,730.1	−1.9
1994	24.0	$5,599.5	23,350.0	−5.6
1995	24.0	$5,716.8	23,818.0	2.0
1996	24.0	$5,679.1	23,660.0	−0.7
1997	24.0	$5,743.4	23,929.2	1.1
1998	24.0	$5,559.2	23,163.4	−3.2
1999	24.0	$5,193.1	21,637.9	−6.6
2000	24.0/34.0[2]	$6,230.3	21,325.0	−1.4
2001	34.0	$7,071.8	21,250.0	−0.4
2002	39.0	NA	NA	NA
Annual average change 1976–2001		4.4%	−1.5%	

[1] Based on year ending June 30.

[2] Rate changed during year.

Source: Orzechowski and Walker, *The Tax Burden on Tobacco: Historical Compilation,* vol. 39 (Arlington, Va.: Authors, 2004).

as well as federal revenues, consumption rates, and the percent change in consumption.

On February 4, 2009, President Barack Obama signed into law the Children's Health Insurance Program Reauthorization Act of 2009 (Public Law 111-3), which increased the federal excise tax by 62¢, the single largest federal tobacco tax hike in history. It took effect April 1, 2009, raising the federal excise tax on a cigarette pack to $1.01. There were also increases to the federal excise tax on other tobacco products.

TOBACCO TAXATION AT STATE AND LOCAL LEVELS

To state governments, tobacco is a financial asset. All 50 states have enacted tax laws affecting cigarettes. Iowa led the way when, in 1921, it became the first state to impose an excise tax on cigarettes, followed in 1923 by Georgia, South Carolina, South Dakota, and Utah. By the end of the 1920s, 6 additional states had enacted cigarette excise tax laws. In the 1940s more than half the states levied taxes on cigarettes. In 1969 North Carolina became the last state to impose an excise tax on cigarettes.

Like the federal government, state taxes on cigarettes have represented attempts to raise revenues rather than lower smoking rates. In 1985, however, Minnesota enacted the first state legislation to use cigarette taxes as a means of discouraging tobacco use. It earmarked a portion of the state cigarette excise tax to support antismoking programs. Other states like California (1988), Massachusetts (1992), and Arizona (1995) have also used increases in cigarette taxes to fund antismoking campaigns and discourage people from smoking. Table 6.2 shows the wide range in state taxes on cigarette packs from $0.07 in South Carolina and $0.17 in Missouri to $2.75 in New York and $2.575 in New Jersey.

In addition to state taxes, some cities and counties have levied taxes on cigarettes as well as noncigarette tobacco products Nationwide, more than 500 local governments in 8 states levy cigarette taxes, mainly in Alabama, Missouri, and Virginia.[5] In Chicago, smokers pay a 68¢ city tax and a $2 Cook County tax as well as state and federal taxes. New York City has imposed a $1.50 cigarette tax.

According to the Institute of Medicine report *Growing Up Tobacco Free,* "Differences in cigarette tax rates among states and localities can create problems in the enforcement of tax laws. There are a variety of tax evasion strategies, including casual smuggling (people buying cigarettes in neighboring states with lower taxes)," buying cigarettes "through tax-free outlets such as military stores and American Indian reservations, commercial smuggling for resale, and illegal diversion of cigarettes within the distribution system by forging tax stamps and underreporting."[6]

Table 6.2 Cigarette federal and state taxes per pack, 2009.

State	State tax	Federal tax	Combined
Alabama	$0.425	$1.0066	$1.43
Alaska	$2.000	$1.0066	$3.01
Arizona	$2.000	$1.0066	$3.01
Arkansas	$1.150	$1.0066	$2.16
California	$0.870	$1.0066	$1.88
Colorado	$0.840	$1.0066	$1.85
Connecticut	$2.000	$1.0066	$3.01
Delaware	$1.150	$1.0066	$2.16
District of Columbia	$2.000	$1.0066	$3.01
Florida	$0.339	$1.0066	$1.35
Georgia	$0.370	$1.0066	$1.38
Hawaii	$2.000	$1.0066	$3.01
Idaho	$0.570	$1.0066	$1.58
Illinois	$0.980	$1.0066	$1.99
Indiana	$0.995	$1.0066	$2.00
Iowa	$1.360	$1.0066	$2.37
Kansas	$0.790	$1.0066	$1.80
Kentucky	$0.600	$1.0066	$1.61
Louisiana	$0.360	$1.0066	$1.37
Maine	$2.000	$1.0066	$3.01
Maryland	$2.000	$1.0066	$3.01
Massachusetts	$2.510	$1.0066	$3.52
Michigan	$2.000	$1.0066	$3.01
Minnesota	$1.504	$1.0066	$2.51
Mississippi	$0.180	$1.0066	$1.19
Missouri	$0.170	$1.0066	$1.18
Montana	$1.700	$1.0066	$2.71
Nebraska	$0.640	$1.0066	$1.65
Nevada	$0.800	$1.0066	$1.81
New Hampshire	$1.330	$1.0066	$2.34
New Jersey	$2.575	$1.0066	$3.58
New Mexico	$0.910	$1.0066	$1.92
New York	$2.750	$1.0066	$3.76
North Carolina	$0.350	$1.0066	$1.36
North Dakota	$0.440	$1.0066	$1.45
Ohio	$1.250	$1.0066	$2.26
Oklahoma	$1.030	$1.0066	$2.04
Oregon	$1.180	$1.0066	$2.19
Pennsylvania	$1.350	$1.0066	$2.36
Puerto Rico	$1.230	$1.0066	$2.24
Rhode Island	$2.460	$1.0066	$3.47

(Continued)

Table 6.2 *Continued*

State	State tax	Federal tax	Combined
South Carolina	$0.070	$1.0066	$1.08
South Dakota	$1.530	$1.0066	$2.54
Tennessee	$0.620	$1.0066	$1.63
Texas	$1.410	$1.0066	$2.42
Utah	$0.695	$1.0066	$1.70
Vermont	$1.990	$1.0066	$3.00
Virginia	$0.300	$1.0066	$1.31
Washington	$2.025	$1.0066	$3.03
West Virginia	$0.550	$1.0066	$1.56
Wisconsin	$1.770	$1.0066	$2.78
Wyoming	$0.600	$1.0066	$1.61

FEDERAL EXCISE TAXES ON TOBACCO PRODUCTS AND IMPACT ON LOW-INCOME AND YOUTH POPULATIONS

Today, the public health community, physicians, and tobacco-free advocates consider pricing policy on tobacco products one of the most important health policy strategies, especially in regard to two populations: lower-income people and young people. The policy has been a subject of intense debate since the early 1970s.

In March 1973 Sen. Frank Moss (D-UT) made a statement about federal excise taxes, fixed at 8¢ a pack for the preceding 22 years. While generally supportive of an increase in taxes on cigarettes, his statement showed his concern that the impact of a federal excise tax on the poor would be "somewhat regressive." In simple terms, a regressive tax imposes a greater burden (relative to resources) on the poor than on the wealthy:

> Any increase in cigarette taxes, regardless of form, will be somewhat regressive. Although the middle class and the wealthy spend more on tobacco than the poor, this expenditure is a smaller proportion of their income. However, a tar and nicotine tax should be less regressive than a customary flat rate tax: the poor consumer can escape the tax entirely by switching to low tar brands, and if the tax does force him to switch, the net result of health cost savings might even prove quite progressive.[7]

The first surgeon general's report in 1964 determined that smoking was more prevalent among lower- or working-class people, but less prevalent among the unemployed poor. National surveys over the years have continued to show a consistent pattern of higher smoking rates among lower-socioeconomic populations. However, in 2007, the *Morbidity and*

Mortality Weekly Report, published by the Centers for Disease Control and Prevention, reported that smoking among adults whose incomes were below the poverty line was 28.8 percent compared to 2 to 3 percent for people whose incomes were at or above the poverty line. Frank Lester, spokesperson for Reynolds American, said that the federal increase would "fall on those who can least afford it." He said one in four smokers live at or below the poverty line.[8]

Since the poor smoke proportionately more than other population groups, they are more greatly affected by health issues related to tobacco use. It is also known that cancers caused by smoking are higher in lower-income populations and that the related medical costs disproportionately impact poorer people.[9]

In 1993 the Institute of Medicine, chartered in 1970 by the National Academy of Sciences to engage in scientific and engineering research for the general welfare, enlisted experts to look at a range of public health policy issues. A committee was put together to undertake an 18-month study on preventing nicotine dependence among children and youth. The committee's 1994 report, *Growing Up Tobacco Free,* found that "the regressiveness of tobacco taxes is a valid concern. On the other hand, the burden of illness and death caused by tobacco is borne to a greater extent by the poor. For the poor as a class the hardship imposed by steep increases in tobacco prices produced by higher tobacco taxes is arguably outweighed by the reduction in suffering and premature death resulting from lower consumption of tobacco. Moreover, revenues generated through higher tobacco taxes could be earmarked for health care for the indigent thus offsetting the regressivity of tobacco taxes." The Institute of Medicine report also found that "evidence ... lead[s] the Committee to the conclusion that pricing policy is perhaps the single most important element of an overall comprehensive strategy to reduce tobacco use, and particularly to reduce use among children and youth."[10]

In October 2007 the Campaign for Tobacco-Free Kids argued that "those who stop smoking in response to cigarette tax increases greatly improve their own health, which significantly reduces health costs. Smokers die younger than nonsmokers, but because of their higher rates of illness and disability they still have substantially higher annual and lifetime health care costs."[11] According to the Campaign for Tobacco-Free Kids, the health of low-income people who smoke and their families is actually improved by increases in taxes, which, in turn reduces their health care costs. Because poor or low-income people are especially sensitive to price increases, they are also more likely not to start smoking due to the higher costs of tobacco products, or they may quit or reduce their tobacco consumption at a higher rate than other population groups. In addition, the amount of secondhand smoke impacting family members and friends is reduced, thus positively impacting their health.[12]

As a result of quitting or cutting back on smoking, low-income people have additional income available to spend. According to Eric Lindblom's report on misleading and inaccurate cigarette company arguments against state cigarette tax increases, published by the campaign for Tobacco-Free Kids, "Smokers who quit or cut back because of a tax increase not only stop paying any cigarette taxes but also stop spending any of the other amounts they previously paid for cigarettes. Calculating the monetary savings for a pack-a-day smoker (or a two packs-a-day smoker who cuts back to one pack) is quite revealing with average savings ranging from $1,000 to $2,500 per year, depending on the state."[13] It can be argued that the financial benefit in terms of increased availability of money to poor individuals who quit smoking and to their families is significant.[14]

According to Eric Lindblom's piece "Federal Tax Increases Will Benefit Lower-Income Households," published by the Campaign for Tobacco-Free Kids, lower-income youth are especially sensitive to cost of tobacco products, and higher prices might deter teens from starting more so than those in higher income populations: "Cigarette tax increases offer one of the best ways to help low income families that suffer from direct and secondhand smoking to escape from the smoking-caused health risks, disease, and related cost, and lower income smokers and families will be much more likely to have those harms and costs eliminated or reduced by a cigarette tax increase than families with higher incomes."[15]

According to the Campaign for Tobacco-Free Kids, in poll after poll, lower-income Americans (along with all other Americans) strongly support higher tobacco product taxes. A 2007 nationwide survey found that voters with yearly incomes less than $30,000 supported a 75¢ increase in the federal cigarette tax nearly two-to-one.[16]

> Differences of opinion exist on what the ultimate impact will be on low income or poor people after excise taxes on cigarettes and other tobacco products were increased after April 1, 2009. Studies have shown that raising taxes on cigarettes reduces consumption among both adults and youth.[17] Price increases impact prevalence of smoking as well. Studies have also shown that adolescents are more likely than adults to be impacted by the price of cigarettes in terms of reducing use, quitting or not even starting.[18]

The tobacco industry has promulgated the concept that excise taxes on tobacco are regressive. In 1985 the Tobacco Institute produced for state lobbyists a document entitled "Excise Taxes: The Fairness Issue." The document stated that "from an economic perspective, excise taxes are unfair: they place the heaviest burden on families at the lowest end of the income scale. The cigarette excise is the most regressive of all selective consumption taxes currently levied by state and federal governments. Its burden on consumers increases drastically as income decreases. Excise taxes are also inequitable with respect to business and public policy ... They single out particular industries to bear the brunt of raising general revenues ... [and] impose a moral judgment on consumers of selected goods."[19]

The industry played a key role in forming and funding the Consumer Tax Alliance in 1989. This advocacy group used the media to target middle-class and labor audiences to build opposition to excise taxes.[20] The National Center for Policy Analysis also questioned the fairness of hiking taxes that have been known to disproportionately burden poor families.[21]

CHILDREN, TEENS, AND TOBACCO TAXATION

According to a study conducted by Pacific Institute for Research and Evaluation and the Roswell Park Cancer Institute, the greatest benefit from a $1 increase in the cigarette excise tax would be to youth smokers who are, as a group, the most sensitive to price fluctuations.[22] Tax increases also provide additional revenues, which can be used to help fund tobacco control programs, prevention/cessation programs, additional health care, and other beneficial programs for low-income communities.[23] In 2007 the Democratic leadership of Congress proposed a massive expansion of the State Children's Health Insurance Program (SCHIP), established by the federal government 10 years ago to provide health insurance to children in families at or below 200 percent of the federal poverty line. The SCHIP expansion would extend federal health insurance coverage to children in families making as much as $82,600 per year, which ultimately would have made 71 percent of America's children eligible for federal health insurance assistance, a form of welfare. Congressional leadership proposed funding this dramatic expansion with an increase in the tobacco tax. The House and Senate approved the Children's Health Insurance Program Reauthorization Act of 2007, HR 976, but it was vetoed by President George W. Bush on October 3, 2007.

The Heritage Foundation, a conservative organization, weighed in on the issue of expanding the SCHIP through a major increase in taxes on cigarettes. It said that the increased taxes would fall heavily on poor people, low-income families, and the young: "Around half of smokers are in families in the income class that SCHIP and Medicaid are trying to help. Furthermore, smokers are more likely to be poor or low income than wealthy. With an expanded tobacco tax, SCHIP expansion to higher income levels would largely be funded by lower income persons, those who can least afford it ... placing the burden of expanding this program on the shoulders of any small subset of the population is unfair. Neither low income families nor young adults should be held responsible for funding an unnecessary expansion of SCHIP."[24]

The Heritage Foundation also expressed concern that an increase in taxes would result in a dwindling number of smokers, a reduction in purchases of cigarettes, less income from excise taxes, and less funding for SCHIP.[25] The Campaign for Tobacco-Free Kids countered this argument by stating that "the higher tax rate per pack brings in more new revenue than is lost from the drop in the number of packs sold."[26]

On February 4, 2009, President Barack Obama signed the Children's Health Insurance Reauthorization Act of 2009 (Public Law 111–3), expanding the program to an additional four million children and pregnant women, including for the first time legal immigrants without a waiting period. The law, which took effect April 1, 2009, increased the federal excise tax from 39¢ a pack to $1.01, which will help pay for the health insurance expansion.

In addition to the federal tax, law makers in more than a dozen states have considered raising their cigarette taxes to fund a number of health programs across the states. For instance, Arkansas passed a 56¢ increase to pay for a statewide trauma system and expanded health programs.

Public health experts, physicians, and others have long felt that raising prices on cigarettes and other tobacco products, especially through increasing federal excise taxes, would reduce use of these products, especially among teenagers. They believe that the more expensive one makes cigarettes, the fewer will be purchased and consumed. In 2007 the Institute on Medicine said:

> It is well established that an increase in price decreases cigarette use and that raising tobacco excise taxes is one of the most effective policies for reducing use, especially among adolescents in the United States. The rise in youth smoking in the early 1900s has been attributed to declines in cigarette prices. Furthermore increases in excise taxes were determined to be effective in preventing tobacco use among adolescents and young adults, according to the June 2006 NIH state-of-the-science panel on tobacco use.[27]

The day President Obama signed the Children's Health Insurance Reauthorization Act, which raised the federal excise tax on tobacco, the Campaign for Tobacco-Free Kids listed a number of benefits for public health and related health care costs savings, including an increase in the total number of kids who will not became smokers, the number of adult smokers who will quit, the number of smokers saved from smoking-related deaths, health care savings from fewer smoking-affected pregnancies and births, and fewer smoking-caused heart attacks and strokes.[28]

Opponents of taxes as a means, via increasing costs of cigarettes and other tobacco products, to combat smoking among children and youth have taken a different approach. Robert A. Levey of the Cato Institute explained his opposition in March of 2009: "Ask yourself why 44 million adult consumers of a perfectly legal product should have to fork up because retailers and 1 million kids break laws against sales to minors that are on the books in all 50 states. The way to keep cigarettes from kids is to enforce those laws-demand proof of age, prosecute offending retailers and prohibit vending machine sales where youngsters are the primary customers. If instead we depend on price hikes to dissuade teenagers, we can count on illegal dealings dominated by criminal gangs hooking underage smokers on adulterated products without the constraints on quality that a competitive market normally affords."[29]

TAX EVASION AND SMUGGLING

The issue of tax evasion and smuggling has become more prominent as more and more states—and the federal government—increase taxes on tobacco products as a means both of reducing use of such products and raising much needed revenue for tobacco control and other programs. Those opposed to tax increases on tobacco products lay out a range of concerns centered on the belief that higher prices will motivate smokers to avoid paying the increased costs by purchasing cigarettes through tax-free outlets, on the black market, through the Internet, in other countries such as Canada, or on American Indian reservations.

Smuggling of tobacco products ultimately impacts health. The public health community and economists have determined that the price of products is a big deterrent to preventing teens from starting to smoke as well as motivating others, especially low-income individuals and the impoverished, to reduce or stop all together. Smugglers who sell tobacco products without federal, state, and local excise taxes charge consumers less for their products than if consumers bought them from a retailer or other "legal" source. Because state and local excise taxes are used in part for tobacco control and health programs, less funds are available due to smuggling.

Cigarette smuggling exists in the United States and around the world. On the international level, it is estimated that "one-third of all cigarette exports in the world disappear into the lucrative black market for tobacco products."[30] With smoking on the rise, especially in Asia and Eastern Europe, the impact of smuggling on health becomes severe. The level of smuggling varies widely from state to state with those states/municipalities having the highest state-local cigarette tax rates facing the biggest problem, most notably Chicago and New York City. The vast majority of states with lower actual or proposed cigarette tax rates and less-established smuggling infrastructures or tax-evasion patterns do not have a large problem. A 2008 Campaign for Tobacco-Free Kids study showed that in Chicago and New York City, smuggling accounted for a small percentage of cigarette sales and that each city has gained substantial new revenues from its cigarette tax increases.[31] In the aggregate, researchers state that cigarette smuggling among individuals has been a relatively small problem, not exacerbated by excise tax increases.

In one of their arguments against cigarette tax increases (especially by states), cigarette companies and their allies have argued that they will not provide "substantial amounts of new state revenues because of enormous surges in cigarette smuggling and smoker tax evasion."[32] But in its June 27, 2008, report, the Campaign for Tobacco-Free Kids countered that every single state with increased cigarette tax rates has seen substantial increases in state revenues. Many of the states allocate at least a portion of the revenues to tobacco control and other health programs. The Campaign for Tobacco-Free Kids argued that research studies and surveys have shown that "smuggling and tax evasion not only fails to eliminate revenue gains from cigarette tax increases but is also a much smaller problem than the cigarette companies and their allies claim (especially when compared to the additional new revenues, public health benefits, and smoking-caused cost reductions from state cigarette tax increases)."[33]

The Campaign for Tobacco-Free Kids has argued that "there are simple, low-cost, steps a state can take to minimize revenue reductions from cigarette smuggling or smoker tax evasion."[34] To combat smuggling, states can implement a high-tech stamp that cannot be counterfeited and enables enforcement officials to readily identify smuggled cigarettes. After California introduced a high-tech stamp, it saw its cigarette tax revenues go up in the following 20 months, without a rate increase. In June 2007 the California tax collection agency announced that annual cigarette tax evasion had dropped by 37 percent because of increased enforcement and the new high-tech tax stamps, gaining the state $120 million in additional tax revenue.[35]

In August 2008 the Campaign for Tobacco-Free Kids published "Measures to Make Smuggling & Tobacco Tax Avoidance More Difficult," listing 14 ways to sharply reduce both organized cigarette smuggling, which accounts for the majority of untaxed sales, and smoker tax avoidance. Their recommended measures were as follows:

1. Improve state tobacco tax stamps.
2. Require state tax-exempt stamps on all cigarettes and other tobacco products sold in state that are not subject to the state's tobacco taxes.
3. Forbid the sale, purchase or possession in the state of any tobacco products that are not marked with state tobacco stamps or other state tax payment indicia establishing that all applicable state tobacco taxes have already been paid—other than small personal—use amounts and those held by or transported between licensed cigarette manufacturers, distributors/wholesalers, retailers, or other licensed tobacco product businesses.
4. Require better record keeping by distributor/wholesalers.
5. Require better record keeping by retailers.
6. Block retail sales clearly not for personal use.
7. Educate smokers about existing state laws restricting smuggling and tax avoidance.
8. Publicize toll-free hot lines to encourage reports of smuggling or tax avoidance activities.
9. Protect "whistleblowers."
10. Work with neighboring states.
11. Put pressure on states with extremely low cigarette tax rates to raise them.
12. Enter into treaties with in-state Indian tribes to eliminate tobacco product price disparities.
13. Support federal antismuggling legislation
14. Coordinate enforcement with efforts to stop illegal sales to youth.[36]

Authors of a 2007 study, "Interstate Cigarette Smuggling," published by the Mackinac Center for Public Policy, concluded that states should think twice before raising excise taxes on cigarettes. They argued that increasing cigarette taxes in recent years has furthered the growth of two types of cigarette smuggling: *casual,* in which smokers save money by buying their cigarettes in low-tax states or countries, and *commercial,* in which large-scale operations buy cigarettes in bulk in a low-tax area and sell them tax-free in high-tax areas. The authors estimated that from 1990 to 2006, the states with the "top five average smuggling import rates as a percentage of their total estimated in-state cigarette consumption, including both legally and illegally purchased cigarettes" were California, New York, Arizona, Washington, and Michigan. In 2006, the authors found that Rhode Island, New Mexico, and the state of Washington had the highest estimated cigarette smuggling import rates; all three raised their cigarette taxes "significantly" since 2003. They reported that commercial import rates were highest in New Jersey, Massachusetts, and Rhode Island; casual smuggling import rates were highest in New York, Washington, and Michigan. The authors also reviewed cigarette smuggling in Michigan, New Jersey, and California and suggested that "cigarette smugglers can realize large profits, tens of thousands of dollars for a single vanload of cigarettes, and hundreds of thousands of dollars for a single truckload. These sums represent a loss in estimated tax revenues to a state's treasury."[37]

The authors suggested that state policy makers reassess the value of cigarette taxes as a revenue and public health tool: "States with high cigarette taxes ... may want to consider reducing these taxes to reduce the smuggling incentive and the attendant ancillary crime. States with lower cigarette tax rates should be cautious about increasing the taxes, especially with an apparent growth in international smuggling."[38]

Business and public policy researcher Richard McGowan has suggested that some states have purposely not raised taxes in order to attract smokers from neighboring states with higher rates: "Rather than raising their own cigarette excise taxes to raise additional revenue, many states are maintaining or even lowering their cigarette excise tax rate to attract smokers from neighboring states that have substantially increased their cigarette excise tax."[39]

Federal agencies are involved with efforts to combat illicit sales of tobacco products. The U.S. Bureau of Alcohol, Tobacco, Firearms and Explosives (ATF) is the federal agency charged with dealing with smuggling, Internet sales, and any other illicit activity designed to avoid payment of excise taxes on tobacco products. The ATF made 35 arrests for tobacco trafficking in 2003 and 162 such arrests in 2005, according to Philip Awe, chief of the alcohol and tobacco enforcement branch. Awe also said ATF has refined "its national strategy for fighting cigarette trafficking and has substantially expanded its investigations, opening up some 700 new cases in the past five years."[40]

Section 723 of the Children's Health Insurance Program Reauthorization Act of 2009 dealt with smuggling. The act required that by one year after its enactment the secretary of the treasury conduct a study concerning the magnitude of tobacco smuggling in the United States and submit to Congress recommendations for the most effective steps to reduce tobacco smuggling. The study must also review the loss of federal tax receipts due to illicit tobacco trade in the United States and the role of imported tobacco products in the illicit tobacco trade in the United States.

AMERICAN INDIAN TRIBAL RETAILERS AND TOBACCO PRODUCT TAXATION

Cigarette prices include a federal excise tax and a state excise tax. Although American Indian retailers include the federal excise tax on all sales, their prices usually do not include the state excise tax. Unless the American Indian retailer and/or the tribal government agree to keep prices close to those offered off-reservation, American Indian retailers hold a competitive advantage over businesses located near tribal lands; without state excise taxes added on, tribal tobacco product prices are lower than those of nontribal retailers.

Cigarette sales on tribal lands to tribal members are exempt from state excise taxes. But non-Indian buyers are supposed to pay state taxes on their tobacco product purchases. When they buy in shops in Indian country, they seldom pay them unless American Indian retailers keep records of purchasers or collect the state taxes due. Federal courts have found that cigarette sales to non-Indians are not exempt from state taxation unless a specific exemption is granted. The courts also have ruled that tribes are obligated to help collect the state taxes due on sales to non-Indians. New York State has a long history of unsuccessful attempts to collect taxes on cigarettes sold by retail stores on sovereign American Indian reservations to non-Indian consumers. American Indians have successfully argued in the past that their reservations are sovereign nations, and they have the legal right to not apply state, and even federal, excise taxes on tobacco products sold on their reservations.

According to J. C. Seneca, a Seneca Nation tribal councilor, "you cannot force the nation to be the state's tax collectors."[41] States and tribes have employed varied arrangements for cigarette and tobacco tax collection. In the 1980s and early 1990s, tribes all across the country entered into various forms of tax compacts that dealt with tobacco and many other tax issues. Generally the result of tobacco tax compacts was that the state and tribe shared tobacco tax revenues. Most of these compacts required tribes to put some form of state tax stamp on cigarette packs that they sold.

In Washington State, the governor was authorized to enter into cigarette-only sales tax contracts that provided for tribal cigarette taxes and stamps in lieu of the state tax. The state made at least 12 such agreements with American Indian tribes since negotiations began in 2001. In 2004, the Yakama Nation and the state of Washington signed a cigarette taxation agreement under which the Yakama imposed a tax on purchases by non-Indians equal to the combined state cigarette and sales tax. In exchange the state did not impose its tax on cigarettes purchased by non-Indians from reservation smokeshops. Revenue from the tax supported the Yakama Nation's government services. In 2008, Washington State terminated the cigarette tax agreement with the Yakama Nation, citing complaints that cigarettes had been sold to non-Indians without proper tax stamps. As a result, the state considered any cigarettes sold on the Yakama Reservation to non-Indians illegal without proper state tax stamps. According to the state Revenue Department, it wrote a letter to Tribal Council Chairman Ralph Sampson that the department "will advise the tribe in advance what state officials decide to do about enforcing state tax laws in absence of a compact."[42]

Under written agreements, tribes and the state of Oregon have agreed to sell only stamped cigarettes. Taxes have been precollected by distributors, and the state annually refunds tribes a dollar amount based on membership per capita plus consumption. The precollection of taxes by distributors has ensured that non-Indians' obligation to pay the taxes is covered, and the tribal members' rights to exemptions have been protected.[43]

Tribes and the state of Minnesota have written agreements under which they have agreed to purchase cigarettes from licensed distributors, who collect the applicable taxes. The state has refunded a portion of the tax collections on a per capita basis annually. Montana Indian reservations have quotas of tax-free cigarettes, and taxes are precollected on all cigarettes that enter tribal lands. Cigarette wholesalers apply for refunds or credits on tribal sales. Florida, Nevada, and New Mexico exempt sales on tribal lands from state tax obligations.[44]

INTERNET SALES OF TOBACCO PRODUCTS

Sales of tobacco products over the Internet have increased. In the 1990s, there were a handful of Web sites that sold tobacco products. According to a report about Internet tobacco sales by substance-abuse policy researchers, in January 2000 there were 88 Internet cigarette vendors; in 2005 there were more than 500; and in January 2006 there were 772 Internet cigarette vendors located within and outside the United States.[45] According to the same study, "much of the growth in Internet cigarette vendors has occurred among international vendors that market primarily to customers in the United States." By 2005 most of the vendors were located in Switzerland, Spain, the United Kingdom, and Indonesia. Among domestic vendors, "63 percent were Native American affiliated," and "more than three-quarters of the Native American Internet cigarette sites were run by Seneca Indians located on two reservations near Buffalo, New York."[46]

The Internet makes it especially easy for children and teens to buy tobacco products, even though they are younger than 18 years of age when the products can be legally purchased. The Internet also makes it relatively easy for adults and youngsters to pay lower prices for tobacco products by avoiding payment of excise taxes, an attraction for smokers of any age. The Internet study reported that "smokers living in states and cities with high cigarette excise taxes are more likely to purchase cigarettes online than smokers in low tax jurisdictions." The study also pointed out that "the availability of lower-cost, tax-free cigarettes online undermines the public health benefit of raising cigarette taxes to curb smoking rates." Tax evasion from Internet cigarette sales also deprives state government and public health programs of revenues that fund tobacco prevention and control programs.[47]

The 1949 Jenkins Act, a federal law, requires tobacco vendors who ship cigarettes out of state to register with the tax authorities in every state in which they have customers and to file monthly reports with each state tax collector listing "the name and address of the person to whom the shipment was made, the brand, and the quantity thereof."[48] The Jenkins Act requires all Internet sellers, including Native American vendors, to provide each state with monthly reports listing state residents who have purchased cigarettes from Internet sellers. This enables states to go after in-state consumers to collect state taxes owed on the sales. Besides the fact that federal officials rarely enforce the act, three-quarters of all Internet tobacco sellers explicitly have said that they will not report cigarette sales to tax collection officials, which violates the Jenkins Act, according to the U.S. General Accounting Office. Internet sales totaled 14 percent of the U.S. market in 2005, and states lost $1.4 billion in uncollected taxes through Internet sales, according to a study by Forrester Research Inc., a private research firm.[49]

Some states have slightly increased the Internet sellers' compliance rate by contacting them and demanding the reports. A few states have initiated lawsuits against some Internet sellers to force them to comply. But given the fact there are hundreds of Internet sellers and vendors who do not comply with the law, state efforts have not been that successful. According to the Campaign for Tobacco-Free Kids, "even when Internet vendors comply with the Jenkins Act and provide the states with the customer information, going after each individual customer to collect taxes is an inevitably time consuming and ineffective process."[50]

The Campaign for Tobacco-Free Kids has identified a few ways to combat the problem of Internet sales of tobacco products and to establish more effective tax collection strategies. These include implementing "new state laws banning or restricting Internet tobacco product sales," supporting "new federal laws to minimize Internet-based tax evasion," and "subjecting Internet and other mail order sellers of tobacco products to the same anti-smuggling measures and other state laws that apply to regular in-state retailers of tobacco products."[51]

CHAPTER 7

Filtered ("Low-Tar/Nicotine") Cigarettes, Advertising, and Health Risks

During the 1930s and 1940s, people smoked unfiltered cigarettes. It was a time when there was a growing perception that cigarettes might be harmful, but there was no proof. It was a time when the public was mainly concerned about symptoms like smoker's cough and throat irritation. It was also a time when some cigarette companies spent a lot of money on "negative" health-related advertising themes, based on coughs and throats, what the business press called "fear advertising."[1]

In the early 1950s, health concerns were vastly increased by news from numerous scientific studies informing the public that cigarette smoking was linked to lung cancer and other serious diseases. The May 1950 *Journal of the American Medical Association* reported how medical researchers found cigarette smoking to be an important factor in bronchiogenic cancer. The December 1952 issue of *Readers Digest,* a magazine with arguably the largest circulation in the nation, republished Roy Norr's "Cancer by the Carton," an article from the *Norr Newsletter about Smoking and Health.* In 1953, researchers at New York's Memorial Center for Cancer and Allied Diseases announced that they had produced cancer in mice by injecting them with tar condensed from cigarette smoke. *Consumer Reports* published a report on the tar and nicotine content of cigarette smoke and other health hazards of smoking. By the mid-1950s, clinicians and researchers had collectively reached an important conclusion about the connection between smoking cigarettes and lung cancer, based on clinical observations, dozens of studies, and laboratory experiments with animals.

"NEGATIVE" HEALTH-RELATED CIGARETTE ADVERTISING IN THE 1940s

Julep: "Smoke all you want without unpleasant symptoms of over-smoking! A smoking miracle? Yes, it's the triple miracle of mint. (1) Your mouth doesn't get smoke-weary! (2) Your throat doesn't get that harsh, hacking feeling! (3) Your breath avoids tobacco-taint! Get Juleps today."

Pall Mall: "Now, at last—thanks to modern design—a truly fine cigarette provides in fact what other cigarettes claim in theory—a smoother, less irritating smoke—Pall Mall."

Philip Morris: "Smoke of the Four Other Leading Popular Brands Averaged More Than Three Times as Irritating—and Their Irritation Lasted More Than Five Times as Long—as the Strikingly Contrasted PHILIP MORRIS!"

Raleigh: "Now! Medical Science Offers Proof Positive! No other leading cigarette is safer to smoke. No other gives you less nicotine, less throat irritants than the NEW smoother, better tasting Raleigh."

Cigarette sales slumped. Tobacco companies were naturally concerned about numerous scientific studies suggesting that smoking could have serious health consequences. Faced with declining profits, tobacco companies needed to rework the messages they had used to sell cigarettes in the 1930s and 1940s. They began to develop cigarettes they internally referred to as "health reassurance" brands in an effort to keep smokers in the market.[2]

To make cigarettes safer, tobacco companies began to produce filter-tipped cigarettes to decrease the amount of tar, nicotine, and other particles inhaled while smoking. Filter tips were nothing new. They had been around since the 1800s, when cork mouthpieces served as filters. In 1936 Viceroy cigarettes first appeared in the markets of United States containing a cardboard tube filled with cotton tufts and folded wads of paper. In 1952 the first filter-tipped cigarette that was highly promoted was Kent Cigarettes, launched by P. Lorillard Company and named for its president, Herbert A. Kent. The company promoted Kent as the brand for "the 1 out of every 3 smokers who is unusually sensitive to tobacco tars and nicotine." A massive print and television advertising campaign hailed Kents as the "Greatest Health Protection in Cigarette History." A clear response to the health risks, Kent ads boasted a new "micronite" filter tip that re-moved more nicotine and tars than any other cigarette. Smokers found Kents hard to smoke and tasteless, so the filters were loosened up to let more flavor through. This made them easier to smoke, but nicotine and tar levels went up. In 1957, without publicity, Kent abandoned its original micronite filter.[3]

After Kent filter tips appeared on the market, other cigarette makers developed competing filters. Filter brands multiplied, and the compet-ing brands all claimed the best combination of good taste with low tar and nicotine. L & M appeared in 1953 with a "Pure White Miracle Tip of Alpha-Cellulose." Winston appeared in 1954 and became the leading filter brand by 1956. Marlboro filters were introduced in 1954 and so, too, was Herbert Tareyton with a "new Selective Filter" containing charcoal. In 1954, Viceroy changed its hollow tube to a cellulose acetate filter, the ma-terial that quickly became the normal filter throughout the industry. Salem, the first filter-tipped menthol cigarette, was introduced in 1956. Newport, another filter-tipped menthol brand, appeared in 1957. That year, filter tips accounted for almost 50 percent of all cigarette sales. Most smok-ers switched to filter tips because they believed the filters would provide health protection.

Filter-tip brands were supposed to reduce the amount of tar and nicotine in smoke that gets sucked directly into the lungs. Tobacco companies at-tempted to assure smokers that cigarettes with filters provided a level of security. They outdid one another in making these claims for their filter-tip brands. In expensive advertising campaigns, each company tried to dif-ferentiate its brand from competing ones. Expenditures in selected media jumped from more than $55 million in 1952 to an estimated $150 million in 1959. In 1950 filter-tipped cigarettes accounted for 0.6 percent of ciga-rette sales. By 1956 filter tips zoomed to almost 50 percent of sales. By 1975 filters accounted for 87 percent of cigarette sales.[4] Filtered cigarettes held 99 percent of the market in both 2004 and 2005.[5]

Eventually, these advertising campaigns led the Federal Trade Com-mission (FTC) to prevent the tobacco industry from making false and misleading claims. In fall of 1954, the FTC circulated a draft set of "Cigarette Advertising Guides," which prohibited all references to "either the presence or absence of any physical effect of smoking."[6] The new rules prohibited all references to "throat, larynx, lungs, nose or other parts of the body," or to "digestion, energy, nerves or doctors." By 1955 phony testimonials and any medical approval of cigarette smoking were barred from advertisements. The guides also prohibited all tar and nicotine claims "when it has not been established by competent scientific proof . . . that the

---

FILTERED CIGARETTE ADS IN THE 1950s

Hit Parade Cigarettes, 1958: "Now Hit Parade has America's best filter! Over 400,000 Filter Traps! Up to 43% Higher Filtration!"

Kent, 1954: "And remember, KENT and *only* KENT has the Micronite Filter, made of a pure, dust-free, completely harmless material that is not only so effective, but *so safe* that it actually is used to help filter the air in operating rooms of leading hospitals."

L&M, 1954: "To All Smokers of Filter Tips ... This Is It! 'Just What The Doctor Ordered.' Effective Filtration, From a Strictly Non-Mineral Filter Material-Alpha Cellulose. Exclusive to L&M Filters, and entirely pure and harmless to health."

Marlboro, 1958: "Mild-burning Marlboro combines a prized recipe (created in Richmond, Virginia) of the world's great tobaccos with a cellulose acetate filter of consistent dependability."

Parliament, 1954: "Parliament's extra-absorbent built-in- filter mouthpiece and superb tobacco mean filtered smoking at its best. More pleasure comes through—more tars are filtered out."

Salem, 1957: "The freshest taste in cigarette flows through Salem's pure white filter ... rich tobacco taste with a surprise softness and menthol-fresh comfort."

Tareyton, 1955: "Yes, here's the best in filtered smoking—all the full, rich taste of Tareyton's famous quality tobacco and real filtration, too! That's because Tareyton's new Selective Filter is the only filter with the world-famous purifying agent, Activated Charcoal."

Viceroy, 1955: "What do Viceroys do for you that *no other* filter tip can do? Only Viceroy Gives You 20,000 Filter Traps in every Viceroy tip to *Filter-Filter-Filter* Your Smoke While the Rich, Rich Flavor Comes Through."

Winston, 1954: "Winston is the new, easy-drawing filter cigarette real smokers can enjoy! Winston brings you real flavor–full, rich, tobacco flavor. Along with finer flavor, you get Winston's finer filter."

---

claim is true, and if true, that such difference or differences are significant." At the same time, the guides explicitly permitted the advertising of taste and pleasure.

The FTC made clear its intention to attack advertising that violated the guides. Within months, cigarette advertising changed to conform with

FTC guidelines. Advertisements disappeared that referred to the fears of smoking or even improved cigarettes, replaced with ads featuring good taste, flavor, and pleasure.[7]

In March 1957 Consumers Union tested 33 brands of cigarettes for the nicotine and tar content in their smoke. After test results showed very little difference in the nicotine and tar content of filtered and unfiltered smoke, the FTC and cigarette companies made a voluntary agreement barring from all ads any mention of filters and tar and nicotine levels. Earl W. Kintner, then FTC chairman, stated that in "the absence of a satisfactory uniform testing method and proof of advantage to the smoker, there will be no more tar and nicotine claims in advertising." On December 17, 1959, the FTC sent a letter to manufacturers: "We wish to advise that all representations of low or reduced tar or nicotine, whether by filtration or otherwise, will be construed as health claims ... Our purpose is to eliminate from cigarette advertising representations which in any way imply health benefit." Kintner called the end of tar and nicotine claims "a landmark example of industry-government cooperation in solving a pressing problem."[8]

Following the publication of the first surgeon general's report on smoking and health in 1964 and the passage of the Federal Cigarette Labeling and Advertising Act of 1965, "the FTC developed a machine for measuring tar and nicotine yield of cigarettes and provided, in the annual report to Congress, the yields of tar and nicotine of the most popular brands. The system was not designed to predict actual tar and nicotine intake among humans, only to provide a relative measure between brands."[9] In 1981 the system was modified to include carbon monoxide.

To prevent government regulation, cigarette makers agreed, under a 1971 consent agreement with the FTC, to disclose in cigarette ads and labels tar and nicotine measurements provided through the FTC measuring system. The industry took over the job of testing in 1987, under the FTC's oversight. It used a smoking machine that smoked cigarettes down to near the butt and then filtered out the tar and nicotine for measurement.

The FTC method of estimating tar and nicotine levels was based on the amount of smoke obtained by cigarette-smoking machines. The machines tested filtered cigarettes that had a band of microscopic air vents. These vents diluted cigarette smoke with air when light cigarettes were puffed on by smoking machines, causing the machines to measure artificially low tar and nicotine levels. Researchers have found that many smokers, who switched to lower-tar, mild, light, or ultralight brands for a smoke less harmful to their health than regular or full-flavor cigarettes, compensated by taking more frequent puffs, inhaling smoke more deeply, holding smoke in their lungs longer, covering cigarette ventilation holes with their fingers or lips, or smoking more cigarettes.

Many smokers never knew that their cigarette filters had vent holes. In a report about light cigarettes, the National Cancer Institute explained that "the filter vents are uncovered when cigarettes are smoked on smoking machines. However, filter vents are placed just millimeters from where smokers put their lips or fingers when smoking. As a result, many smokers block the vent—which actually turns the light cigarette into a regular cigarette."[10] In addition, "some cigarette makers increased the length of the paper wrap covering the outside of the cigarette filter, which decreases the number of puffs that occur during the machine test. Although tobacco under the wrap is still available to the smoker, this tobacco is not burned during the machine test. The result is that the machine measures less tar and nicotine levels than is available to the smoker."[11]

For decades tobacco companies have marketed and promoted their low-tar/low-nicotine cigarettes using descriptors like *light, ultralight, mild,* and *medium* and claims of *low tar and nicotine* to suggest that these products were safer than regular cigarettes. The industry made health-benefit claims regarding filtered cigarettes when it either lacked evidence to substantiate the claims or knew that they were false. Millions of pages of internal documents of major tobacco companies, made available through litigation brought by the National Association of Attorneys General that resulted in the Master Settlement Act of 1998, reveal that the companies never had adequate support for their claims of reduced health risk from filtered cigarettes. Rather the documents confirm their awareness by the late 1960s and early 1970s that filtered cigarettes were unlikely to provide any health benefit to smokers compared to regular cigarettes. The tobacco company documents show that it was known that smokers of filtered cigarettes with reduced yields of nicotine modified their behavior in order to obtain an amount of nicotine sufficient to satisfy their need. Concurrently, smokers of light cigarettes boosted their intake of tar, thus negating what tobacco companies have long promoted as a "primary health-related benefit of light cigarettes: lower tar intake."[12]

Besides the tobacco industry's false health claims about filtration, there are other health issues involving the filter itself. In 2002 researchers systematically reviewed 61 documents of Philip Morris, which disclosed the fall-out of carbon particles and cellulose acetate fibers from filters manufactured by Philip Morris and its competitors. In 1985 Philip Morris defined *fall-out* to mean "loose fibers (or particles) that are drawn out of the filter while puffing a cigarette." The researchers concluded that their analysis of Philip Morris documents "showed that filter fibres and carbon particles were discharged from the filters of all types of cigarettes tested." The researchers also identified other companies that tested for defective filters and pointed out that "simple, expedient, and inexpensive technologies for decontaminating cigarette filters of loose cellulose acetate fibres and particles from the cut surface of the filter have been developed." The investigators stated that the results of tobacco industry investigations substantiating defective filters were concealed from smokers and the health community. Finally, they established that "the tobacco industry has been negligent in not performing toxicological examinations and other studies to assess the human health risks associated with regularly ingesting and inhaling non-degradable, toxin coated cellulose acetate fragments and carbon microparticles and possibly other components that are released from conventional cigarette filters during normal smoking."[13]

Today the public health and scientific communities recognize what tobacco companies have long known internally: there is no meaningful reduction in disease risk in smoking filtered low-tar/low-nicotine cigarettes as opposed to regular cigarettes.[14]

In a 2001 National Cancer Institute monograph covering the years during which the "decreased risk" cigarettes were developed and marketed by tobacco companies, the authors showed that "the tobacco companies set out to develop cigarette designs that markedly lowered the tar and nicotine yield results as measured by the Federal Trade Commission (FTC) testing method. Yet, these cigarettes can be manipulated by the smoker to increase

---

DEFECTIVE FILTERS

In 2002 a group of cancer immunologists and an epidemiologist reported on their review of tobacco company writings that documented the existence of defective filters:

"Nearly all filters consist of a rod of numerous plastic-like cellulose acetate fibers. During high speed cigarette manufacturing procedures, fragments of cellulose acetate that form the mouthpiece of a filter rod become separated from the filter at the end face. The cut surface of the filter of nearly all cigarettes has these fragments. In smoking a cigarette in the usual manner, some of these fragments are released during puffing. In addition to the cellulose acetate fragments, carbon particles are released also from some cigarette brands that have a charcoal filter. Cigarettes with filters that release cellulose acetate or carbon particles during normal smoking conditions are defective."[15]

the intake of tar and nicotine. The use of these 'decreased risk' cigarettes has not significantly decreased the disease risk." According to the report, "the use of these cigarettes may be partly responsible for the increase in lung cancer for long term smokers who have switched to the low-tar/low-nicotine brands." Switching to these cigarettes may have provided smokers with "a false sense of reduced risk, when the actual amount of tar and nicotine consumed may be the same as, or more than, the previously used higher yield brand."[16]

Medical researcher Peter G. Shields, M.D., found that when people smoke low-tar/low-nicotine cigarettes, they modify their behavior or compensate by inhaling more deeply; taking larger, more rapid, or more frequent puffs; or smoking a few extra cigarettes each day to get enough nicotine to satisfy their craving. These adaptive behaviors may cause lung cancers farther down inside the lung.[17]

The American Cancer Society and Massachusetts Institute of Technology conducted a study of the smoking habits of nearly one million adults, aged 30 and older, for six years. The researchers found that "people who smoked low tar cigarettes had the same lung cancer risk as those who smoked regular cigarettes."[18]

In a National Cancer Institute Fact Sheet, researchers pointed out that "although smoke from light cigarettes may feel smoother and lighter on the throat and chest, light cigarettes are not healthier than regular cigarettes." Researchers also found "that the strategies used by the tobacco industry to advertise and promote light cigarettes are intended to reassure smokers, to discourage them from quitting, and to lead consumers to perceive filtered and light cigarettes as safer alternatives to regular cigarettes." They concluded that "there is no evidence that switching to light or ultra-light cigarettes actually helps smokers quit."[19]

The disclosure of tobacco industry deception about the harmful nature of smoking light cigarettes has led to litigation around the country. The tobacco industry faces numerous class-action lawsuits from smokers and ex-smokers who seek billions of dollars in damages and claim they were fooled by the marketing, advertising, and distribution of light and low-tar cigarettes.

An important step in the legal arena took place on December 15, 2008, when the U.S. Supreme Court ruled that tobacco companies can be sued by smokers who claim they were deceived about the health risks of smoking light cigarettes. In 2005 longtime smokers of Marlboro Lights cigarettes, Stephanie Good, Lori Spellman, and Allain Thibodeau, who live in Maine, filed a class action against Altria Group Inc. and Philip Morris USA Inc., claiming that Altria and Philip Morris deliberately deceived them about the true and harmful nature of light cigarettes, therefore violating the Maine Unfair Trade Practices Act and enriching themselves unjustly. The three plaintiffs sought to represent all buyers of Marlboro Light or Cambridge Light cigarettes, for a period up through November 2002.

The lawsuit asserted that the three individuals had smoked light cigarettes for at least 15 years and claimed that Philip Morris, the manufacturer, had used unfair and deceptive practices in making, promoting, and marketing Cambridge Light and Marlboro Light cigarettes with statements that they were light because they were lower in tar and nicotine. The lawsuit contended that the company knew all along that the cigarettes would not deliver less tar or nicotine when actually used by smokers. According to the lawsuit, the low yields of the test method were offset by the actual smoking habits of the users: they compensated by taking deeper puffs, holding the smoke in their lungs longer, or smoking more cigarettes. The lawsuit did not seek compensatory damages, but rather a return of the money smokers had paid for light cigarettes, along with a claim for punitive damages and recovery of their attorneys' fees.

Philip Morris tried to get the case dismissed, arguing that state law claims had been displaced by the Federal Cigarette Labeling and Advertising Act of 1965, which required a package warning label "Caution: Cigarette Smoking May Be Hazardous to Your Health." The act required the FTC to report to Congress annually on the effectiveness of cigarette labeling, advertising, and promotion.

Philip Morris made two claims of preemption of state law claims: the tobacco company said the state law was expressly pushed aside by the 1965 federal law and an implied preemption by the FTC's four-decades-long effort to implement a uniform policy on disclosing the health risks of smoking. The U.S. District Court of Maine dismissed the lawsuit, ruling that federal law preempted the plaintiffs' causes of action and granted summary judgment in favor of Philip Morris. The First U.S. Circuit Court of Appeals in Boston reinstated it, ruling that the lawsuit was based on claims of false statements about the two brands' tar and nicotine content. It said that the suit was not based on health-hazard claims that are regulated by federal law, but rather on the duty not to deceive consumers, a duty imposed by state law. That ruling disposed of the federal law preemption claim. The circuit court also said the FTC's actions did not amount to a formal regulation of the use of tar and nicotine yields, rejecting the implied FTC preemption claim.

The merits of the dispute did not reach the Supreme Court, since the lower court had granted summary judgment in favor of the cigarette manufacturer on the ground that the plaintiffs' state law claims were preempted by the federal labeling act. The First Circuit reversed that judgment, and in light of a conflicting decision from the Fifth Circuit, the Supreme Court granted certiorari (a written order from a higher court requesting records of a case tried in a lower court).[20]

In October 2007, Philip Morris, joined by its parent company, Altria Group, filed its appeal in the Supreme Court. "The lower courts," the petition said, "have reached conflicting decisions on whether claims like these are preempted by federal law. ... A definitive answer to this question will significantly impact the outcome of dozens of pending lawsuits in which the plaintiffs are alleging billions of dollars in potential liability." Philip Morris argued that the disagreement among the federal appeals courts would "obliterate the [federal] Labeling Act's objective of establishing national uniformity in the regulation of cigarette advertising and promotion." Philip Morris also argued that because the case presented both levels of the preemption question (preemption by federal law and implied preemption by FTC actions since 1996), the case was the "ideal vehicle" for resolving the conflicting views.[21]

The smokers, responding to the appeal, stressed the claim that their lawsuit was based only on the state law duty not to deceive, not on any law contradicting federal marketing regulation, and the assertion that the Supreme Court has never held that the federal cigarette labeling law has any implied preemptive effect. Their response noted that they were not seeking damages for any health-related injuries, but only "economic damages."[22]

On January 18, 2008, the Supreme Court granted review of the case, which suggested a clash between the Federal Cigarette Labeling and Marketing Act of 1965 and FTC actions on one side, and Maine's Unfair Trade Practices Act on the other. The justices heard arguments on whether cigarette makers defrauded smokers with claims about light and low-tar cigarettes. The federal government opted to get involved in the case in mid-June, filing a brief supporting the Maine smokers only on the meaning and impact of what the FTC had done, in the beginning and since—that is, the question of whether state law claims are preempted by implication. Three weeks after that brief was filed, the solicitor general's office notified the Supreme Court that the FTC had proposed to rescind its 1966 guidance that had provided legal cover for the industry's light cigarette claims for more than four decades. The FTC said it had been concerned "for some time" that the machine testing method might be producing "misleading" information "to consumers who rely on the yields as indicators of the amount of tar, nicotine, and carbon monoxide they actually will get from smoking a particular cigarette. In fact, the current yields tend to be relatively poor indicators of tar, nicotine, and carbon monoxide exposure, and do not provide a good basis for comparison among cigarettes."[23]

The appeal drew the pro-business and manufacturing groups on Philip Morris' side, and the antismoking community and consumers' advocates on the other, with the state of Maine defending its own law's validity.

On October 6, 2008, the first day of the 2008 term, the Supreme Court heard arguments on whether the tobacco industry can be held liable for allegedly perpetrating a massive fraud on the smoking public. In the December 15 ruling, Justice Stevens delivered the opinion of the Court in which justices Kennedy, Souter, Ginsburg, and Breyer joined. They rejected Philip Morris' claim that federal law prevented the case from going forward. The lawsuit was remanded to the trial court below.[24]

The *Altria Group Inc. v. Good* ruling had immediate impact on other pending litigation. In 2003 Minnesotans Michael S. Dahl and David Scott Huber sued the cigarette manufacturer R. J. Reynolds Tobacco Company "on behalf of all people in the state who smoked their 'light' brands over the years." The men did not claim that their health suffered as a result of their tobacco use, "but rather that they were deceived by the company's advertising and marketing about the nature and effect of smoking 'light' cigarettes."[25] The decision from the U.S. Supreme Court in *Altria Group Inc. v. Good* in late 2008 allowed the men and many other plaintiffs to move forward again in their lawsuits.

On June 22, 2009, President Barack Obama signed the Family Smoking Prevention and Tobacco Control Act of 2009, historic legislation granting authority over tobacco products to the U.S. Food and Drug Administration (FDA). The law provided that as of June 22, 2010, tobacco manufacturers could no longer use the terms "light," "low," and "mild," which have been present on about half the packages of cigarettes sold in the United States. The words suggest to some consumers that some cigarettes were safer than others. In a 2009 survey conducted by David Hammond and four other Canadian health researchers, their results showed that "adults and youth were significantly more like to rate [cigarette] packs with the terms 'smooth', 'silver', and 'gold' as lower tar, lower health risk'. ... For example, more than half of adults and youth reported that brands labelled [sic] as 'smooth' were less harmful compared with the 'regular' variety."[26]

The law, which does not stop companies from making light cigarettes, bars cigarette manufacturers from using "light" and similar words in marketing. Anticipating the new rules, Philip Morris renamed Marlboro Lights, the nation's best-selling brand, Marlboro Gold, and changed Marlboro Ultra Lights to Marlboro Silver, "according to a flier the company sent to distributors."[27] R. J. Reynolds changed Salem Ultra Lights to Silver Box. The tobacco companies also use colors on their packages to market different product lines to customers. David M. Sylvia, a spokesmen for Altria, the parent company of Philip Morris, said, "colors are used to identify and differentiate different brand packs. We do not use colors to communicate whether one product is less harmful or more harmful than another."[28]

Critics disagree. Matthew L. Myers, president of Campaign for Tobacco-Free Kids, said cigarette companies had responded to bans of terms like "light" and "low tar" in at least 78 countries by color-coding their packaging to convey the same ideas.[29] He said that "if the FDA concludes that either the new wording or color coding is misleading consumers, then the FDA has authority to take corrective action." Hammond's cigarette packaging survey showed that "plain packs significantly reduced false beliefs about health risk."[30]

CHAPTER 8

The Food and Drug Administration, Tobacco Regulation, and Health

Whether tobacco should be regulated as a drug has been controversial long before the creation of the Food and Drug Administration (FDA), a consumer protection group. Its origins date back to 1820, when the *U.S. Pharmacopoeia* was founded. Physicians and scientists wanted to standardize drugs and prevent adulterated drugs from entering the United States from abroad. At first only 217 drugs that met the criteria of "most fully established and best understood" were admitted. In 1906 Congress passed the Pure Food and Drugs Act, which established the Bureau of Chemistry, a predecessor to the FDA. The 1906 act defined drugs as "all medicines or preparations recognized in the United States Pharmacopoeia or National Formulary," which is an official listing of substances that effect the functioning of the human body in any way.[1] The Bureau of Chemistry was charged with enforcement of the act. The bureau delegated control to the newly formed Food, Drug, and Insecticide Administration in 1927, which was later renamed the Food and Drug Administration in 1930.

In the 1890 edition of the *U.S. Pharmacopoeia,* tobacco was listed as a drug. It was widely used during the colonial period as a medicine because of the properties of nicotine. "Nicotine therapy" was used an analgesic, an expectorant, a laxative, and a salve. During the 19th century, the medical uses of tobacco declined, but it remained in the *U.S. Pharmacopoeia* until it was dropped from the publication in later editions published prior to the passage of the 1906 act. In 1906 tobacco was dropped from the eighth edition, the same year the Pure Food and Drug Act became law. Since nicotine in tobacco was no longer considered a drug, it was not subject to supervision by the Bureau of Chemistry. There has been speculation that legislators from states where tobacco was grown got tobacco removed from the national drug list to avoid regulation in return for their support of the 1906 act. No deal, however, was mentioned in the *Congressional Record* or the papers of Dr. Harvey Washington Wiley, a physician/pharmacist who headed the precursor of the FDA. In 1914 the Bureau of Chemistry proclaimed that because tobacco was not labeled as a therapeutic agent, it could not be regulated as a drug.[2]

In 1929 Sen. Reed Smoot (R-UT) reminded Congress that the bureau should be provided with explicit authority to regulate tobacco, but the move failed to become law. He said: "In the past tobacco has been listed in the pharmacopoeia as a drug, but was dropped in the last revision of this work with the following explanation, which makes the reason for omissions self evident: Tobacco, the leaves of *Nicotiana tabacum,* was official in former pharmacopoeias, but was dropped in the last revision. It was formerly highly esteemed as a vulnerary [used in the healing or treating of wounds], but is little used as a drug by intelligent physicians. A decoction of tobacco in which corrosive sublimate has been dissolved makes a satisfactory bedbug poison."[3]

Smoot further argued: "Although tobacco is thus officially banned as a remedy, despite the claims of the American Tobacco Company that it promotes the health of the user, the fact remains that tobacco contains many injurious drugs, including nicotine, pyridin, carbolic acid, ammonia, marsh gas, and other products ... tobacco, the abuse of which has become a national problem, is not included within the regulations of the food and drugs act, for the merely technical reasons that since modern medical practice has abandoned it as a remedy it is no longer listed in the pharmacopoeia."[4] He proposed amending the 1906 food and drugs act to include tobacco.

Critics of Smoot argued that his bill would be difficult to enforce and promoted black markets. Others condemned the bill as "unjust in its deprivation of inalienable personal liberty ... attempting to force the masses to act in accord with the whims and peculiar views of certain groups."[5]

Owing to shortcomings in the 1906 law and a therapeutic disaster in 1937 in which more than 100 people died after taking an untested product, President Franklin D. Roosevelt signed the Food, Drug, and Cosmetic Act on June 25, 1938. The new law, which repealed the 1906 act, brought cosmetics and medical devices under its control, and it required that drugs be labeled with adequate directions for safe use. Moreover, it mandated premarket approval of all new drugs; manufacturers would have to prove to

EXCERPT FROM THE FEDERAL FOOD AND DRUGS ACT OF 1906

"An act for preventing the manufacture, sale, or transportation of adulterated or misbranded or poisonous or deleterious foods, drugs, medicines, and liquors, and for regulating traffic therein, and for other purposes."

Sec. 6. Definitions

"That the term "drug," as used in this Act, shall include all medicines and preparations recognized in the United States Pharmacopoeia or National Formulary for internal or external use, and any substance or mixture of substances intended to be used for the cure, mitigation, or prevention of disease of either man or other animals."

EXCERPT FROM THE FEDERAL FOOD, DRUG AND COSMETIC ACT OF 1938

§ 201 (21 U.S.C. 321)

"(1) The term 'drug' [as used in this act] means (A) articles recognized in the official United States Pharmacopoeia, official Homoeopathic Pharmacopoeia of the United States, or official National Formulary, or any supplement to any of them; and (B) articles intended for use in the diagnosis, cure, mitigation, treatment, or prevention of disease in man or other animals; and (C) articles (other than food) intended to affect the structure or any function of the body of man or other animals ...

"The term 'device' ... means an instrument, apparatus, implement, machine, contrivance, implant, in vitro reagent, or other similar or related article, including any component, part, or accessory, which is (1) recognized in the official National Formulary, or the United States Pharmacopeia, or any supplement to them, (2) intended for use in the diagnosis of disease or other conditions, or in the cure, mitigation, treatment, or prevention of disease, in man or other animals, or (3) intended to affect the structure or any function of the body of man or other animals."

the FDA that drugs were safe before they could be sold. The 1938 revised law and subsequent amendments have given consumers greater protection from dangerous and impure foods and drugs. An important tenet of the act, that a drug or device is subject to regulation if its manufacturer intends that it affect the structure or function of the body when used, came into play in the late 1990s in federal court rulings regarding the issue of the FDA's authority to regulate tobacco products.

Despite its mandate to protect consumers, the FDA has not been a well-regarded agency. For years it has been criticized by congressional committees, public interest groups, and executives of industries it has tried to regulate. A 1990 advisory committee, appointed by secretary of Health and Human Services, Dr. Louis W. Sullivan, reported that the FDA operated on a threadbare budget, with a shortage of inspectors and laboratories in abysmal condition, and without a clear-cut mission. Under the leadership of the FDA's new commissioner, Dr. David Kessler, who brought a new sense of purpose to the agency when he took the position in November of 1990, the FDA began restoring its credibility.

In spring of 1991, Jeffrey Nesbit, an FDA spokesperson, told Kessler that if the FDA was a public health agency, it ought to protect public health by taking on tobacco, a politically explosive issue. He showed the FDA committee many years' worth of petitions containing hundreds of thousands of signatures calling for the agency to regulate tobacco products as drugs.[6] Kessler, aware that the Coalition on Smoking OR Health, a Washington group of health lobbyists, had been pressing the government to regulate cigarettes since the late 1980s, assigned several dozen FDA scientists, lawyers, and other staffers to collect data. By the end of 1994, the FDA had collected enough information to begin work drafting a proposed rule that would give the agency the authority to regulate nicotine as a drug and cigarettes as drug-delivery devices.

On August 10, 1995, President Bill Clinton became the first president in U.S. history to assert authority over the tobacco companies when he ordered FDA regulation of cigarettes, only with respect to minors, not adults. The proposals would create strict limits on the advertising, sale, and distribution of cigarettes. Under the federal regulatory process, the FDA was required to take public comment for 90 days, but the agency extended the period until January 1, 1996. More than 700,000 comments on its finding of jurisdiction and on its proposed regulations were sent to the FDA, more comments than had been received about any other federal rule in history.

On the last day of the comment period, 32 senators declared their opposition to the FDA regulatory proposal. A survey of 1,500 people by Republican pollster Linda DiVall, showed that "a majority of people did not see tobacco as a threat to teenagers comparable to violence, illegal drugs, and pregnancy ... Almost two thirds of the respondents strongly agreed that 'tobacco should not be regulated by the FDA like pacemakers, allergy medication, and insulin, but an aggressive campaign against teenage smoking should be waged.'"[7] People opposed to FDA regulation argued that the agency couldn't do its current job properly because the workforce did not have the capacity or the capability and it was too mismanaged to deal with limiting youth access to tobacco products. They also argued that FDA regulation would trample free-speech rights of tobacco producers, enhance federal government power over private life, and lead to a total ban of cigarettes. Rather than increased FDA regulation over tobacco products, legislators, civil libertarians, tobacco growers, and others called for tax increases; national education programs about smoking, addiction, disease, and death; funding for state and local community antismoking programs; and enforcement of state laws banning sales to minors.

On August 25, 1996, President Clinton authorized the final FDA rule to regulate tobacco products. The rule, the most far-reaching measure ever instituted to reduce tobacco use by young people, differed in some ways from those the FDA initially proposed. It allowed more leeway for sales of tobacco products clearly aimed at adult purchasers and dropped language that called for a $150 million annual fund given by the tobacco industry to conduct a national education campaign. In response to business complaints, the president changed one of the FDA proposals to ban all vending machine sales of cigarettes to locations where children have access, and he rejected another proposal to prohibit tobacco sales through the mail. The final rule permitted color imagery in ads only in adults-only areas such as bars and nightclubs, provided the image cannot be seen from the outside and cannot be removed easily.

The authority asserted by the FDA to regulate tobacco products was challenged immediately by the tobacco companies in the Federal District Court in Greensboro, North Carolina. They charged that the administration overstepped its authority and was heading down the path toward prohibition of all tobacco products. Trade associations representing advertising agencies and convenience stores, distributors, and others filed a lawsuit claiming the FDA violated the commercial free-speech interpretation of the First Amendment. Judge William L. Osteen, Sr., ruled on April 25, 1997, that the FDA had jurisdiction under the Food, Drug, and Cosmetic Act of 1938 (FDCA) to regulate nicotine-containing cigarettes and smokeless tobacco. The court held that tobacco products fit within the act's definitions of *drug*" and *device,* and that the FDA could regulate cigarettes and smokeless tobacco products as drug-delivery devices. Osteen found that Congress never expressly excluded the agency from controlling nicotine in cigarettes. Besides finding that nicotine alters the bodily function just as other drugs do, he said cigarettes delivered nicotine and so were drug-delivery devices. The court upheld all restrictions involving youth access and labeling, including two provisions that went into effect on February 29, 1997: (1) the prohibition on sales of cigarettes and smokeless tobacco products to children and adolescents under 18 years of age, and (2) the requirement that retailers check photo identification of customers who were under 27 years old. The court upheld access and labeling restrictions scheduled to go into effect in August of 1997, including a prohibition on self-service displays and the placement of vending machines where children have access to them.[8]

Judge Osteen's decision was immediately appealed by both sides to the U.S. Court of Appeals for the Fourth Circuit, which overturned it on August 14, 1998. In a 58-page opinion, Circuit Judge H. Emory Widener noted that from 1914 until its attempts to regulate tobacco in 1996, the FDA had consistently said tobacco products were outside its authority. He found that in the 60 years following the passage of the FDCA in 1938, at least 13 bills were introduced in Congress between 1965 and 1993, which would have given the FDA jurisdiction over tobacco products. None of these bills were enacted even though Congress was well aware of the dangers of tobacco products and of the FDA's position that it had no jurisdiction over tobacco products. Congress did not take steps to overturn the FDA's interpretation of the act. Judge Widener found that "Congress did not intend its jurisdictional grant to the FDA to extend to tobacco products." He also found that "based on our examination of the regulatory scheme created by Congress, we are of opinion that the FDA is attempting to stretch the Act beyond the scope intended by Congress."[9] Because the majority of the court found that the agency lacked jurisdiction, it invalidated the FDA's August 1996 regulations that restricted the sale and distribution of tobacco products to children and adolescents.

Circuit Judge K.K. Hall, a dissenting judge, argued, however, that tobacco products fit comfortably into the FDCA's definitions of *drug* and *device*. He said the FDCA was written broadly enough to accommodate both new products and evolving knowledge about existing ones, and it was written that way on purpose. He felt that since cigarettes and smokeless tobacco were responsible for illness and death on a vast scale, there should be FDA regulations aimed at curbing tobacco use by children. Judge Hall referred to the rule making record, which contained voluminous evidence of the pharmacological effects of nicotine as highly addictive, a stimulant, tranquilizer and appetite suppressant. He did not understand the majority saying otherwise because nicotine clearly "affect[s] the structure or function of the body of man."[10]

The dissenting judge also wanted to permit the use of recently disclosed evidence, including heretofore-secret company documents, that established that the tobacco companies had known about the addictive qualities of their products for years and that cigarettes were deliberately manipulated to create and sustain addiction to nicotine. He said the agency's current position was a response to the increasing level of knowledge about the addictive nature of nicotine and the manufacturer's deliberate design to enhance and sustain the additive effect of tobacco products. Judge Hall said that when the early tobacco-specific statutes were being debated in Congress, the essential link between tobacco and illness had not yet been proven to the satisfaction of all. Under the facts found by the FDA during the rule-making process, he felt with certainty that it was now a scientific certainty that nicotine is extremely addictive and that a large majority of tobacco users use the product to satisfy that addiction. Even more important to his mind was the new evidence that the manufacturers designed their products to sustain such addiction. He concluded that the administrative record in this case was a perfect illustration of why an agency's opportunity to adopt a new position should remain open.[11]

The Clinton administration appealed the court of appeals decision to the Supreme Court, which heard the case in December 1999. On March 21, 2000, the Supreme Court issued its decision in *Food and Drug Administration, et al., v. Brown & Williamson Tobacco Corporation et al.,* ruling by 5–4 that the FDA did not have jurisdiction to regulate tobacco because Congress developed a separate regulatory structure outside the FDA and it never intended to give the agency regulatory authority over tobacco.

Justice Sandra Day O'Connor delivered the opinion of the Court, joined by Justices Rehnquist, Scalia, Kennedy, and Thomas. The majority felt that Congress intended to exclude tobacco products from the FDA's jurisdiction. A fundamental precept of the FDCA is that any product regulated by the FDA that remains on the market must be safe and effective for its intended use. Justice O'Connor explained that in its rule-making proceeding, the FDA exhaustively documented that "tobacco products are unsafe," "dangerous," and "cause great pain and suffering from illness ... These findings logically imply that, if tobacco products were 'devices' under the FDCA, the FDA would be required to remove them from the market" because, as the agency asserted in House committee hearing in 1964 and

1972, "it would be impossible to prove they were safe for their intended use[s]." According to the Court, "Congress stopped well short of ordering a ban. Instead it has generally regulated the labeling and advertisement of tobacco products, especially providing that it is the policy of Congress" that "commerce and the national economy may be ... protected to the maximum extent consistent with" consumers "be[ing] adequately informed about any adverse health effects ... A ban of tobacco products by FDA would therefore plainly contradict congressional policy." O'Connor wrote that the FDA recognized the dilemma and had concluded that "tobacco products are actually 'safe' within the meaning of the FDCA. Banning tobacco would cause a greater harm to public health than leaving them on the market." (In 1996, the FDA found that current tobacco users could suffer from extreme withdrawal, the health care system and pharmaceutical industry might fail to meet their treatment demands, and a black market might develop that sold cigarettes more dangerous than those sold legally.) Justice O'Connor concluded: "The inescapable conclusion is that there is no room for tobacco products within the FDCA's regulatory scheme. If they cannot be used safely for any therapeutic purpose, and yet they cannot be banned, they simply do not fit."[12]

The court found that contrary to the agency's position between 1914 until 1995,

> the FDA has now asserted jurisdiction to regulate an industry constituting a significant portion of the American economy. In fact, the FDA contends that, were it to determine that tobacco products provide no "reasonable assurance of safety," it would have the authority to ban cigarettes and smokeless tobacco entirely. Owing to its unique place in American history and society, tobacco has its own unique political history ... It is highly unlikely that Congress would leave the determination as to whether the sale of tobacco products would be regulated, or even banned, to the FDA's discretion in so cryptic a fashion. Given this history and the breadth of the authority that the FDA has asserted, we are obliged to defer not to the agency's expansive construction of the statute, but to Congress' consistent judgment to deny the FDA this power.[13]

According to the court, no matter how important, conspicuous, and controversial the issue, an administrative agency's power to regulate in the public interest must always be grounded in a valid grant of authority from Congress. Congress, however, has foreclosed the removal of tobacco products from the market. A provision of the U.S. Code currently in force states that "the marketing of tobacco constitutes one of the greatest basic industries of the United States with ramifying activities which directly affect interstate and foreign commerce at every point, and stable conditions therein are necessary to the general welfare."[14]

The Court then referred to the history of tobacco-specific legislation, which to it demonstrated that Congress had spoken directly to the FDA's authority to regulate tobacco products. Since 1965 Congress has enacted six separate statutes addressing the problem of tobacco use and human health:

Federal Cigarette Labeling and Advertising Act (FCLAA), 1965
Public Health Cigarette Smoking Act of 1969
Alcohol and Drug Abuse Amendments of 1983
Comprehensive Smoking Education Act of 1984
Comprehensive Smokeless Tobacco Health Education Act of 1986
Alcohol, Drug Abuse, and Mental Health Administration Reorganization
    Act 1992

According to the Court's majority, when Congress enacted these statutes, the adverse health consequences of tobacco use were well known, as were nicotine's pharmacological effects. Justice O'Connor wrote that "in adopting each statute, Congress acted against the backdrop of the FDA's consistent and repeated statements that it lacked authority under the FDCA to regulate tobacco absent claims of therapeutic benefit by the manufacturer. In fact, on several occasions over this period, and after the health consequences of tobacco use and nicotine's pharmacological effects had become well known, Congress considered and rejected bills that would have granted the FDA such jurisdiction." Under these circumstances, Congress' tobacco-specific statutes effectively ratified the FDA's long-held position that it lacked jurisdiction under the FDCA to regulate tobacco products. The Court argued that "Congress has created a distinct regulatory scheme to address the problem of tobacco and health, and that scheme, as presently constructed, precludes any role for the FDA. Therefore, it was left to Congress to make policy determinations regarding further regulation of tobacco through congressional action, not by an agency made up of appointed officials."[15]

Justice Stephen Breyer delivered the opinion of the dissenters, joined by Justices Stevens, Souter, and Ginsburg. They wanted to uphold FDA jurisdiction over tobacco products. The dissent referred to the history of the 1938 FDCA, in which Congress expanded the FDCA's jurisdictional scope significantly with the added definition of drugs: "articles (other than food) intended to affect the structure or any function of the body." It also added a similar definition in respect to a *device*. The dissent said that the broad language was included deliberately, so that jurisdiction could be had over "all substances and preparations, other than food, and all devices intended to affect the structure or any function of the body."[16] Contrary to the majority decision, four justices argued that the FDCA was broad enough to include tobacco within the meaning of the statutory definition of drugs and devices because such products were intended to affect the structure and function of the body.

The dissenters also argued that the purpose of the FDCA—to protect the public health—also supported the conclusion that the FDA was authorized to regulate tobacco products. The dissent said that the majority did not deny that tobacco products (including cigarettes) fall within the scope of this statutory definition and that cigarettes achieve their mood-stabilizing effects through the interaction of the chemical nicotine and the cells of the central nervous system. Both cigarette manufacturers and smokers alike have known of, and desired, that chemically induced result. Therefore, according to this line of reasoning, cigarettes are "intended to affect" the body's *structure* and *function,* in the literal sense of these words. (The tobacco companies' principal argument was focused upon the statutory word *intended.* The companies say that the statutory word *intended* means that the product's maker has made an express claim about the effect that its product will have on the body. According to the companies, the FDA's inability to prove that cigarette manufacturers made such claims is precisely why that agency historically has said it lacked the statutory power to regulate tobacco.)

The dissent also said that the statute's basic purpose—the protection of public health—supported the inclusion of cigarettes within its scope because unregulated tobacco use causes more than 400,000 people to die each year from tobacco-related illnesses, such as cancer, respiratory illnesses, and heart disease.

The dissent argued that the FDA obtained scientific and epidemiological evidence that "permitted the agency to demonstrate that the tobacco companies knew nicotine achieved appetite-suppressing, mood-stabilizing, and habituating effects through chemical (not psychological) means, even at a time when the companies were publicly denying such knowledge. Moreover, scientific evidence of adverse health effects mounted, until, in the late 1980's, a consensus on the seriousness of the matter became firm."[17] Convincing epidemiological evidence began to appear mid-20th century, with the first surgeon general's report of 1964 that documented the adverse health effects from tobacco use and the surgeon general's report of 1988 establishing nicotine's addictive effects. By the mid-1990s, the emerging scientific consensus about tobacco's adverse, chemically induced, health effects doubtless convinced the agency that it should spend its resources on this important regulatory effort. At each stage, the health conclusions were the subject of controversy. The dissent asserted that although earlier administrations may have hesitated to assert FDA jurisdiction, nothing in the law prevents the FDA from changing its policy.

The Supreme Court's decision made it clear that Congress would have to enact legislation giving the FDA authority over tobacco products. Legislators drafted language regarding FDA jurisdiction in the 105th Congress (1997–1998) and 107th Congress (2001–2002), but there was no legislative action.

Early in the 107th Congress, in March 2001, Philip Morris, the tobacco industry's sales leader, released a white paper supporting legislation giving FDA new authority to regulate cigarettes, as long as new legislation recognized cigarettes as legal products and respected the decision of adults to smoke. Earlier, the company opposed the FDA rule on the grounds it would have left the agency with no choice but to ban the sale of cigarettes. Philip Morris argued that regulation "would provide greater consistency in tobacco policy, more predictability for the tobacco industry, and an effective way to address issues that are of concern ... These issues include youth smoking, ingredient and [smoke] constituent testing and disclosure; content of health warning on cigarette packages and in advertisements; use of brand descriptions such as 'light,' and 'ultra light'; good manufacturing practices for cigarettes; and standards for defining, and for the responsible marketing of any reduced risk or reduced exposure cigarettes."[18]

Philip Morris opposed proposals that would give FDA the authority to ban cigarettes outright or to achieve de facto prohibition by imposing lower tar and nicotine levels that would render the product unpalatable to adult smokers. Both Philip Morris and the FDA reasoned that banning tobacco would encourage cigarette smuggling and the development of a black market supplying smokers with unregulated and potentially more dangerous products. Unlike Philip Morris, other tobacco companies have criticized various legislative proposals. R. J. Reynolds and Lorillard fear that new regulations, especially restrictions on marketing, will benefit Philip Morris, by allowing it to lock in its leading market share.

A partnership of leading antitobacco organizations and the Campaign for Tobacco-Free Kids developed a set of elements that it wants incorporated into regulatory legislation. While the Campaign and Philip Morris generally agree on several areas over which the FDA should be granted authority (youth access and marketing, ingredient testing and disclosure, good manufacturing practice, and reduced-risk products), "they fundamentally disagree on whether any limitations should be placed on that authority. ... The Campaign argues that FDA should be granted broad and unrestricted regulatory authority to take those actions it deems necessary to protect public health." The Campaign for Tobacco-Free Kids insists that the "FDA should have the authority to evaluate scientifically and, through a notice-and-comment rulemaking process, decide whether to reduce or eliminate harmful and addictive components of all tobacco products in order to protect the public health."[19] Legislation empowering the FDA to regulate tobacco passed in the Senate in 2004, but saw no action in either chamber. In July 2008 HR 1108, the Family Smoking Prevention and Tobacco Control Act, passed the House, with support from Philip Morris, a number of medical societies and public health organizations, and the Campaign for Tobacco-Free Kids, but it never became law. On April 2, 2009, the House passed HR 1256, the Family Smoking Prevention and Tobacco Control Act (FSPTCA), to protect public health by providing the FDA with certain authority to regulate tobacco products. The Senate approved the bill on June 11. On June 22, 2009, President Obama signed the FSPTCA into law, empowering the FDA to regulate tobacco.

The law requires that larger warning labels cover the top 50 percent of the front and rear panels of the cigarette packages by July 2011; that tobacco companies be prohibited from using terms such as *low tar, light,* or *mild* by July 2010; that tobacco companies no longer sell candy-flavored and fruit-flavored cigarettes; that tobacco company no longer put logos on sporting, athletic, or entertainment events, or on clothing and other promotional items; and that outdoor tobacco ads are banned within 1,000 feet of schools and playgrounds. The law empowered the FDA to create a new Center for Tobacco Products to oversee the science-based regulation of tobacco products in the United States.[20] In August 2009, Dr. Lawrence R. Dyton was named as the first director of the newly created Center for Tobacco Products. Dr. Margaret A. Hamberg, FDA Commissioner, said Dr. Deyton was "the rare combination of public health expert, administrative leader, scientist, and clinician."[21]

Less than three months after the FSPTCA granted the FDA power to regulate tobacco products, several of the largest tobacco companies filed suit in Kentucky claiming that the law "individually and collectively violate their free speech rights under the First Amendment, their Due Process rights under the Fifth Amendment; and effect an unconstitutional Taking under the Fifth Amendment."[22] On January 4, 2010, in a 47-page ruling, Judge Joseph H. McKinley, Jr., overturned two of the marketing restrictions in the FSPTCA, ruling that tobacco companies could not be forced to limit their marketing materials to only black text on a white background.

The judge said the companies could use images and colors to "communicate important commercial information about their products, i.e., what the product is and who makes it."[23] The judge also agreed with the plaintiffs who argued that "the ban on mentioning the FDA regulation of tobacco products" is unconstitutional.[24] Judge Joseph upheld other restrictions of the law including a ban on forms of tobacco marketing that might appeal to youngsters and a ban on free samples, and he upheld the warning requirements that "include color graphics that depict the negative health consequences of smoking to accompany the label statements."[25] He said: "The government's goal is not to stigmatize the use of tobacco products on the industry's dime; it is to ensure that the health risk message is actually *seen* by consumers in the first instance."[26]

CHAPTER 9

Preventing/Reducing Tobacco Use by Children and Teens

Physicians, educators, legislators, public health groups, parents, and other antitobacco activists have been debating ways to discourage and/or prevent tobacco use among children and teens since the 1890s. At the turn of the century and in the early 1900s, tobacco was used predominantly for chew, snuff, pipes, and cigar smoking; mass-produced cigarettes were growing in popularity.

The disagreements about goals and tactics continue today. The question is not whether cigarettes, smokeless tobacco, and cigars have been harmful to young people. Opinion over the past 100+ years has been nearly uniform that tobacco products have been hazardous to their health. But opinion has differed over the best approaches to take to prevent or reduce tobacco use in all its forms by kids under 18. Over the past decades, antitobacco advocates have considered health education programs, regulatory efforts (tobacco advertising and promotions, and reducing teen access), excise taxes, and mass media campaigns.

Between 1885 and 1902, cigarettes gained popularity in the United States, especially with young boys, because they were inexpensive, easy to use, and a milder form of tobacco. By 1900 some 7.4 total pounds of tobacco were consumed per capita by youngsters 15 years and older in the United States: 2 percent as cigarettes, 4 percent as snuff, 27 percent as cigars, 19 percent as smoking tobacco (pipe and roll-your-own), and 48 percent as chewing tobacco.[1]

The American Tobacco Company and several other manufacturers created a demand for paper smokes by packaging them in brightly colorful cigarette packs with attention-grabbing names and images. Advertisements were placed on billboards and on posters tacked to fences, walls, and storefronts, even in small towns.

Between 1885 and 1912, dozens of manufacturers inserted small color-picture cards ("trade" cards) in each box to attract cigarette buyers to their brands. Every possible subject was pictured on them from birds, dogs, flags, and flowers to actresses, great American Indian chiefs, presidents, and baseball players. Collecting cards showing pretty women and baseball players, the new national heroes, became a national craze for old and young. These cardboard cards slipped between two rows of cigarettes did more than stiffen the paper cigarette packages. Cigarette manufacturers encouraged customers to collect complete sets. The trade cards made sales zoom up, and they made cigarettes big business.

Around the turn of the century, cigarette sellers began attracting young male customers just starting to smoke by breaking open packs of cigarettes and selling single cigarettes called *loosies*. Children of ages 8 or 9 went into stores and bought them from the shopkeepers. On August 6, 1913, the *New York Times* reported that in New York City, a squad of boys ranging in age from 10 to 12 conducted a sting of neighborhood stores. They were able to buy cigarettes from 200 shopkeepers. Since the law required that no cigarettes be sold to children under 16 and made it a misdemeanor for them to smoke in public, the boys turned the names of the lawbreakers over to the East Side Protective Association.

By the 1920s, cigarette-smoking boys were a common sight in cities and rural areas. However, before the advent of systematic surveillance of cigarette smoking by the federal and state governments and private organizations like the American Cancer Society, no surveys existed to convey the extent of youthful tobacco use. More than 60 years later, during the 1980s, the surgeon general of the Public Health Service (PHS) and National Cancer Institute researchers reconstructed the prevalence of cigarette smoking among 10- through 19-year-olds in the United States from 1920 until 1980.[2] According to the report, in 1920 almost 17 percent of white male boys were smoking, higher than among African American males (12.5%), African females (2.5%), and white females (1.0%). Parents worried that excessive cigarette smoking by their sons would lead to weakening of eyesight, stunted growth, sterility, dulled ambition, or moral dissipation. (Women and girls became the object of antismoking efforts decades later.) Populist health reformers worried that any stimulant was unhealthy. These antitobacco critics worried that tobacco caused ailments ranging from cancer and heart disease to other illnesses.

The strong outcry about childhood smoking by parents, teachers, physicians, social and health reformers, and others led to public or private efforts to prevent or discourage tobacco use. State legislators responded: During the 1890s, 26 states (of the 45 states in the Union at the time) passed laws prohibiting the sale or giving away of cigarettes to minors. As defined by states, *minor* could range anywhere from 14 to 21.

Cigarette prohibition began with Washington State in 1893 when the legislature made it illegal to "manufacture, buy, sell, give or furnish to anyone cigarettes, cigarette paper or cigarette wrapper."[3] Three months after the law was enacted, a federal court in Seattle declared it unconstitutional on the grounds that it improperly restrained interstate trade. The June 15, 1893, issue of the *New York Times* endorsed the court's decision, commenting that "the smoking of cigarettes may be objectionable, as are many other foolish practices and it may be more injurious than other modes of smoking tobacco, but it is an evil which cannot be remedied by law."[4] The law was repealed in 1895 and reenacted in 1907. Another law banning the sale, manufacture, and possession was enacted in 1909 and repealed in 1911. By 1909 some 14 states and 1 territory (Oklahoma) banned the sale and, in some cases, possession of cigarettes. By 1920, minors could legally buy cigarettes only in 2 of the 48 states: Virginia and Rhode Island. By 1930 there were 37 states and territories that had considered legislation to ban the sale, manufacture, possession, and/or use of cigarettes altogether; 15 states adopted these prohibitive laws, and all 15 states subsequently repealed them.[5] Legislative records, newspaper reports, and other sources show that towns and cities also limited the sale or use of cigarettes.

State and local laws forbidding the sale of cigarettes to minors were fairly useless. Since evasion was easy for retailers and smokers, enforcing the antismoking laws was nearly impossible. Cigarette vendors continued to attract young customers. Some educators took matters into their own hands. In 1893 Charles B. Hubbell, president of the New York Board of Education, began a crusade against cigarettes in public schools because he felt the cigarette habit was "more devastating to the health and morals of young men than any habit or vice that can be named."[6] He formed an anticigarette smoking league in every boys' school in New York City. The first one was established in 1894, and eventually, 25,000 New York schoolboys belonged to leagues established in almost all of the 63 male grammar schools. When boys joined a league, they signed a pledge not to smoke until they were 21. They received diamond-shaped badges of solid silver whose face bore the words: "The cigarette must go." If a member was caught smoking, he turned in his badge and was barred from the league for six months. After he returned, he got his badge back and was given another chance to be a member.

In Chicago, Lucy Page Gaston, a Women's Christian Temperance Union worker and an implacable foe of cigarettes, began her anticigarette crusade in the late 1890s. Traveling throughout the Midwest, Gaston administered the New Life Pledge to thousands of boys and girls who promised to abstain from tobacco and alcohol. She founded the Anti-Cigarette League (ACL) in 1899 whose objective was "to combat and discourage, by all legitimate means, the use of and traffic of cigaretts [sic]." The organization, which claimed a membership of 300,000 by 1901, primarily wanted to enact legislation and prosecute violators.[7] Special officers hired by the league arrested anyone under 18 who was found smoking in public. Gaston, who linked cigarette smoking to alcohol abuse, believed it was in the public interest that state legislatures ban cigarettes. She had little faith in the value of education as a means of stamping out tobacco use by children (or adults). Between 1908 and 1917, the Illinois legislature considered 12 bills to ban the manufacture, use, sale, and giving away of cigarettes, each one promoted by Gaston and the ACL.[8] Gaston, who signed letters to supporters "Yours for the extermination of the cigarette," was eventually forced to resign by the ACL in 1919. A few months after another anti-cigarette board of directors fired her in 1921, it noted that her tactics were "no longer the most effective means of fighting the cigarette evil."[9]

In addition to the ACL, the No-Tobacco League and a new organization, the Anti-Cigarette Alliance, founded in 1927, focused on youth, emphasizing education over the coercive methods that had been advocated by Gaston and her followers. Group members visited classrooms as guest lecturers showing slides depicting diseased organs. One of the demonstrations they did involved "soaking a cigarette in water, straining the liquid through a white handkerchief ... and dramatically identifying the resultant yellow stain as nicotine."[10] The stain was actually caused by tar.

HEALTH EDUCATION CAMPAIGNS

Educational approaches to smoking prevention, like those undertaken by the ACL, other antitobacco organizations, as well as programs designed from the late 1920s until the present day, have been based on an assumption that adolescents would refrain from cigarette smoking if they were supplied with adequate information demonstrating that this habit and other tobacco products cause serious harm to the body. The public has looked to schools to educate children about the hazards of tobacco use. A number of states have enacted laws that mandate education about smoking and health in schools. States like Massachusetts require that the dangers of tobacco be included in every school's health education curriculum.[11] A Nebraska state code mandates a comprehensive health education program, which includes instruction that emphasizes physiological, psychological, and sociological aspects of tobacco abuse.[12] In part, the emphasis on school-based education has long reflected a belief that education is the most effective way to discourage children from smoking.

Contemporary educational techniques to raise awareness of the health effects of smoking have included lectures, demonstrations, films, posters, books, curriculum, and teaching aids like an inflatable smokers' lungs that show the impact of tobacco use; Mr. Gross Mouth, a hinged model of the teeth, tongue, and oral cavity, which shows the effects of using smokeless tobacco; and Smoky Sue, a simulation doll, which shows how smoke inhalation by a mother can damage a fetus.

Although education programs have increased knowledge among youngsters about the health risks of tobacco use, large numbers of young people still smoke or chew. Each day in the United States, approximately 4,000 young people between the ages of 12 and 17 initiate cigarette smoking, and an estimated 1,140 young people become daily cigarette smokers.[13] In 2007, 2.5 million youths aged 12 to 17 used cigarettes, and 1.1 million used cigars. That year, 1.8 percent of 12- or 13-year-olds, 8.4 percent of 14- or 15-year-olds, and 18.9 percent of 16- or 17-year-olds were current cigarette users.[14] Young people also use smokeless (spit) tobacco. The CDC 2006 Youth Tobacco Survey reported that, of middle school students, 4 percent of the boys and 1 percent of the girls reported using smokeless tobacco at least once in the 30 days before the survey.[15] According to a 2007 survey by the Centers for Disease Control and Prevention (CDC), more than 13 percent of male high school students and 2 percent of female high school students were using smokeless tobacco.

REGULATORY EFFORTS: ADVERTISING AND PROMOTIONS

In the late 1880s and 1890s, the antismoking movement focused on restricting children's access to cigarettes. In 1888 a New York citizen complained, "There is no question that demands more public attention than the prevailing methods of cigarette manufacturers to foster and stimulate smoking among children. At the office of a leading factory in this city you can see any Saturday afternoon a crowd of children with vouchers clamoring for the reward of self-inflicted injury."[16] The children were exchanging the coupons they found in cigarette packets for prizes such as pocketknives. According to an issue of the *New York Times* printed on Christmas Day, 1888, "Every possible device has been employed to

---

SCHOOL TEXTBOOKS AND TOBACCO
EDUCATION, 1894–1930

1894. School health booklet for primary grades states: "When we eat or drink anything poisonous, it is taken up by the blood and carried to all parts of the body, bones and all. Tobacco is a poison. Although we do not eat it, its poison surely affects us, if we smoke it, chew it, or take it into our nostrils in the form of snuff." (Joseph Chrisman Hutchison, *Our Wonderful Bodies and How to Take Care of Them.* New York: Maynard, Merrill & Company Publishers, 1894)

1910. An elementary school textbook stated: "The cells of the brain may become poisoned from tobacco … The will power may be weakened, and it may be an effort to do the routine duties of life … The memory may be impaired … The reason for this is plain. The mind of the habitual user of tobacco is apt to lose its capacity for study or successful effort. This is especially true of boys and young men. The growth and development of the brain having been once retarded, the youthful user of tobacco has established a permanent drawback which may hamper him all his life." (Albert F. Blaisdell. *Our Bodies and How We Live.* New York: Ginn and Company, 1910)

1919. A junior high textbook used from 1919 to 1936 states: "The harmful substance in tobacco is nicotine, which is a narcotic … its effect is distinctly poisonous." (C. E. Turner. *Community Health.*)

1930. A state-approved health education textbook in New York stated: "Tobacco, too, is a habit forming narcotic. It contains a deadly drug called nicotine, part of which is absorbed, when tobacco is used." (William E. Burkhard, Raymond L. Chambers, and Frederick W. Maroney, *Health and Human Welfare: A Health Text for Secondary Schools.* Chicago: Lyons and Carrahan, 1931)

---

interest the juvenile mind, notably the lithographic album … many a boy under 12 years is striving for the entire collection, which necessitates the consumption of nearly 12,000 cigarettes."[17]

Around 1912 tobacco companies inserted small silk rectangles in cigarette boxes. Female smokers bought the cigarettes and collected the *silks,* which they stitched together and sewed onto pillows and bedspreads. Small silk rugs were also the perfect size for a child's dollhouse.

Since the 1890s, an era rife with tobacco promotions that especially appealed to young boys, the potential influence of tobacco advertising and promotion on children and teens has been a subject of concern and debate. According to the 2000 surgeon general's report, a "contentious debate has persisted about whether marketing induces demand and what the appropriate role of government is in protecting the consumer."[18]

The concern over the influence of advertising on youngsters led to regulation of tobacco by federal government agencies. The fairness doctrine of the Federal Communications Commission (FCC), introduced in the United States in 1949, required broadcasters to devote some of their airtime to discussing controversial matters of public interest and to air contrasting views regarding those matters. The FCC required all radio and television stations broadcasting cigarette commercials to donate "significant" free airtime to antismoking messages. Over the objections of tobacco companies and broadcasters, Lee Loevinger, FCC commissioner, said that "suggesting cigarette smoking to young people, in the light of present-day knowledge, is something very close to wickedness."[19] Between July 1, 1967, and December 21, 1970, antismoking messages were aired at no cost alongside paid commercials promoting cigarette smoking. Surveys of teenagers exposed to the messages showed a sharp decline in the number taking up cigarettes. In April of 1970, President Richard Nixon signed the Public Health Cigarette Smoking Act of 1969, which banned cigarette advertising on TV and radio as of January 1, 1971, thus ending the exposure of children and teens to thousands of commercials that glamorized smoking. According to syndicated newspaper columnist Jacob Sullum, these regulatory efforts and others "can be viewed as responses to anxiety about the 'constant seduction' of children."[20]

During the late 1980s, a cartoon character named Joe Camel stirred up a great deal of controversy. In 1988 RJR Nabisco launched the "smooth character" advertising campaign featuring "Old Joe," often referred to as Joe Camel, who appeared in ads and on promotional merchandise like mugs and lighters as well as on clothing and sunglasses. In 1991 the "Camel Cash" promotion offered coupons resembling $1 bills in every pack of filtered Camel cigarettes. Consumers could redeem the coupons for flip-flops, towels, hats, T-shirts, all featuring images of Joe Camel. Health professionals who worried that Old Joe caught the attention of children did studies to determine the campaign's influence on children. Dr. Paul Fisher's landmark study, one of three published in the December 11, 1991, issue of the *Journal of the American Medical Association,* showed that 30 percent of 3-year-olds correctly matched the "Old Joe" cartoon camel with a picture of a cigarette. The study also showed that 91 percent of 6-year-olds recognized "Old Joe." In a *Washington Post* column on May 9, 1991, Courtland Milloy said that "packaging a cartoon camel as a 'smooth character' is as dangerous as putting rat poison in a candy wrapper." Other critics argued that the cartoon character had a substantial influence on smoking among underage youth.[21] According to surveys of the Monitoring the Future project and the National Household Survey on Drug Abuse, teenage smoking declined during the first five years of the Joe Camel campaign, then began to rise in 1993.

During the early 1990s, there were some calls to end the Joe Camel campaign. In 1992 Surgeon General Antonia Novello and the American Medical Association called on Reynolds to withdraw the Joe Camel campaign. In 1997 the Federal Trade Commission (FTC) filed a complaint that the Joe Camel campaign illegally promoted cigarettes to minors.

R. J. Reynolds retired Joe Camel from its domestic marketing in July of 1997. Reynolds and other tobacco manufacturers agreed to stop using cartoon characters as part of a proposed tobacco settlement. The FTC ultimately dismissed its complaint as no longer necessary after the November 23, 1998, Master Settlement Agreement (MSA) banned the use of all cartoon characters, including Joe Camel, in the advertising, promotion, packaging, and labeling of any tobacco product.

Although the process of legally regulating tobacco advertising and promotion had been under way for decades, significant developments took place in the summer of 1995. For the first time since the enactment of the original Food and Drugs Act in 1906 and the modern Food, Drug, and Cosmetic Act in 1938, the Food and Drug Administration (FDA) asserted authority to regulate tobacco products on August 10, 1995. The FDA published a proposed rule that included several restrictions on the sale, distribution, and advertisement of tobacco products to children and adolescents. The rule was designed to reduce the availability and attractiveness of tobacco products to young people. A public comment period followed, during which the FDA received over 710,000 submissions, "the largest outpouring of public response in the agency's history."[22] On August 28, 1996, the FDA issued a final rule entitled "Regulations Restricting the Sale and Distribution of Cigarettes and Smokeless Tobacco to Protect Children and Adolescents."

Based on the deleterious health effects associated with tobacco use, and evidence that the prevalence of youth smoking and smokeless tobacco had recently increased, the FDA argued that "tobacco use, particularly among children and adolescents, poses perhaps the single most significant threat to public health in the United States."[23] Based on the agency's findings

Figure 9.1 Cover of the 1994 surgeon general's report, focused specifically on children and teens.

that "nicotine addiction usually begins in adolescence or before," the FDA became convinced that the appropriate policy was "to stop children and adolescents from using tobacco in the first place."[24] The FDA promulgated regulations concerning tobacco products' promotion, labeling, and accessibility to children and adolescents as well as reducing the appeal (through advertising) of tobacco products to minors.

The promotion regulations required that "only black-and-white text advertising would be permitted in publications for which more than 15 percent of the readership is under age 18 and in publications with more than 2 million young readers," unless the publication in which the advertising appeared was read almost exclusively by adults; prohibited outdoor advertising "within 1,000 feet of schools and playgrounds"; prohibited the distribution of T-shirts or hats bearing the manufacturer's brand name; and prohibited the "sponsorship of sporting or entertainment events using specific brand names or product identification ... although the use of company names would not."[25]

A group of tobacco manufacturers, retailers, and advertisers filed suit in U.S. District Court for the Middle District of North Carolina challenging the regulations. Among its findings, the court held that the 1938 Food, Drug, and Cosmetic Act authorized the FDA to regulate tobacco products as customarily marketed and that the FDA's access and labeling regulations were permissible, but the FDA's advertising and promotion restrictions exceeded its authority. The Court of Appeals for the Fourth Circuit overturned the lower court decision in August 1998, holding that Congress had not granted the FDA jurisdiction to regulate tobacco products.

In 1999 the Justice Department filed a petition with the U.S. Supreme Court to review the Fourth Circuit ruling and find that the FDA has full statutory authority to regulate tobacco products and to issue all the provisions of the FDA Tobacco Rule, some of which addressed tobacco advertising and marketing to children. The Supreme Court's 5–4 ruling on March 21, 2000, said that Congress had not given the FDA adequate jurisdiction to regulate cigarettes and smokeless tobacco products or related marketing practices. As a result, the FDA no longer had regulatory authority to enforce its final rule issued in 1996.

In the absence of congressional action, on November 23, 1998, eleven tobacco companies executed a legal settlement with 46 states, the District of Columbia, and 5 commonwealths and territories. In addition to the monetary payments from the tobacco companies to states, the MSA contained provisions regarding marketing restrictions on the industry by prohibiting direct advertising and promotions aimed at young people, and by limiting brand-name sponsorship at concerts, team sporting events, or events with a significant youth audience. The MSA banned cartoon characters in tobacco advertising, packaging, and promotions; the use of tobacco brand names in stadiums and arenas; payments to promote tobacco products in movies; and distribution and sale of merchandise with brand-name tobacco logos. The MSA banned transit and outdoor advertising, including billboards. At industry expense, states could substitute advertising discouraging youth smoking.[26]

Not everyone agrees that restrictions on tobacco advertising and promotions will work to reduce or prevent children and teens from smoking. Writer Jacob Sullum argues that "restrictions on the advertising and promotion of cigarettes might also have the perverse effects of making these products more appealing. The attempt to shield kids not only from cigarettes but from *images* of cigarettes-even from articles of clothing carrying brand names-is bound to pique curiosity and foster rebellion."[27] He also argues that "exposure to advertising does not independently predict the decision [of teenagers] to smoke."[28]

REGULATORY EFFORTS: REDUCING ACCESS TO TOBACCO

The policy of restricting children's access to cigarettes was the focus of the antismoking movement in the late 1880s and 1890s. More than 100 years later, it became the focus again. A 2001 study stated that making it as difficult and inconvenient as possible for children and teens to get cigarettes would reduce the number of young people who smoke. About half of all young smokers reported that they usually bought their cigarettes from retailers or vending machines, or by giving money to others to purchase the cigarettes for them. Minimizing the number of retailers who were willing to illegally sell cigarettes to kids would also reduce smoking by young people, according to the researchers.[29]

Success in reducing youth access to tobacco depends on merchant compliance with state laws prohibiting tobacco sales to minors; the extent of active compliance checking by minors who, under adult supervision, periodically try to purchase tobacco; and enforcement of fines for merchants who violate the law. Other issues may also impact success in reducing young people's access to tobacco. One study's findings suggest that "tests of compliance ... underestimate young people's access to tobacco ... the rate of compliance by merchants might not reflect actual access to tobacco. Even if one store in a community sells tobacco to minors, young people who know about it could obtain tobacco easily."[30]

Efforts to curb illegal sales to minors have occurred at the federal level. According to the 2000 surgeon general's report, "The most sustained and widespread attention to the issue of minors' access laws and their enforcement" was taken by the "U.S. Congress in 1992 when it adopted the Synar Amendment (42 U.S.C. § 300x-26) as part of the Alcohol, Drug Abuse, and Mental Health Administration Reorganization Act (Public Law

102–321, sec. 1926)." The amendment, whose regulations were finalized in 1996, "requires states (at the risk of forfeiting federal block grant funds for substance abuse prevention and treatment)" to adopt laws prohibiting "any manufacturer, retailer, or distributor of tobacco products from selling or distributing such products to any persons under the age of 18"; to enforce the law, to "conduct annual, random, unannounced inspections to ensure compliance with the law"; to show "an inspection failure rate of less than 20 percent among outlets accessible to underaged youth"; and "to submit an annual report detailing the state's activities in enforcing the law, the success achieved, methods used, and plans for future enforcement." According to the 2000 surgeon general report, "twenty-two states and two U.S. jurisdictions modified their youth access laws within a year of implementing Synar inspections."[31]

The 2000 report also noted that "in spite of some advances in enforcement of youth access laws, states also encountered difficulties" while trying to comply with Synar regulations. Synar does not fund enforcement, a problem for states where youth access laws have not been a priority. Other obstacles include "fear of lawsuits from cited vendors," "liability issues associated with working with young people," and opposition to conducting enforcement from state and local officials, law enforcement, and the general public in regions of the country where the economy is tied to the production of tobacco.[32]

Laws on the minimum age for tobacco sales have been part of many state statutes for decades. Today all 50 states and the District of Columbia prohibit tobacco sales to minors. Most states define minors as persons under 18 years of age. Four states—Alabama, Alaska, New Jersey, and Utah—define minors as under 19 years of age. Thirty-eight states and the District of Columbia require retailers to post signs at the point of purchase stating that selling tobacco products to minors is illegal. Eighteen states and the District of Columbia require a person selling tobacco products to check the identification of a purchaser who appears to be under the age of 18. All 50 states and the District of Columbia prohibit the distribution of tobacco products to minors. Forty-eight states and the District of Columbia restrict the placement of tobacco product vending machines.[33] Despite minimum-age laws, a 2008 national survey of teens aged 12 to 17 interviewed in March of 2008 revealed that, among 15- to 17-year-olds, 76 percent thought it was easy to buy cigarettes.[34]

Although some policy makers, public health officials, and tobacco control advocates believe that penalizing children has not been proved to be an effective technique to reduce underage tobacco usage, 45 states penalize minors for tobacco-related offenses. Twenty-five states order minors who are guilty of a tobacco-related offense to perform community service as well as, or in lieu of, a fine. Nine states may suspend the driver's license of a minor who violates their youth access law. Sixteen states require minors to attend smoking education/cessation programs in addition to or in lieu of other penalties for tobacco-related offenses.[35]

Some antitobacco advocates argue that these state laws (as well as local laws) deflect responsibility for illegal tobacco sales away from retailers to underage youth. They also argue that sanctions against minors are more difficult to enforce than those against retailers. Other advocates insist that youthful purchasers must accept some responsibility.

REGULATORY EFFORTS: TAXATION

Because of state and local enforcement, penalties, and other issues involving teen access to tobacco products, not everyone feels that banning the sale of tobacco to minors is as effective as it should be. Some studies and experience in dozens of states show that raising cigarette taxes is one of the most effective ways to reduce smoking among both youth and adults. Forty-four states and the District of Columbus have increased cigarette taxes since January 1, 2002. According to the June 2006 National Institutes of Health State-of-the-Science Panel on tobacco use, "It is well established that an increase in price decreases cigarette use and that raising tobacco excise taxes is one of the most effective policies for reducing use, especially among adolescents ... increases in excise taxes were determined to be effective in preventing tobacco use among adolescents and young adults."[36]

Proponents of higher tobacco taxes argue that most smokers start before the age of 18 and that teens are sensitive to price increases. Critics, however, argue that higher taxes impose a burden on all smokers to deter a small minority who are not legally permitted to buy cigarettes, smokeless tobacco, and other tobacco products in the first place. Sullum and others maintain that "since every state prohibits the sale of cigarettes to minors, a serious effort to enforce these laws seems a more appropriate response to underage smoking."[37]

The numbers of teens buying cigarettes online has been rising, especially as access to cigarettes becomes more difficult in retail stores. These teens have circumvented excise taxes by buying cigarettes from Internet cigarette vendors who sell cigarettes at much lower prices because they do not charge excise taxes. Since few Internet vendors check the age and identity of their customers, these sites are attractive options for underage youngsters. Although all U.S. states have laws that ban cigarette sales to minors and cigarette retailers are required to verify the age of customers, Internet vendors do not comply with these laws. (See chapter 6, "Tobacco Excise Taxation and Health Policy," for further discussion about tobacco taxation.)

COMPREHENSIVE PROGRAMS

In December 2006, the National Institutes of Health State-of-the-Science Conference stated that "previous reviews have identified three effective general population approaches to preventing tobacco use in adolescents and young adults: 1) increased prices through taxes on tobacco products; 2) laws and regulations that prevent young people from gaining access to tobacco products, reduce their exposure to tobacco smoke, and restrict tobacco industry advertising; and 3) mass media campaigns. Previous reviews show that school-based intervention programs aimed at preventing tobacco use in adolescents are effective in the short term. Comprehensive statewide programs have also reduced overall tobacco use in young adults."[38]

In 2009 the American Legacy Foundation (ALF) recommended mass media campaigns at the national level. Created in 1999 out of the landmark MSA between the tobacco industry and 46 state governments and 5 U.S. territories, ALF states that "a national, evidence-based, independent and well-funded media campaign is a proven effective and necessary component of youth prevention efforts." While noting that a national media campaign is expensive, requiring "at least $100 million per year, the ALF trusts that it is the most cost effective way to reach teens across the country."[39]

It is clear that none of the approaches taken alone, health education campaigns and several regulatory efforts, can substantially reduce smoking by teens and children. But as the CDC suggested in 2007, a comprehensive approach, "one that optimizes synergy from applying a mix of educational, clinical, regulatory, economic, and social strategies"[40] stands a better chance of reducing or preventing tobacco use among children and teens.

CHAPTER 10

Environmental Tobacco Smoke and Health Risks

Environmental tobacco smoke (also known as sidestream smoke, second-hand smoke, passive smoke, and involuntary smoking) has been an issue for at least 100 years. Long regarded as an irritant, it took decades before scientists regarded it as a health threat to nonsmokers. In the early 20th century, many people advocated for the rights of nonsmokers by calling for restrictions on smoking in public places. In 1910 New York attorney and antismoking advocate Twyman Abbott penned an article titled "The Rights of the Nonsmoker." He asked: "In all fairness, is it not reasonable to demand that some limitation be placed upon the indulgence of this habit?"[1] He claimed smoking in public was worse than drinking alcohol because it created toxic fumes. He wanted dining rooms, railways, and public buildings to provide adequate accommodations for nonsmokers.

Some antismoking advocates founded organizations to lobby for bans on smoking in public places. In 1910 the *New York Times* reported that Charles Pease, a New York physician, founded the Non-Smokers Protective League. In a November 10, 1911, letter to the *New York Times,* he explained his group's position: "The right of each person to breathe and enjoy fresh and pure air—air uncontaminated by unhealthful or disagreeable odors and fumes—is a constitutional right, and cannot be taken away by legislatures and courts, much less by individuals pursuing their own thoughtless or selfish indulgence." In 1913 the *New York Times* noted that "the relaxed regulations which allow smoking in almost all public places, such as hotel dining rooms and theaters, inconvenience sufficiently those to whom smoking is generally offensive." In an editorial "To Smoke or Not

Figure 10.1 An 1886 wood carving showed the public's reaction to environmental smoke (secondhand smoke) as an irritant. Some antismoking advocates argued it was a constitutional right to breathe clean air. (Courtesy of the National Library of Medicine)

Source: Image appeared in *Good Health* 21 (1886): 257.

to Smoke," the paper opposed a petition to create smoking cars in public subways.[2]

The Non-Smokers Protective League convinced New York State's Public Service Commission to prohibit smoking on railroads, streetcars, and ferries, and in waiting rooms. The decision came after a public hearing at which people aired their grievances against smokers. Cigarettes were described as a nuisance, a fire hazard, and a public health hazard. According to a report in the June 19, 1913, issue of the *New York Times,* a few smokers who tried to speak on their own behalf were ridiculed. One smoker said: "Spare a little of our vices. We shall be a long time dead. They have a constitutional right to breathe fresh air; haven't we got a constitutional right to the pursuit of happiness?" Despite the work of the Non-Smokers Protective League, a decade later, health reformer John Harvey Kellogg wrote: "Smoking has become so nearly universal among men, the few nonsmokers are practically ignored and their rights trampled upon."[3]

The issue of public smoking erupted in the Senate in 1914. Weakened by strokes, Sen. Benjamin Tillman (D-SC) followed a health regimen that included avoiding tobacco. According to an "Historical Minute Essay" on the U.S. Senate Web site, "Concerned for his own well-being, along with that of his colleagues, in the often smoke-filled chamber that he likened to a 'beer garden,'" Tillman introduced a resolution to ban smoking in the Senate chamber. "Noting the high death rate among incumbent senators—within the previous four years fourteen had died, along with the vice president and sergeant at arms—he surveyed all members. Nonsmokers responded that they would like to support him, but worried that their smoking colleagues would consider this a selfish gesture."[4] Sen. Charles E. Townsend (R-MI) would not support the proposal despite a letter from Tillman describing the effects of tobacco smoke on the old and the sick.[5] The essay reported that "the majority of smokers however, saw no reason why an old and sick senator should be driven from the chamber, his state deprived of its full and active representation, merely for the gratification of 'a very great pleasure.' In this spirit, the Senate adopted Tillman's resolution." On March 9, 1914, the Senate unanimously agreed to ban smoking in its chamber. Following Tillman's death four years later, the Senate kept the restriction in force. The language of the Senate rule was drafted broadly. It prohibits the actual act of smoking and the carrying into the chamber of "lighted cigars, cigarettes, or pipes."

The same year as the Senate smoking ban, Dr. Daniel H. Kress, secretary of the Anti-Cigarette League, predicted that "the time is not far distant when there will be a universal protest against (smoking in public) and protection will be afforded on our street cars and other public places for those

---

THE U.S. SENATE SHOPS AND SALES OF
TOBACCO PRODUCTS

U.S. Senate shops, long known as a source for discount cigarettes, stopped selling all tobacco products on January 1, 2008. Senate Rules Chairman, Sen. Dianne Feinstein (D-CA), and ranking Republican member, Sen. Bob Bennett (UT), issued the tobacco sales ban at the request of six Democratic senators, including Frank Lautenberg (NJ), Tom Harkin (IA), Dick Durbin (IL), Sherrod Brown (OH), and Jack Reed (RI). Tobacco products had always been cheaper when purchased from shops, restaurants, and vending machines in the U.S. Capitol complex, where District of Columbia and federal taxes do not apply.

Sale of tobacco on Capitol grounds has been an ongoing source of discomfort for government leaders who publicly endorse nationwide "stop smoking" efforts. In a 1998 sting operation, for example, the American Lung Association reported that five out of nine attempts by two undercover 15-year-old girls to buy cigarettes from snack bars and shops on the Capitol grounds were successful.[6]

who are liberal enough to permit others to smoke, but do not wish to inhale the smoke at second hand."[7]

Some states debated whether or not to restrict smoking in public: Maryland considered bills in 1916, 1918, and 1920 to restrict public smoking. South Carolina considered a" bill to ban smoking in public eating places" in 1920.[8] Minnesota considered a bill to ban smoking in theaters, streetcars, railway coaches, train stations, buses, taxis, barbershops, and all state-owned buildings. Neither South Carolina nor Minnesota's bills made it into laws. Some city leaders also debated the public smoking issue. In 1923 three men were arrested for smoking in a restaurant in Salt Lake City, Utah, and briefly detained in a local jail.[9]

In 1929 Emil Bogen, M.D., became one of the first physicians to write about the harm, rather than the annoyance, of sidestream smoke. In "The Composition of Cigarets and Cigaret [sic] Smoke," published in the *Journal of the American Medical Association (JAMA),* Bogen suggested that sidestream smoke emitted from the burning tip of a cigarette would harm nonsmokers. He concluded that "simply holding a lighted

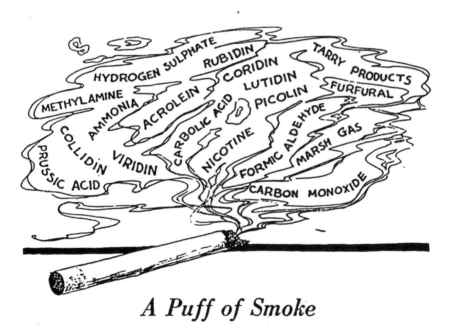

A Puff of Smoke

Figure 10.2 A 1922 image depicted the chemicals found in a puff of smoke long before the 2006 surgeon general's report, *The Health Consequences of Involuntary Exposure to Tobacco Smoke,* stated that scientific evidence indicated that there is no risk-free level of exposure to secondhand smoke. (Courtesy of Frances E. Willard Memorial Library, Evanston, Illinois)

cigarette in the hand ... produces more toxic materials in the room air than result from active smoking."[10]

The U.S. Public Health Service (PHS) first became engaged in the environmental tobacco smoke (ETS) issue in June 1956 when a study group reviewed "sixteen independent studies from five countries, concluding that a direct causal relationship indeed existed between exposure to cigarette smoking and cancer of the lung." Impressed by the findings, Surgeon General LeRoy Burney issued two major statements between 1957 and 1959, in which he stated it was the official position of the U.S. PHS that "cigarette smoking particularly was associated with an increased chance of developing lung cancer."[11]

In November of 1971, Surgeon General Jesse Steinfeld, convinced that scientific evidence indicated a possible risk to nonsmokers, called for a national bill of rights for the nonsmoker that included bans on smoking in restaurants, public transportation, and theaters. He received thousands of letters in support of smoke-free air. Steinfeld's 1972 surgeon general's report, *Health Consequences of Smoking,* for the first time identified exposure of nonsmokers to cigarette smoking as a health hazard.[12] Steinfeld's report was mentioned in an article "Non-Smokers Arise!" by Max Wiener in the November 1972 issue of *Reader's Digest.* The writer suggested that "smoking should be confined to consenting adults in private. It is time for you, the innocent bystander, to assert your rights."

Armed with the official approval of the PHS and scant scientific evidence, antitobacco advocates pushed for prohibitions on smoking in a variety of public places in the 1970s. The shift in social attitudes toward public smoking was shaped, in part, by a broader emerging environment movement and a new health consciousness. For some people, there was little or no annoyance from cigarette smoke. For others, however, cigarette smoke smelled bad, irritated their eyes and throats, burned their noses, made them nauseous, and gave them headaches. For people, with allergies, asthma, and angina, tobacco smoke was a serious health threat. According to Allan M. Brandt, "Nothing spurred the effectiveness of this new anticigarette movement so powerfully as the recognition of the so-called 'innocent victim' of 'secondhand smoke.' The old ambivalence about preaching to smokers about their individual behavior disappeared; now one could talk about the impact their self-destructiveness had on others."[13]

Antitobacco advocacy groups and new grassroots organizations, influenced by environmental groups, civil rights, and antiwar organizations, recruited volunteers to advocate for the rights of nonsmokers. Group Against Smoking (GASP), founded in 1971 by Clara Gouin, printed flyers, manufactured buttons, and mailed a newsletter to local lung associations, growing the organization to 56 local chapters by 1974. GASP's local chapters actively pushed for local and state ordinances regulating smoking in offices, public buildings, and restaurants. And, according to Brandt, GASP, like similar organizations, "reveled in controversy, deliberately seeking media attention to sustain their cause."[14]

The notion of the innocent bystander promoted the federal government's interest in regulating behavior previously outside its purview. Federal regulatory agencies responded to the issue of secondhand smoke in the early 1970s. Richard Kluger, author of *Ashes to Ashes: America's Hundred-Year Cigarette War, the Public Health, and the Unabashed Triumph of Philip Morris,* credited Ralph Nader with launching, at the end of 1969, what came to be called the nonsmokers' rights movement when he petitioned "the Federal Aviation Administration (FAA) to ban the use of cigarettes, cigars, and pipes on all passenger flights, arguing that the smoke annoyed nonsmokers, distracted the flight crew, and posed a danger to health and a fire hazard for all aboard." John Banzhaf, founder of Action on Smoking and Health, called for separate seating for smokers and nonsmokers on all domestic flights.[15] In 1972 the Civil Aeronautics Board responded to a Nader petition to require separate passenger sections because 60 percent of all passengers said they were bothered by smoke.[16] In 1981 when the deregulatory Reagan administration rolled back reforms, cigars and pipes were permitted in smoking sections. During 1974 the Interstate Commerce Commission established separate seating on buses and railroads.

State legislatures also became active in regulating smoking in public places. In 1973 Arizona became the first state to restrict smoking in some public places to protect nonsmokers. Proponents of the law noted that people suffering from lung ailments had come to Arizona for its healthy air. In 1974 Connecticut became the first state to restrict smoking in restaurants. In 1975 Minnesota passed a comprehensive state law that prohibited smoking in public spaces and at public meetings, except in designated smoking areas. By the end of 1975, some 31 states had approved legislation establishing or extending smoking restrictions, transforming what Jacob Sullum called "quiet resentment into vocal political action."[17] In 1977, Berkeley, California, became the first local community to limit smoking in restaurants and other public places.

In 1978 the tobacco industry, worried about the emerging nonsmokers' rights movement, engaged the Roper Organization to conduct a secret study for the tobacco industry. The Roper study concluded that a majority of Americans believed it was probably hazardous to be around people who smoked, even if they were not smoking themselves. It reported that a majority of people wanted separate smoking sections in public places.

The study concluded that "what the smoker does to himself may be his business, but what the smoker does to the non-smoker is quite a different matter." The Roper Organization also concluded that "passive smoking" posed a hazard to the viability of the tobacco industry.[18]

At the time, little scientific evidence existed about the health effects of secondhand smoke on nonsmokers. Scientists were not ready to say with certainty that exposure to tobacco smoke caused serious illnesses. In 1975 Cuyler Hammond of the American Cancer Society stated that there was "no shred of evidence" yet that nonsmokers would contract cancer from ETS. The same year, Gary Huber, a physician, who later became a sharp critic of the developing public health consensus on the risks of tobacco smoke to nonsmokers, wrote that questions centering on the potential biological effect of exposure to ETS "remain unanswered." Ernst Wynder, a respected medical investigator, said, "Passive smoking can provoke tears or can be otherwise disagreeable, but it has no influence on health [because] the doses are small."[19]

In 1978 James L. Repace, a physicist and clean-air and antismoking activist who suffered from asthma, especially aggravated by exposure to cigarette smoke, did field research with Alfred H. Lowrey, a theoretical chemist. They developed a model for estimating the amount of "respirable suspended particulates (RSPs) from cigarette smoke in confined environments and then measured actual levels of smoke in bars, restaurants, bowling alleys, and other sites using a handheld device."[20] An employee at the Environmental Protection Agency (EPA), Repace found that the risk of exposure to lung cancer from ETS levels he obtained in public spaces to be 250 to 1,000 times above the acceptable level as set down by federal guidelines for carcinogens in air, water, and food. Repace and Lowrey published their findings in *Science* in May 1980. Five years later a peer-reviewed study about lung cancer risk and passive smoking was published in *Environmental International*. The Tobacco Institute issued a 43-page rebuttal pamphlet entitled *Tobacco Smoke in the Air* a few months after the 1985 article's publication, charging it with too many theoretical or unwarranted assumptions. The institute argued that a calculation developed by James Repace and Alfred Lowrey, who claimed that cigarette smoke in the air was responsible for 500 to 5,000 lung cancer deaths per year among U.S. nonsmokers, was derived from highly controversial "risk assessment models," data from their own questionable 1980 report on particulates in the air in various buildings, and data from other equally questionable epidemiologic studies. The institute also argued that the authors were not unbiased researchers because they were longtime, highly vocal antismoking activists.

More studies followed in the 1980s, some of which suggested that exposure to cigarette smoke had health consequences. The 1981 study by epidemiologist Takeshi Hirayama of the Tokyo National Cancer Center Research Institute made the front pages of newspapers around the world. His study showed that nonsmokers who were married to smokers who smoked 14 cigarettes a day had a 40 percent greater risk of lung cancer than women married to nonsmokers.[21] Criticisms of the study appeared in the letters section of several issues of the *British Medical Journal* during 1981. The tobacco industry responded with a multimillion-dollar advertising campaign in major newspapers and magazines, in which it criticized Hirayama's study.

Gauging the health hazards of ETS was difficult. In 1985 *Consumer Reports* examined the literature to date and reported that evidence against ETS was "spare" and "often conflicting."

By the time the PHS issued its surgeon general report, *The Health Consequences of Involuntary Smoking,* at the end of 1986, it confirmed findings of a National Academy of Science report earlier that year, as well as over a dozen epidemiologic studies existed in peer-reviewed literature on ETS and lung cancer. In his 1986 report, Surgeon General C. Everett Koop wrote that "the relative abundance of data reviewed in this Report, their cohesiveness, and their biological plausibility allow a judgment that involuntary smoking can cause lung cancer in nonsmokers. ... It is certain that a substantial proportion of the lung cancers that occur in nonsmokers are due to ETS exposure; however more complete data on the dose and variability of smoke exposure in the nonsmoking U.S. population will be needed before a quantitative estimate of the number of such cancers can be made."[22] Despite inconclusive scientific data about the health effects of secondhand smoke, Koop justified his forceful stance against ETS as the way to capture the public's attention. He said: "Critics often express that more research is required, that certain studies are flawed, or that we should delay action until more conclusive proof is produced. As both a physician and a public health official it is my judgment that the time for delay is past, measures to protect the public health are required now."[23] Koop withheld judgment on the possibility that ETS caused cardiovascular disease, saying more research was required. (Shortly after the EPA report was released in 1992, studies linking ETS and heart disease accumulated, suggesting that secondhand smoke exposure was graver than previously supposed.)

In his history of America's hundred-year cigarette war, Richard Kluger pointed out that "although the belief in secondhand smoke as a serious menace had become the most potent contributor to the nation's deepening war on cigarettes, just how real a peril it was had not been definitely determined. The three authoritative reports in 1986—by the U.S. surgeon general, the National Academy of Sciences, and the congressional Office of Technology Assessment—had all agreed that further serious research was needed before a true appraisal of the ETS risk could emerge."[24]

Smoke-free advocates did not wait for definitive evidence. At a 1986 antismoking conference in October 1986, Stanton Glantz, professor of medicine with a doctorate in engineering and economics, explained that "although the nonsmokers' rights movement concentrates on protecting the nonsmoker ... clean air indoor legislation reduces smoking because it undercuts the social support network for smoking by implicitly defining it as an antisocial act."[25]

During the 1980s, it was widely accepted that secondhand smoke, called ETS by public health people, was harmful to nonsmokers. Smokers found themselves "more and more under assault everywhere they turned—by their loved ones, their friends, their doctors, their employers, and workmates, the schools and churches in their communities, the media, and the government."[26] The idea that secondhand smoke endangered health gave a boost to the movement to restrict tobacco use in public places. More local ordinances prohibited smoking on public transportation, at workplaces and sporting events, and in theaters, restaurants, and shops. By the mid-1980s, most large corporations developed smoking policies with no prompting from the government. By the end of 1985, a total of 89 cities and counties had limited public smoking, and by 1986, some 41 states and the District of Columbia had enacted statutes that imposed restrictions on smoking. More restrictions followed in 1987, when the U.S. Department of Health and Human Services established a smoke-free environment in all its buildings nationwide. In 1988 Congress imposed a smoking ban on all U.S. domestic flights two hours or less. Two years later the ban was extended to flights of six hours or less. By 1988 some "400 local ordinances restricting smoking had been enacted in the United States." By the end of the 1980s, "about half of all U.S. companies had established some sort of smoking rules on their premises."[27]

The Tobacco Institute responded to the smoke-free movement by creating a Center for Indoor Air Research (CIAR) in 1988 to fund studies to counter findings that ETS threatened the health of nonsmokers. Some CIAR projects tried to prove that other factors besides ETS, such as faulty ventilation systems and other contaminants besides smoke, caused problems with indoor air. As William Murray, vice chairman of the board of Philip Morris explained, "Our principal defense has been the position ... that there are many other things to blame for poor indoor quality, and tobacco smoke is only a small part of the problem." He urged that "we must find stronger arguments to support our position on ETS."[28]

The institute also tried to transform the issue of restrictive policies from one centered on health risks associated with ETS to one focused on American values of liberty. According to public health researchers, "The industry fostered and then underwrote smokers' rights and activities and publications." The smokers' rights publications, which characterized regulatory efforts to restrict smoking as intrusive and unnecessary, proposed as an alternative the virtues of courtesy and mutual respect between smokers and nonsmokers.[29]

The tobacco industry portrayed restrictions on smoking as massive government intrusion into personal behavior. As Stanley Scott, vice president and director of corporate affairs for Philip Morris explained: "The basic freedoms of more than 50 million American smokers are at risk today. Tomorrow, who knows what personal behavior will become socially unacceptable, subject to restrictive laws and public ridicule?"[30]

In late 1992, the first ever scientific assessment of the health effects associated with exposure to tobacco smoke to be undertaken by an agency was published. The EPA officially declared ETS a hazard in *Respiratory Health Effects of Passive Smoking: Lung Cancer and Other Disorders.* It declared ETS to be a human lung carcinogen, responsible for approximately 3,000 lung cancer deaths annually. EPA placed ETS in the same category as asbestos, benzene, and radon. The EPA said ETS has significant effects on the respiratory health of nonsmoking adults. Among its findings, the report estimated that 250,000 to 300,000 cases annually of lower respiratory tract infections were linked to ETS in children younger than 18 months. The study stated that the condition of 200,000 to 1 million asthmatic children was worsened by exposure to tobacco smoke. In his preface to the EPA report, Dr. Samuel Broder, Director, National Cancer Institute, wrote that "while the report will have a profound effect on framing the debate concerning restrictions on smoking in worksites and other public settings, its most lasting impact may well be to change the way we, as a society, view smoking as a socially acceptable behavior ... As a Federal official ... I strongly recommend the implementation of comprehensive policies that will protect innocent bystanders in all public places to the fullest extent possible."[31]

The tobacco industry responded by criticizing the EPA for inadequate data and poor analysis, calling the study "another step in the long process characterized by preference for political correctness over sound silence."[32] Despite the fact that the EPA did not issue any regulations pursuant to the report, in June 1993, the tobacco industry filed a lawsuit in federal court in Greensboro, North Carolina, requesting that the court declare the report to be invalid. (Eventually, the district court ruled in 1998 that the EPA overstated the link between secondhand smoke and cancer and based its findings on insufficiently rigorous statistical tests. The decision had no direct legal impact on regulations and ordinances enacted around the country restricting smoking in public buildings, workplaces, and restaurants.)

In response to the EPA study, a *New York Times* editorial claimed that "the evidence is now overwhelming that smokers endanger all those forced to inhale the lethal clouds they generate. That makes smokers at least a small hazard to virtually all Americans." The editorial agreed with the Tobacco Institute's contention that two-thirds of 30 or more studies reviewed by the EPA showed no "statistically significant" increase in lung cancer risk, but countered that "one-third of the studies do show significance, and the combined results are persuasive."[33]

Not everyone agreed that the scientific evidence was conclusive. A 1994 *Wall Street Journal* editorial stated that "the anti-smoking brigade relies on proving that secondhand smoke is a dangerous threat to the health of others. 'Science' is involved in ways likely to give science a bad name ... [t]he health effects of secondhand smoke are a stretch."[34] The Congressional Research Service weighed in as well, that "statistical evidence does not appear to support a conclusion that there are substantial health effects from passive smoking."[35] In a March 1994 issue of *Reason,* Jacob Sullum, managing editor of the conservative journal, drew attention to the limitations behind EPA's scientific methods. He argued that newspapers accepted the EPA findings in order to advance the agenda of the smoking control movement. In his 1998 book, *For Your Own Good: The Anti-Smoking Crusade and the Tyranny of Public Health,* he questioned the existence of a lung cancer risk from ETS in a lengthy chapter, suggesting that "not only is the estimated risk from ETS small when compared to the risk from smoking, but it's small in absolute terms as well." He said that there was "scant evidence that exposure to ETS on the job increases the risk of lung cancer." And "contrary to the impression created by [public health] messages, there is no evidence that occasional encounters with tobacco smoke pose a significant risk."[36]

A year after the release of the EPA report, thousands of businesses banned smoking. The report also prompted the number of local ordinances restricting smoking to grow dramatically. By the end of 1998, the American Lung Association calculated that there were more than 800 ordinances restricting smoking.

Despite the number of ordinances enacted around the United States, in 2006 the surgeon general's report—*The Health Consequences of Involuntary Exposure to Tobacco Smoke*—concluded that many millions of Americans, both children and adults, were still exposed to secondhand smoke in their homes and workplaces despite substantial progress in tobacco control. The report also stated that scientific evidence indicated that there is no risk-free level of exposure to secondhand smoke. It advocated that by eliminating smoking in indoor spaces, nonsmokers would be protected from exposure to secondhand smoke, whereas separating smokers from nonsmokers, cleaning the air, and ventilating buildings would not eliminate exposures of nonsmokers to secondhand smoke.[37]

In January 2009, the Americans for Nonsmokers' Rights, an organization that has tracked, collected, and analyzed tobacco control ordinances since the early 1980s, published on its Web site a summary of smoke-free laws in the United States. According to Americans for Nonsmokers' Rights, across the nation, 16,505 municipalities were covered by a 100 percent smoke-free provision in workplaces, and/or restaurants, and/or bars, by either a state, commonwealth, or local law representing 70.2 percent of the U.S. population. Thirty states, Puerto Rico, and the District of Columbia have laws in effect that require 100 percent smoke-free workplaces and/or restaurants and/or bars. A total of 15 states, Puerto Rico, and Washington, D.C., have a state law in effect that requires workplaces, restaurants, and bars to be 100 percent smoke free.[38] In January 2010, North Carolina, one of the nation's leading tobacco producers, banned smoking in restaurants and bars. According to the American Lung Association (ALA), North Carolina became the only southern state where smoking is not permitted in both types of establishments. But the ALA also said the state must also prohibit smoking in workplaces, stores, and places of public recreation.

Some communities have moved beyond bans in public settings like restaurants and bars and have restricted outdoor smoking on beaches and in public transit waiting areas, parks, and zoos. Still others have restricted smoking in cars and, in some cases, homes. According to the National Resource Center for Family-Centered Practice and Permanency Planning, in 2005 at least 13 states had prohibited smoking around foster children in homes or cars or both.[39] In more than a dozen states, judges who determine parental rights have ordered a parent not to smoke around a child. Tenants in apartments have occasionally succeeded in curtailing secondhand smoke from neighboring apartments.

While some public health smoke-free activists find stringent limitations on public tobacco use acceptable, others worry that the movement has begun "to take on the taint of moralism and authoritarianism."[40] In their study about the campaign against ETS, two public health research-ers concluded that "the strictures imposed by the cultural and ideological antipathy to paternalism may serve as an impediment to the further de-velopment of policies designed to alter the normative and public context of smoking in America. ... It may well be necessary to directly address public smoking as a matter of protecting not only nonsmokers, but smok-ers themselves."[41]

PART III

References and Resources

Timeline of Tobacco Use and Health

1492	Christopher Columbus and his crew reported seeing people who "drank smoke."
1560–1561	Jean Nicot de Villemain, France's ambassador to Portugal, learned that court physicians prized tobacco for its curative powers. In 1561 Nicot presented some tobacco plants to the Queen, Catherine de Medici. Nicot's name was later used to name nicotine, an element in tobacco.
1604	King James I of England issued "A Counterblaste to Tobacco," calling smoking "a custom loathesome to the eye, hateful to the nose, harmful to the brain, dangerous to the lungs."
1614	In June, John Rolfe of the Virginia Colony shipped his first cargo of Virginia tobacco to London, where it became an immediate success. The popularity of the tobacco crop made the colony, near financial collapse, economically viable.
1769	Pierre Lorillard established a plant in New York City for processing tobacco, the first tobacco company in the colonies.
1794	The U.S. Congress passed its first tobacco tax. It applied only to snuff.
1839	Tobacco manufacturers in North Carolina used charcoal for the first time in the process of flue curing tobacco leaves, turning them into a *bright leaf* and making tobacco milder in taste when smoked.
1847	Philip Morris opened a shop in England to sell Turkish cigarettes.
1870s–1910	Cigarette manufacturers inserted series of colorful picture cards with every possible subject, especially baseball, into cigarette packs. Used to stiffen packs, the cards were also a marketing device to attract buyers who wanted to collect all the images in

	a series. Hand rolling of cigarettes was done by skilled female *rollers* in Virginia factories who rolled four to five cigarettes a minute.
1875	Richard Joshua Reynolds founded R. J. Reynolds Tobacco Company in Winston, North Carolina, to make chewing tobacco.
1881	James Albert Bonsack, a Virginian, patented a cigarette-rolling machine that produced more than 70,000 cigarettes in a 10-hour day.
1884	On April 30, 1884, referred to as the birthday of the modern cigarette, the Bonsack machine successfully operated for a full day turning out 120,000 cigarettes, the equivalent of 40 hand rollers rolling 5 cigarettes a minute for 10 hours.
1890	James Buchanan Duke formed the American Tobacco Company, a monolithic tobacco enterprise that gobbled up competitors. • Anticigarette leagues were organized in the American heartland.
1892	Portable matches were invented that permitted smokers to light up whenever and wherever they wished.
1893	State legislatures began to pass anticigarette laws. Some states totally outlawed the sale, manufacture, possession, advertising, and/or use of cigarettes; others outlawed sales to minors.
1902	British tobacco companies united to fight James Buchanan Duke by forming the Imperial Tobacco Group.
1906	Brown & Williamson Tobacco Corporation was formed by a group of farmers in Winston-Salem, North Carolina. It made plug, snuff, and pipe tobacco. • The Food and Drug Act of 1906, the first federal food and drug law, made no express reference to tobacco products. The definition of a drug included medicines and preparations listed in the U.S. Pharmacoepia or National Formulary.
1911	The U.S. Supreme Court ruled that the American Tobacco Company violated the 1890 Sherman Anti-Trust Act and ordered James Buchanan Duke to break up his company.
1912	Liggett & Myers introduced Chesterfield cigarettes.
1913	On October 13, R. J. Reynolds Tobacco Company introduced Camels, the first modern blended cigarette, and launched the first national cigarette advertising campaign in the nation.
1914	The Federal Trade Commission Act was empowered to "prevent persons, partnerships, or corporations ... from using unfair or deceptive acts or practices in commerce."
1917–1918	During World War I, soldiers smoked cigarettes that were part of their daily rations.
1921	Iowa became the first state to levy a tax on cigarettes. Cigarettes became the main form of tobacco consumed, beating out pipes, snuff, chewing tobacco, and cigars.

1927	State anticigarette laws were all repealed. • British-American Tobacco bought Brown & Williamson Tobacco Corporation.
1928	George Washington Hill and Albert Lasker, advertising executives, launched one of most profitable ad campaigns in advertising history, "Reach for a Lucky Instead of a Sweet." Sales of Lucky Strike zoomed up by 47 percent two months after radio listeners first heard commercials on the air.
1933	On May 12, President Franklin Delano Roosevelt signed the Agricultural Adjustment Act, the first law aimed at providing immediate relief to growers of basic crops such as wheat and tobacco and preventing crop prices from collapsing. • Brown & Williamson introduced Kool menthol brand of cigarettes.
1938	The Wheeler-Lea Act gave the Federal Trade Commission (FTC) power to regulate "unfair or deceptive acts or practices in commerce." Since 1938, the FTC has acted over fifty times against tobacco companies. • The Food, Drug, and Cosmetic Act of 1938 defined *drug* as "articles intended for use in the diagnosis, cure, mitigation, treatment, or prevention of disease in man or other animals" and "articles (other than food) intended to affect the structure or any function of the body of man or other animals." • On February 16, the Agricultural Adjustment Act gave relief to tobacco farmers by controlling the number of acres planted and setting quotas on crops to be marketed.
1940s	Almost 20 percent of the cigarettes produced in the United States were shipped to soldiers overseas, as well as added to Army K-rations. A domestic shortage resulted.
1941	A study by Alton Ochsner, a renowned thoracic surgeon, and Michael DeBakey, renowned heart surgeon, concluded that "it is our definite conviction that the increase of pulmonary carcinoma is due largely to the increase in … cigarette smoking.
1947	Lucky Strikes began sponsoring televised college football games.
1948	Camels sponsored the televised "Camel News Caravan."
1950	American scientists Ernst L. Wyndner and Evarts A. Graham published a report stating that 96.5 percent of lung-cancer patients were moderate-to-heavy smokers.
1952	Reacting to lung cancer publicity, Lorillard introduced its new Micronite filter-tip Kent cigarettes in full-page advertisements. Filters were supposed to protect smokers from nicotine and tar. Competing brands soon developed their own filter brands.
1953	A landmark study by Ernst L. Wyndner showed that painting cigarette tar on the backs of mice created tumors.
1954	The tobacco industry established the Tobacco Industry Research Council (later renamed the Council for Tobacco Research).

On January 4, it issued a "Frank Statement" to the public, a nationwide two-page advertisement that stated cigarette makers did not believe their products were injurious to a person's health. • "On Campus with Max Shulman," a column by humorist Shulman, appeared in 132 college newspapers. The following line appeared at the bottom of the column: "This column is brought to you by the makers of Philip Morris, who think you would enjoy their cigarette." • Philip Morris hired attorney David Hardy to defend the company in litigation, beginning the company's association with Shook, Hardy & Bacon. Philip Morris won the first case handled by Hardy.

1955   In January the Marlboro Man appeared for the first time in ads.

1957   Philip Morris began diversifying by acquiring Milprint Inc., a packaging products firm. The same year, R. J. Reynolds established a diversification committee.

1958   Major cigarette manufacturers formed the Tobacco Institute to counter the adverse effects of health studies as well as to emphasize the inconclusiveness of the research on smoking and disease, the contribution of tobacco products to the national economy, and the individual rights of smokers. • Philip Morris Inc. made its first grant to support the arts. The tobacco company now operates the leading corporate arts support program in the world.

1962   Every one of the 20 teams in Major League Baseball had either tobacco or alcoholic-beverage sponsorship, or both.

1964   On January 11, U.S. Surgeon General Luther Terry issued the first report on smoking and health. The landmark report linked smoking to cancer and increased mortality and identified it as a contributing factor in several diseases. • Leo Burnett, advertising genius, changed the Marlboro image from "Mild as May" to the "Marlboro Man." At the time, Marlboro cigarettes only had 1 percent of the U.S. market. Philip Morris decided to concentrate on the cowboy as the only Marlboro Man. The image now is the most widely recognized advertising image in the world. • State Mutual Life Assurance became the first company to offer life insurance to nonsmokers at discounted rates.

1966   The Cigarette Labeling and Advertising Act of 1965 took effect January 1, requiring a nine-word health warning on cigarette packages: "Caution: Cigarette Smoking May Be Hazardous to Your Health." The act prohibited labels on advertisements for three years. The act required the FTC to report to Congress annually on effectiveness of cigarette labeling and current cigarette advertising and promotion practices. The act required

	the Department of Health, Education and Welfare to report annually to Congress on the health consequences of smoking.
1967	The Federal Communications Commission ruled that the fairness doctrine applied to cigarette advertising. Stations broadcasting cigarette commercials had to donate airtime to antismoking messages.
1968	Philip Morris introduced Virginia Slims, a cigarette strictly for women. Soon after, other cigarettes for women appeared on the market.
1969	The Public Health Cigarette Smoking Act of 1969 required a package label "Warning: The Surgeon General Has Determined That Cigarette Smoking Is Dangerous to Your Health." Other health warnings on advertisements were prohibited. The act prohibited cigarette advertising on television and radio after January 1, 1971. The act prevented states or localities from regulating or prohibiting cigarette advertising or promotion for health-related reasons.
1970s	Tobacco industry marketed its products to countries in Africa, Asia, and Latin America. • Tobacco sponsorship of sporting events put tobacco ads back on television.
1970	The Controlled Substances Act of 1970 excluded tobacco from the definition of a *controlled substance.*
1971	The Public Health Cigarette Smoking Act went into effect banning cigarette ads from television and radio at midnight, January 1. Print ads zoomed up after the ban. • The fairness doctrine antismoking messages ended when cigarette advertising ended on television and radio. •Surgeon General Jesse Steinfeld called for a national Bill of Rights for the Nonsmoker, touching off the environmental tobacco smoke (ETS) movement. During the 1970s, nonsmoking sections began to appear on buses, airplanes, and trains, and in other public places.
1972	Cigarette advertising warnings in print ads began. • The Consumer Product Safety Act of 1972 did not include tobacco or tobacco products.
1973	Arizona became the first state to pass a comprehensive law protecting nonsmokers by prohibiting smoking in select public places. • The Little Cigar Act banned little cigar advertisements from television and radio. • The Civil Aeronautics Board required no-smoking sections on all commercial airline flights.
1975	The military stopped providing cigarettes in K-rations and C-rations given to soldiers and sailors.
1976	The Toxic Substances Control Act of 1976 did not include tobacco or any tobacco products.

1977	Berkeley, California, enacted the first modern ordinance limiting smoking in restaurants and other public places. • The American Cancer Society sponsored its first national Great American Smokeout.
1978	Utah enacted the first state law banning tobacco ads on any billboard, streetcar sign, or bus.
1979	Minneapolis and St. Paul, Minnesota, became the first cities to ban free distribution of cigarette samples in the streets. • Cigarettes were the most advertised product in some women's magazines, with as many as 20 ads in a single issue.
1980s	Studies by the American Council on Science and Health showed that magazines with tobacco ads rarely carried articles about health dangers of smoking.
1980	The surgeon general's report was devoted to the health consequences of smoking for women.
1982	Surgeon General C. Everett Koop's report on smoking and cancer made headlines: "Cigarettes Blamed for 30 Percent of All Cancer Deaths." • Congress doubled the federal excise tax on cigarettes to 16¢ per pack.
1983	The FTC determined that its testing procedures may have "significantly underestimated the level of tar, nicotine, and carbon monoxide that smokers received from smoking" certain low-tar cigarettes. • The FTC prohibited Brown & Williamson Tobacco Company from using the tar rating for Barclay cigarettes in advertising, packaging, or promotions because of problems with the testing methodology and consumers' possible reliance on that information. • San Francisco, California, enacted the first strong smoke-free workplace protections, including a ban on smoking in private workplaces.
1984	On January 13, the FDA approved Nicorette® Gum, a nicotine gum, as a smoking cessation product. Once available only by prescription, its sale was now restricted to those over 18 of age. • On October 12, President Ronald Reagan signed the Comprehensive Smoking Education Act of 1984 instituting four rotating health warning labels on cigarette packages and advertisements (all listed as surgeons general warnings): smoking causes lung cancer, heart disease and may complicate pregnancy; quitting smoking now greatly reduces serious risks to your health; smoking by pregnant women may result in fetal injury, premature birth, and low birth rate; cigarette smoke contains carbon monoxide. The act preempted other package warnings. The act created a Federal Interagency Committee on Smoking and Health. The act required the cigarette industry to provide a confidential list of cigarette additives.

The Cigarette Safety Act of 1984 passed to determine the technical and commercial feasibility of developing cigarettes and little cigars that would be less likely to ignite upholstered furniture and mattresses.

1985   Aspen, Colorado, became the first city to ban smoking in restaurants. • Philip Morris bought General Foods; R. J. Reynolds purchased Nabisco Brands Inc.

1986   Surgeon General C. Everett Koop crusaded against smokeless tobacco and passive smoking. His report said that secondhand smoke could cause lung cancer and other disorders. • The Comprehensive Smokeless Tobacco Health Education Act of 1986 instituted three rotating health warnings on smokeless tobacco packages and advertisements: this product may cause mouth cancer; this product may cause gum disease and tooth loss; this product is not a safe alternative to cigarettes. The act preempted other health warnings on packages or advertisements, except billboards. The act prohibited smokeless tobacco advertising on television and radio. The act required the FTC to report to Congress on smokeless tobacco sales, advertising, and marketing. The act required smokeless tobacco companies to provide a confidential list of additives and a specification of nicotine content in their products.

1987   A workplace smoking ban went into effect at the Department of Health and Human Services, the first smoke-free federal agency. • Public Law 100–202 banned smoking on domestic airline flights scheduled for two hours or less. • The first World No Tobacco Day was celebrated on April 7. Since then, it has been observed on May 31 of every year.

1988   R. J. Reynolds Tobacco Company launched its "Old Joe" ad campaign featuring a "smooth character" cartoon camel. • Surgeon General C. Everett Koop declared nicotine a highly addictive substance. • The 15th Winter Olympic games in Calgary, Canada, were the first to have a smoke-free program. • The Canadian government passed the Tobacco Products Control Act, which banned tobacco advertising in Canada. It was struck down by the Canadian Supreme Court in 1995. • On February 1, a Newark, New Jersey, federal district court ruled, for the first time in history, that cigarette manufacturers were liable for the death of a smoker, Rose Cipollone who died of lung cancer in 1984. Liggett & Myers was ordered to pay Cipollone's family $400,000 in compensatory damages. • On April 23, Northwest Airlines became the first nonsmoking airline. It banned smoking on all of its domestic flights in North America regardless of length. • The first World No-Tobacco Day, an internationally coordinated event, was held to discourage tobacco users from consuming tobacco. Now a growing global observance, diverse celebrations take place every May 31. • California voters passed a referendum raising the state cigarette excise tax by 25¢ per pack, the largest cigarette excise tax increase in U.S. history.

1989   Public Law 101–164 banned smoking on domestic airline flights scheduled for six hours or less (except the cockpit) and on intercity buses. • The Minnesota Timberwolves basketball team opened the first major smoke-free stadium in the nation. • The Tobacco Institute launched an antismoking youth campaign, "It's the Law." • Don Barrett, a Mississippi attorney representing Nathan Horton, won the case against the American Tobacco Company, but his client was not awarded money.

1991   Researchers found that Camel cigarette's cartoon camel was as familiar to 6-year-olds as Mickey Mouse.

1992   The Synar Amendment to the Alcohol, Drug Abuse, and Mental Health Administration Reorganization Act required all states to enact and enforce laws prohibiting the sale and distribution of cigarettes to children under 18 years. • The Supreme Court handed down a landmark decision in *Cipollone v. Liggett Group, Inc.,* ruling that the federal Cigarette Labeling and Advertising Act of 1965 does not shield tobacco manufacturers from liability. • *Cigar Aficionado* was launched celebrating the pleasures of cigar smoking. One of the most successful magazine start-ups of the 1990s, it has also been credited with launching the cigar craze.

1993   The Environmental Protection Agency released its final risk assessment report on environmental tobacco smoke (ETS), classifying it as a "Group A" (known human) carcinogen.

1994   In her surgeon general's report (the first devoted solely to young people), Joycelyn Elders reported that most smokers become addicted by age 18, and emphasized the importance of preventing smoking among children and teenagers. • Baltimore, Maryland, became the first city to ban tobacco ads on billboards in most neighborhoods. • The Pro-Children Act of 1994 required all federally funded children's services to become smoke free. • The Department of Defense (DOD) banned smoking in DOD workplaces. • On February 28 ABC's news magazine *Day One* reported that cigarette companies controlled the content of nicotine in cigarettes to keep smokers hooked. • On March 29, a national class-action suit, know as the Castano lawsuit, filed on behalf of nicotine-addicted smokers, evolved into the largest class action in U.S. judicial history. The case was dismissed in May of 1996. • On April 14, in a widely televised broadcast, seven executives of the largest American tobacco companies testified under oath before a House subcommittee that they did not believe cigarettes and nicotine were addictive. • On May 5, the nation's second class-action lawsuit brought by smokers, *Engle v. R. J. Reynolds Tobacco Company et al.,* was filed. The trial started on October 14, 1998. • On May 7, the *New York Times* published its first report on internal tobacco company documents stolen by Merrell Williams, a former employee of a law firm doing work for Brown & Williamson Tobacco Corporation. • On May 23, Mississippi became the first state to file a lawsuit suing tobacco companies for reimbursement of the costs of treating smoking-related illnesses incurred by Medicaid and other public health care programs in the state. • In June 1994, Geoffrey Bible was named Philip Morris' president and chief executive, replacing Michael Miles.

1995   Delta Airlines banned smoking aboard its international flights, the first and only U.S. airline to provide a completely smoke-free environment worldwide. • The Department of Justice reached an agreement with the Philip Morris Companies to remove from sports arenas and stadiums tobacco advertisements seen regularly on telecasts of football, basketball, baseball, or hockey games. • The *New York Times* disclosed that it obtained some 2,000 pages of documents showing that Philip Morris studied nicotine and found it affected the body, brain, and behavior of smokers. • Philip Morris announced a comprehensive program to curb underage smoking. Called "Action against Access," Philip Morris said the program reflected the company's concern about the tobacco industry's negative image caused by young people who smoke. • On July 1, at 12:01 A.M. Pacific standard time, the University of California at San Francisco Library posted documents on the Internet stolen by Merrell Williams from the law firm doing work for Brown & Williamson Tobacco Corporation. • In August, President Bill Clinton announced his support for the Food and Drug Administration (FDA) proposal to regulate tobacco sales, distribution, and marketing aimed at youth under 18. Clinton was the first president in history to make smoking prevention among youth a national priority. • In August the nation's five largest tobacco companies filed a lawsuit in Federal District Court in Greensboro, North Carolina, to block the FDA rule-making procedure. Six trade groups, including the National Advertisers and the American Association of Advertising Agencies, filed separate lawsuits in North Carolina, challenging the FDA's regulations. • In October, Steven Goldstone was named chief executive of

RJR Nabisco Holdings Corporation, after having served as president and general counsel. • In November 1995, Dr. Jeffrey Wigand, a former top scientist at Brown & Williamson Tobacco Corporation, became a whistle-blower, providing tobacco industry secrets to CBS's *60 Minutes* and to Mississippi lawyers. • In December the nation's largest retailer and wholesaler associations announced the "We Card" program to provide training and educational materials to retailers to prevent the sale of tobacco products to underage customers. • In December a federal hearing examiner awarded death benefits to Philip E. Wiley whose wife died from lung cancer. This was believed to be the first award of death benefits in the nation for a workplace injury connected to secondhand smoke.

1996   The *Washington Post* disclosed a 1973 R. J. Reynolds Tobacco Company marketing memo from Claude E. Teague, then RJR assistant director of research and development. The memo proposed marketing cigarettes to underage smokers, suggesting that teenage rebellion might make the risks of smoking more attractive to that market. • In January the *Wall Street Journal* published excerpts of a sealed deposition from Jeffrey Wigand (former Brown & Williamson Tobacco Corporation employee) that was leaked to the paper. Wigand claimed that former Brown & Williamson CEO Thomas Sandefur repeatedly acknowledged that nicotine was addictive, comments that directly contradicted Sandefur's testimony before Congress on April 14, 1994. • In March the Liggett Group became the first tobacco company to settle, unilaterally, out of court, a lawsuit with Castano class-action lawyers and five states suing tobacco companies for the Medicaid costs of treating smoking-related diseases. • In April, Nicorette gum became available for nonprescription sale as a smoking cessation aid. • In May a federal appellate court in New Orleans, Louisiana, disqualified the Castano suit as a national class action on the grounds that it involved too many different state laws and too many plaintiffs. The ruling overturned a 1995 decision that would have allowed almost any smoker in the country to sue the tobacco industry on the grounds that tobacco companies manipulated nicotine levels to addict smokers. • In July the FDA approved the Nicotrol transdermal patch for nonprescription sale. The patch became available over the counter starting July 18. • In August a Florida circuit court awarded $750,000 to 66-year-old Grady Carter, who sued the maker of Lucky Strikes after he lost part of a lung to cancer in 1991, the second time the tobacco industry was ordered to pay damages in a liability case. • On August 23, President Clinton announced the nation's first comprehensive program to prevent children and teens from smoking cigarettes or smokeless tobacco. The provisions of the FDA rule were aimed at reducing youth access to tobacco products and the appeal of tobacco advertising to young people.

1997   On February 28, the FDA ban on tobacco sales to minors went into effect requiring retailers to card all cigarette and smokeless tobacco customers under 27 years of age. • On March 20, the Liggett Group signed a new, broader settlement with 22 states that sued to recoup smoking-related Medicaid costs. As part of a settlement, the Liggett Group, the smallest of the major cigarette companies in the nation, acknowledged that smoking causes cancer and other diseases, that nicotine is addictive, and that it and other major tobacco companies deliberately targeted their products to teens. It provided evidence implicating other tobacco companies. • On April 25, Federal District Judge William L. Osteen, Sr., upheld the FDA's power to regulate nicotine in tobacco as a drug, but he said the FDA lacked authority to control advertising and promotions. The FDA and the tobacco industry appealed the ruling. • On May 28, the FTC filed an unfair advertising complaint against the R. J. Reynolds Tobacco Company alleging that its Joe Camel advertising campaign illegally promoted cigarettes to minors, the first time the FTC accused the tobacco industry of aiming its products at youngsters. • On June 20, the tobacco companies and state attorneys general announced the landmark $368.5 billion settlement agreement in Washington, D.C., the largest proposed payout in U.S. history. The settlement collapsed. • On July 3, Mississippi became the first state to settle its lawsuit against the tobacco industry for $3.4 billion. • On August 25, Florida settled its lawsuit against the tobacco industry for $11.3 billion. • In October, four major tobacco companies settled the first major class-action lawsuit over the effects of secondary smoke by flight attendants known as *Broin v. Philip Morris Companies, Inc.* • President Clinton announced an executive order to make all federal workplaces smoke free.

1998   In January, Texas settled its lawsuit against the tobacco industry for at least $15.3 billion over 25 years. • Tobacco executives testified before Congress that nicotine is addictive and smoking may cause cancer. • On March 30, Sen. John McCain (R-AZ) offered a comprehensive tobacco bill that would toughen the June 1997 settlement reached with state attorneys general and public health groups. The bill was killed in the Senate in June. • On May 8, Minnesota settled its lawsuit against the tobacco industry for $6.5 billion. As a result of the suit, the Council for Tobacco Research was disbanded. • On November 14, 1998, the attorneys general of 46 states and 5 territories and the nation's four biggest cigarette companies reached agreement on a $206 billion tobacco settlement, the biggest U.S. civil settlement in history, now known as the Master Settlement Act (MSA). Unlike the earlier June 1997 tobacco settlement, the 1998 MSA, which settled Medicaid lawsuits, did not need congressional approval.

1999   Patricia Henley was awarded $51.5 million in damages against Philip Morris. A state judge later cut the verdict to $26.5 million. Philip Morris appealed the award. • A jury in Portland, Oregon, awarded the family of Jesse Williams $79.5 million against Philip Morris in punitive damages plus $821,485 in compensatory damages for medical costs and pain and suffering. The judge later reduced the punitive damages to $32 million. Philip Morris appealed the case. • In the first class-action lawsuit to go trial, a Florida jury said five tobacco companies engaged in "extreme and outrageous conduct" in making a defective product. • In September the U.S. Justice Department sued the tobacco industry to recover billions of government dollars spent on smoking-related health care.

2000   The Supreme Court ruled 5–4 against the FDA finding that the agency lacked the authority to regulate tobacco. • California became the first state to ban smoking in bars and restaurants. • Canada unveiled its graphic new cigarette warning labels that covered half of each cigarette box. • RJR marketed its Eclipse cigarette as a healthier alternative. • In February, farmers sued tobacco companies in a $69 billion lawsuit seeking to recover damages they say were caused by the industry's settlement with the U.S. government. • In March a California superior court jury found that the Philip Morris and R. J. Reynolds acted with malice, knew about the health hazards of smoking, and deliberately misled the public about those dangers. It also found that the two companies committed fraud. It ordered the companies to pay $1.7 million in compensatory and $20 million in punitive damages to Leslie Whiteley. Her husband was awarded $250,000 for loss of companionship. Both companies appealed. • In April in the second phase of the landmark Florida class-action trial, the jury awarded two smokers $6.9 million in compensatory damages. The jury awarded a third smoker $5.8 million, but determined that he could not collect because the four-year statue of limitations had run out. • In June the U.S. Department of Transportation banned smoking on all U.S. international flights. • In July a jury ordered the tobacco industry to pay $145 billion in punitive damages to sick Florida smokers, a record-shattering verdict. • The American Legacy Foundation launched its "truth" campaign, led by teens.

2001   President Clinton issued an executive order announcing the U.S. government's leadership on global tobacco control and prevention. • In March, Grady Carter collected $1.1 million from Brown & Williamson Tobacco Corp. The payment, covering a 1996 jury award of $750,000 plus interest, represented the first time an individual collected payment from the tobacco industry for a tobacco-related illness. • In June a California jury awarded Richard Boeken $3 billion in his suit against Philip Morris in Los Angeles. The amount was later reduced to $100 million. • In August, the National Conference of State Legislators report found that only 5 percent of state tobacco settlement monies from the MSA went to tobacco control.

2002   In January, President Bush signed into law the Safe and Drug-Free Schools and Communities Act. In a section titled the "Pro-Children Act of 2001," the new law banned smoking within any indoor facility owned or leased or contracted for and utilized for routine or regular kindergarten, elementary, or secondary education or library services to children. • In September a jury ordered Philip Morris to pay Betty Bullock $28 billion in punitive damages, the largest payment to a single plaintiff in history and the largest single judgment against Philip Morris. (*Bullock v. Philip Morris, Inc.*) The award was slashed to $28 million in December. • In December a federal appeals court upheld a $1.4 million verdict against Olympic Airways in the secondhand-smoke death of Dr. Abid Hanson from an asthma attack, the largest individual secondhand-smoke award in the United States. • In December a ban on smoking became effective throughout the U.S. military, in accordance with President Clinton's 1997 executive order banning smoking in all federal facilities, and after Defense Secretary Cohen's three-year grace period for all Morale, Welfare and Recreational facilities. Barracks and housing remained exempt.

2003   On January 27, Philip Morris Companies stock began trading as Altria Group Inc. Philip Morris USA, Philip Morris International, and Kraft Foods Inc. will keep their names. Altria is derived from the Latin word altus, reflecting a desire to "reach higher." • The World Health Organization's (WHO's) Sixth Framework Convention on Tobacco Control session met in Geneva, finalizing a landmark treaty to stem tobacco use and related disease worldwide. It was formally adopted by 192 nations in May. • In March, New York City banned smoking in all public places. • In March, Illinois Circuit Court Judge Nicholas Byron ruled in *Susan Miles et al. v. Philip Morris Inc.* that Philip Morris had to pay $10.1 billion in damages for misleading smokers into believing that low-tar cigarettes are safer than regular brands. • In July, New Jersey raised its state tax rises 55¢ per pack, bringing New Jersey's total cigarette tax to $2.05 per pack, making it the highest in the nation—the first to break the $2 barrier. Thirty states increased cigarette taxes since January 2002. • In August, 26 state attorneys general wrote the president of the Motion Pictures Association of America, urging him to help reduce smoking in the movies. • In August, R. J. Reynolds paid $196,000 to the estate of Floyd Kenyon, the second time an individual collected payment from the tobacco industry for a tobacco-related illness. This was the first time RJR paid damages in an individual product-liability lawsuit.

2004   On July 30, the nation's second and third largest tobacco companies, R. J. Reynolds and Brown & Williamson, merged, establishing Reynolds American Inc. as the parent company of R. J. Reynolds Tobacco Company, Santa Fe Natural Tobacco Company, Lane Limited, and R. J. Reynolds Global Products.

2005   In February, WHO's Framework Convention on Tobacco Control went into effect in 57 countries that ratified the treaty. One hundred eleven nations signed it but did not ratify it.

In March the Supreme Court refused to hear the Patricia Henley appeal. Henley's $9 million award against Philip Morris stood. The tobacco company paid $10.5 million in compensatory and punitive damages and about $6.2 million in interest to Henley, the second payout for Philip Morris, and the largest. It was also the first punitive damages ever paid to an individual smoker.

R. J. Reynolds won a lawsuit. A jury found that exposure to secondhand smoke in airplane cabins did not cause the chronic sinusitis of Lorraine Swaty, a flight attendant for US Airways.

2006   In May the New Hampshire governor signed a fire-safe cigarette law, making New Hampshire the fifth state to require fire-safe cigarettes. The law went into effect on October 1, 2007. New York (2004), Vermont (2006), California (2007), and Illinois (2008) also had such laws on the books.

On August 17, U.S. District Judge Gladys Kessler issued a final opinion in the U.S. government's landmark lawsuit, initiated in 1999, against the major tobacco companies (except Liggett) under Racketeer Influenced and Corrupt Organizations (RICO). The judge found that the companies violated racketeering laws and defrauded the American people by lying for more than

	50 years about the health risks of smoking and their marketing to children. Besides enjoining the companies from lying in the future, the judge also enjoined them from using *light*-type descriptors. She ordered them to issue corrective statements.
2007	In November, R. J. Reynolds announced that it would stop advertising in newspapers and consumer magazines in 2008.
2009	The largest federal tobacco tax increase in history took effect in April when the cigarette tax jumped from 39¢ a pack to $1.01.

President Barack Obama signed the Family Smoking Prevention and Tobacco Control Act, historic legislation granting authority over tobacco products to the U.S. Food and Drug Administration.

The U.S. Food and Drug Administration banned cigarettes with fruit, candy, or clove flavors.

Dr. Lawrence R. Dyton was named as the first director of the new Center for Tobacco Products.

2010	A U.S. District Court judge overturned two of the marketing restrictions in the Family Smoking Prevention and Tobacco Control Act, but backed most limits on merchandise sales, event sponsorships, and free samples of cigarettes.

The FDA's new Tobacco Products Scientific Advisory Committee met for the first time. What to do about menthol flavorings in cigarettes topped the panel's agenda.

Annotated Primary Source Documents

Document 1: Republican Senator Reed Smoot's Tobacco Regulation Speech in the U.S. Senate, June 10, 1929; *Congressional Record* 71st Congress, 1st Session, pp. 2586–90.

Reed Smoot represented Utah in the U.S. Senate for 30 years. The only Mormon apostle to serve in the U.S. Senate, Smoot addressed tobacco product marketing and advertising aimed at women and children as well as his proposal to extend the Food and Drugs Act to tobacco and tobacco products. These issues still concern the medical and public health communities 80 years later.

Mr. Smoot: Mr. President, 10 years ago, when in certain quarters of our metropolitan cities a saloon flourished on every corner, when red lights marked houses of infamy, when blazing electric signs reminded the passerby that it was time for another drink of whisky, no tobacco manufacturer, despite the vast license permitted, had the temerity to cry to our women, "Smoke cigarettes—they are good for you." When newspapers were filled with cure-all and patent medicines advertisements, no manufacturer of a tobacco product dared to offer nicotine as a substitute for wholesome foods; no cigarette manufacturer was so bold as to fly in the face of established medical and health opinion by urging adolescent boys to smoke cigarettes, or young girls—the future mothers of the Nation—to adopt the cigarette habit.

Not since the days when public opinion rose in its might and smote the dangerous drug traffic, not since the days when the vendor of harmful nostrums was swept from our streets, has this country witnessed such an orgy of buncombe, quackery, and downright falsehood and fraud as now marks the current campaign promoted by certain cigarette manufacturers to create a vast woman and child market for the use of their product.

In bringing to the attention of my colleagues in Congress a situation which demands strong legislative remedy if the health and welfare of the Nation are not to be increasingly undermined by an evil which promises to be greater than alcohol I desire to make it clear that no attack is intended upon the tobacco growers of our country, many of whom are in the grip of pernicious cigarette-manufacturing interests; that I realize that many tobacco manufacturers, with a due sense of their social obligations, have refrained and are refraining from exploiting public health in the sale of their products; and that the use of tobacco as a moderate indulgence by adult people is not in question. I rise to denounce insidious cigarette campaigns now being promoted by those tobacco manufacturing interests whose only god is profit, whose only bible is the balance sheet, whose only principle is greed. I rise to denounce the unconscionable, heartless, and destructive attempts to exploit the women and youth of our country in the interest of a few powerful tobacco organizations whose rapacity knows no bounds.

Whatever may be said of the moderate indulgence in the use of tobacco it is clear that the issue raised before the country in some of the current cigarette campaigns is the issue raised by urging excessive cigarette smoking; by flaunting appeals to the youth of our country; by misrepresenting established medical and health findings in order to encourage cigarette addiction.

These great cigarette campaigns, into which millions are being pored in order to create new armies of cigarette addicts, have been accompanied by a barrage of the most patent hypocrisy. "There is not the slightest basis, either in this company's advertising or radio broadcasting, for any suggestion that this or any other tobacco company is planning to create a vast child market for cigarettes," George Washington Hill, president of the American Tobacco Co., has protested in the newspapers. "I should be as shocked," he has declared, "as anybody else if a tobacco company should undertake to appeal to adolescents."

What is to be said for such a statement, when, at the very moment that this is written, the American Tobacco Co. dares to flaunt on the billboards of the Nation posters showing an adolescent girl smoking cigarettes?

What is to be said about such a statement when the American Tobacco Co. stands self-convicted before the country for broadcasting tainted testimonials from professional athletes, urging cigarettes as aid to physical prowess, although it has since been forced by innumerable protests addressed to radio stations to discontinue these claims on the air.

What is to be said about such a statement when to this very day the American Tobacco Co. attacks public health by urging young women to maintain slender figures by smoking cigarettes?

For months the gigantic machine of deception and fraud set up by pernicious cigarette interests has been gathering momentum. Under cover of alleged competition—the "newer competition," as Mr. Hill describes it in an article in the June issue of World's Work—the campaign to place a cigarette in the mouth of every woman and youth in the United States has now been extended to every town and village in the country. Mr. Hill's account of the accidental observation that led to the present campaign is very illuminating. He writes:

> I was driving home from my office one afternoon last fall when my car was stopped by a traffic light. A very fat woman was standing on the near corner chewing with evident relish on what may have been a pickle, but which I thought of instantly through a natural association of ideas as a sweet.
>
> That had no great significance until a taxicab pulled in between my car and the curb and blocked my view of the fat woman. I found my eyes resting easily on a pretty and very modern flapper whose figure was quite the last word in slimness. The girl took advantage of the halt to produce a long cigarette holder, filled it with a fag, and lighted up.

But pickle or candy—he did not care which—this flash of vision in the brain of the president of the American Tobacco Co. became we are told, the basis of a $12,000,000 advertising effort in which football coaches were hired to tell the American boy that cigarettes put vim and vigor into the most strenuous of all physical exercises; in which the alleged testimonials of opera singers were used to persuade the American public that cigarette smoke was soothing to the throat; in which current celebrities were made to say that the cigarette habit was a social asset; in which moving-pictures actresses, stage stars, and others were paid to tell the American woman that they retained their lovely figures only by smoking cigarettes.

What a pity Mr. Hill's limousine did not take him further afield. He might have traveled to Atlantic City on May 29 and heard the appalling reports made at the annual convention of the National Tuberculosis Association. Here is how the New York Times of May 30 heads its account of the meeting:

> Find tuberculosis gains among girls; physicians of convention lay rise to smoking, late hours, and inadequate diet; victims of "flapper" age; death rate, 50 percent greater than among boys five years ago, now is shown to be 100 percent higher.

In any schoolroom he could have seen the dwarfed body of an habitual boy smoker, ruined in health and morals by being led into the cigarette habit at a tender age.

Mr. Hill might have inquired of any reputable physician who could have told him that intestinal catarrh, ulcer, liver hemorrhages, kidney degeneration, chronic bronchitis, heightened blood pressure, palpitation of the heart, pronounced anemia, Bright's disease, neurasthenia, cancer of the mouth and nose, premature senility are but a few of the ailments of which nicotine poisoning stands convicted by the medical profession.

The evil examples set by the most powerful factor in the American tobacco industry has been quick to bear fruit. A widespread advertising campaign is now under way that actually features cigarettes as a newly discovered nerve tonic. In many women's colleges resentment has been caused by the free distribution of cigarettes designed to start girl undergraduates on the road to cigarette addiction. Another company sends congratulatory birthday greetings with a carton of cigarettes to boys who have reached 16 years of age. Every temptation that greed can devise is thus placed in the path of our boys and girls.

No wonder that the serious social problems presented by this huge campaign of miseducation have stirred so many elements of our national life. In the Journal of the American Association on December 8, 1928, the campaign is condemned in the following words:

> Who would have thought 10 years ago that cigarettes would be sold to the American public ... actually by insistence on the health qualities of certain brands? That American womanhood passed during the last five years through one of those periodic crazes that have afflicted womankind since the world began is not a secret. Indeed, women everywhere began to cultivate sylphlike figures, dieted themselves to the point of destruction; and tuberculosis rates, particularly for young girls, rose in many communities.

At the same time the manufacturers of Lucky Strike cigarettes having secured, they claim, statements from 20,678 physicians that Lucky Strikes were less irritating than other cigarettes, are promulgating a campaign in which they assert that those cigarettes do not cut the wind or impair the physical condition, and that Lucky Strikes satisfy the longing for things that make you fat without interfering with a normal appetite for health foods. To which the simple reply is made, "Hooey."

The human appetite is a delicate mechanism and the attempt to urge that it be aborted or destroyed by the regular use of tobacco is essentially vicious.

The Life Extension Institute, whose board is made up of leading American physicians and public-health authorities, is definitely on record with regard to tobacco. In its bulletin headed What it Costs to Smoke Tobacco, it is declared that among 5,000 smokers examined who showed various physical impairments requiring medical supervision, 6 percent suffered from thickened arteries, 15 percent from rapid pulse, 15 percent from decayed teeth, 13 percent from gum recession, 27 percent from marked pyorrhea. The Life Extension Institute likewise reports college texts which indicate lower scholarship records by students who inhaled tobacco fumes. The bulletin includes the following statement:

> How many deaths have occurred from typhoid and from surgical operations upon those who have injured the nervous mechanism of their circulation by tobacco will never be known. But surgeons have noted instances of failure to rally after operations among cigarette smokers.

No less significant is the fact that at a time when powerful cigarette interests are screaming from every billboard and through millions of radio sets their pernicious advice to the women of our country to maintain a slender figure by smoking cigarettes, the Metropolitan Life Insurance Co. finds it necessary to warn its policyholders as well as the general public against such harmful dieting:

> The desire for extreme slenderness–reads its statement—is bringing serious consequences. When stimulants, sedatives, or drugs are substituted for the food needed to build health or strength the penalty is certain and severe—frequently broken health and sometimes death.

The bibliography of those who have condemned the excessive use of tobacco includes some of the greatest names in medicine and public health in the history of this country—Dr. Alexander Lambert; the late Doctor Janeway, of Johns Hopkins Hospital; Doctor Sheldon, of Cornell University Medical College; Dr. Eugene L. Fisk, medical director of the Life Extension Institute; Professor Pack, of the University of Utah; Prof. M.V. O'Shea, of the University of Wisconsin; Dr. Arthur Deramont Bush, of the University of Vermont; Prof. W. P. Lombard, professor of physiology of the University of Michigan; Dr. Harvey W. Wiley; Dr. Samuel G. Dixon, commissioner of health for Pennsylvania; Dr. J. H. Kellogg, superintendent of Battle Creek Sanitarium; Dr. Francis Dowling; Dr. Elbert H. Burr; Dean Hornell, of Ohio Wesleyan University; Dr. Henry Churchill King, president of Oberlin College; Robert Lee Bates. Of the psychological laboratory of Johns Hopkins University; Dr. Pierce Clark. Consulting neurologist of the Manhattan State Hospital, New York. A host of other investigators might be mentioned.

But a no more pertinent, timely, and measured condemnation of the current cigarette propaganda can be quoted than the statement made on June 7, 1929 by Dr. Hugh S. Cumming, Surgeon General United States Public Health Service. He said:

> The cigarette habit indulged in to excess by women and girls tends to cause nervousness and insomnia. If American women generally continue the habit, as reports now indicate they are doing, the entire Nation will suffer. The physical tone of the whole Nation will be lowered. The number of American women who are smoking cigarettes to-day is amazing. The habit harms a woman more than it does a man. The woman's nervous system is more highly organized than the man's. The reaction is, therefore, more intense. It may ruin her complexion, causing it to become gradually ashen. Propaganda urging that tobacco be used as a substitute for food is not in the interest of public health, and if practiced widely by young persons will be positively harmful.

It was natural that the great voice of the pulpit should rise in indignant protest against the appalling exploitation of the health and welfare of the American family inherent in the current cigarette propaganda.

The board of Christian education of the Presbyterian Church in the United States; the board of temperance, prohibition, and public morals of the Methodist

Episcopal Church; the board of education of the Reformed Church in America, as well as the Congregational Church extension boards, have denounced the insidious cigarette campaign. The United Presbyterian General Assembly, meeting at Pittsburgh on June 4, 1929, protested in a resolution against the "boldness of the tobacco interests in advertising their wares over the radio, in newspapers, and on billboards."...

Nearly every leading organization concerned with the education of our young, with juvenile delinquency, with the maintenance of public morals, has taken some action to protest against the wholesale attempt to nicotinize the youth of our Nation, including the National Education Association, the American Federation of Teachers, the American Eugenics Society, the American Child Welfare Association, and numerous parent-teacher associations throughout the country.

The General Federation of Women's Clubs declared its views on cigarette smoking at its fifteenth biennial convention in a resolution reading as follows:

> Whereas the cigarette is a serious menace to the physical, mental, moral, and spiritual development of the youth of our country: Therefore be it *Resolved,* That the women of the General Federation go on record as favoring an educational propaganda against cigarettes, and further indorsing state legislation prohibiting the furnishing of cigarettes to minors.

The contemptuous term "tainted testimonials," coined by leading advertising men to describe the purchased testimony offered by cigarette interests, is sufficient indication of the way in which American business generally views this campaign. What quackery! Overnight, as it were, the old "coffin nail," against which we solemnly warned our young, became the sovereign good. Are you suffering from a sore throat? Gargle with cigarettes—there is not a cough in them. Would you be slender and charming? Substitute cigarettes for wholesome foods. Would you gain laurels on the football field? Cigarettes will give you vim and vigor. Would you be a great general? Forget that an army marches on its stomach—it marches on cigarette stubs. Would you be a popular sea hero? Throw the life preservers overboard—and place your trust in a package of cigarettes.

It is a high affirmation of American business standards that the Association of National Advertisers, including the most reputable business interests of the country, at its meeting in French Lick, Ind., during the week of May 27, passed the following resolution repudiating the tainted testimonials now used in the nation-wide cigarette propaganda on the billboards and in the magazines:

> Whereas we believe that advertising, in order to be lastingly effective and profitable, must not only be truthful and sincere but must also appear to be; and Whereas, this being our belief, it naturally follows that we view with disapproval the use of the so-called paid testimonials: Therefore be it Resolved, That our members continue carefully to scrutinize their own advertising from this standpoint, and that they express this opinion of the

association on insincere testimonials, gratuitous or paid for, at every opportunity.

It is important to note, also that out of 786 advertising agencies and national advertisers which answered a questionnaire from the National Better Business Bureau, 581 expressed emphatic condemnation of tainted testimonial advertising. The cigarette campaign, it is evident, is a libel—a great libel—upon American business ethics. ...

It will be noted that the consumption of cigarettes in the United States has now reached the enormous total of 102,000,000,000, an increase of 118 percent during the last decade. In 1901, only 3,000,000,000 cigarettes were consumed by the American public. The increase from that figure to the present annual rate of consumption is more than 3,000 percent.

What is the bill which the Nation pays for this huge tobacco consumption? In terms of premature death, of disease, of ill health, of lessened efficiency, of loss through fires started by smoking, the sum is incalculable. In the price paid directly in dollars and cents, the following comparative table, compiled by the National Education Association, for the year 1926, based on United States Treasury Department tax returns, is illuminating:

Cost of public schools, elementary, secondary, and collegiate, in 1926	$2, 255,251,327
Spent for tobacco, 1926	$2,087,110,000
Spent for life insurance, 1926	$2, 624,000,000

It is evident that there is a deeper, more sinister purpose behind the vast machinery of deception created for the cigarette campaign than the "new competition" by which the American Tobacco Co. seeks to cloak its attack upon the public health. The cigarette interests concerned in the present campaign are playing for larger stakes than a mere share of the farmer's, the dairy producer's, the baker's, the ice cream man's, the candy man's, the sugar man's, and the grocer's dollar. All producers and purveyors of raw and manufactured food products are well within their rights in attacking such a campaign of unfair competition, when the American public is urged, on the basis of misleading and destructive health claims, to substitute cigarettes for wholesome foods. Farm groups and farm organizations, at a time when Congress is legislating on important problems of farm relief, are fully justified in denouncing a campaign which seeks to increase harmful and destructive dieting habits that have done so much to reduce the per capita consumption of foodstuffs in the United States.

What pernicious tobacco interests really see is the vacant throne created by the deposition of King Alcohol. And well they may. Let me quote from the second volume of Modern Medicine by Doctors Osler and McCrea:

Many patients (alcoholic) in whom the attack seems to be without exciting cause, if questioned closely, are found to be great tobacco smokers, and the cause of their outbreak is a really recurrent poisoning by tobacco. Usually the history is that they smoke, especially the cigarette smokers, incessantly and to excess. This finally makes them nervous. Then they smoke more to quiet their nervousness until finally they seek another narcotic to quiet them; then they naturally turn to alcohol.

The link between the drink habit and the drug habit inherent in excessive cigarette smoking has been made clear repeatedly by medical authority.

The insidious cigarette campaign now in progress concerns every father and every mother of children in the country; every man and woman responsible for the education of the young; every medical and health authority; every employer of labor; every worker whose efficiency is decreased by the cigarette habit. It concerns every welfare organization, every tuberculosis association, every life and fire insurance company, every property owner, every juvenile protective association. ...

The challenge hurled at public health, public welfare, and business decency by destructive cigarette interests must be fairly and squarely met. State legislation is now attempting to cope with the problem.

In Illinois a bill has been introduced in the general assembly for the restriction of advertising which urges young people to smoke cigarettes. A similar measure is before the senate of that State.

A bill to prevent the advertising of cigarettes through the radio and on the billboards, introduced February 12, is now before the Idaho State Senate.

The laws of the State of Maine have put tobacco in the class with poisons and narcotic drugs.

In the State of West Virginia tobacco is placed by statute in the class with opium.

In Michigan a bill has been offered in the lower house against advertising designed to promote the sale of cigarettes to women.

In the State of Utah billboard and street-car advertising of cigarettes has been made a misdemeanor.

In Mississippi Dr. W.F. Bond, State superintendent of education, is calling for a nation-wide effort to combat the millions of dollars that cigarette manufacturers are spending for propaganda.

In California schools are required by law to instruct children as to the injurious effects of tobacco and the sale of cigarettes is forbidden to any girl or boy under the age of 18.

In practically every other state of the Union public disapproval of cigarettes for minors is expressed by law in one form or another.

At the present time intensive efforts are in progress in various communities against the billboard advertising of the American Tobacco Co., which has dared to feature a poster picturing a girl of tender years actually smoking cigarettes. These community efforts are now in progress in Arkansas, California, Colorado, Idaho, Illinois, Iowa, Massachusetts, Michigan, Minnesota, Mississippi, New

York, North Carolina, North Dakota, Ohio, Oklahoma, Oregon, South Dakota, Texas, Tennessee, Washington, and other States.

But the time has come for the Congress of the United States to take definite action. The sale of cigarettes, promoted upon a national scale, is properly a subject of interstate commerce. Cigarettes and many tobacco products are nationally advertised in media which in most cases are subject only to Federal control.

I am convinced that the present great license assumed by certain cigarette interests would have been impossible if tobacco and tobacco products were subject to the same regulations that apply to basic food products or to drug products, in which latter classification tobacco properly belongs.

Only a fine technicality permits tobacco at the present time to escape proper classification and control. In section 6 of the food and drugs act drugs are defined as "all medicines and preparations recognized in the United States Pharmacopoeia, or National Formulary, for internal and external use."

In the past tobacco has been listed in the pharmacopoeia as a drug, but was dropped in the last revision of the work with the following explanation, which makes the reason for omission self-evident:

Tobacco, the leaves of Nicotiana tabacum, was official in former pharmacopoeia, but was dropped in the last revision. It was formerly highly esteemed as a vulnerary, but is little used as a drug by intelligent physicians. A decoction of tobacco in which corrosive sublimate has been dissolved makes a satisfactory bedbug poison.

Although tobacco is thus officially banned as a remedy, despite the claims of the American Tobacco Co. that it promotes the health of the user, the fact remains that tobacco contains many injurious drugs, including nicotine, pyridin, carbolic acid, ammonia, marsh gas, and other products.

While basic food products upon which our agricultural population is dependent, while any drug and medicines the use or abuse of which may have a bearing upon public health, are under the Food, Drug, and Insecticide Administration of the United States Department of Agriculture, tobacco, the abuse of which has become a national problem, is not included within the regulations of the food and drugs act, for the merely technical reason that since modern medical practices has abandoned it as a remedy it is no longer listed in the pharmacopoeia.

The bill which I now lay before this body, designed to protect public health and public welfare from the further exploitation of irresponsible cigarette interests, provides:

(a) For the inclusion of tobacco and tobacco products within the scope of the food and drugs act,
(b) For the amendment of the food and drugs act so that claims made for food and drug products in any advertising medium subject to interstate-commerce control should be under the same strict regulation now applied

to labels or other descriptive matter on, within, or around the container in which the product is packed.

Public interest, efficiency, and economy require the amendment to the food and drugs act empowering the Food, Drug, and Insecticide Administration to proceed against any manufacturer of a drug or food product whose public sales claims are partly or wholly unjustified by the facts. The Federal Trade Commission, which now cooperates with the Food, Drug, and Insecticide Administration, has no laboratory facilities and no adequate corps of investigators. Procedure is slow, therefore, and in matters affecting public health vast harm may be done before the Federal Trade Commission is ready or able to take action in the premises.

This measure is proposed, therefore, to remedy this situation and in order to avoid duplication, the overlapping of authority, the diffusion of responsibility, and the dual expense to the Government.

The bill which I now send to the Clerk's desk is designed to meet a problem of such great and immediate importance to public health and of such vital interest to our agricultural producers and business men that I am confident it deserves and will obtain support of every Member of Congress.

Document 2: Horace R. Kornegay, president of the Tobacco Institute, *Congressional Record-House*, September 29, 1976, pp. 33754–55.

Mr. Kornegay, a former member of the House of Representatives from North Carolina, addressed the convention of the Tobacco Workers International Union, which represented more than 50,000 men and women from the United States and Canada. In his speech, "Tobacco's Need for Unity," inserted in the Congressional Record *on September 29, 1976, he dealt with what he perceived as manifestations of antitobacco prejudice since 1621, "prohibition bills masquerading as public health bills," and the need for labor, management, and agriculture to unite against antitobacco people who make smokers social outcasts as well as shift the blame for disease and industrial and environmental pollution on tobacco.*

When our president, Rene Rondou [president of the Tobacco Workers International Union], and your secretary-treasurer, Homer Cole, asked me to speak to your convention, I accepted with pleasure. "Avec Plaisir," as those delegates from across our Northern border say.

This is the first time a president of the Tobacco Institute has been given this opportunity and I thank you for it.

I regard it as more than an opportunity, however. I regard it as a necessity, parce que je suis aussi un travailleur du tabac ... because I too am a tobacco worker. And never before is the time more ripe to fight back.

This being our Bicentennial year, we have heard a lot about our Founding Fathers, the Declaration of Independence, the Constitution and the Bill of Rights.

There has been much talk about our unique form of representative democracy, our system of checks and balances, and our government of laws not men.

But one subject has been almost totally omitted.

This being the convention of the Tobacco Workers International Union, I can think of no better place to remedy this omission–and to mention the unmentionable. I refer, of course, to tobacco—which a lot of people are trying to turn into a dirty word.

Tobacco played a vital role in America 200 years ago. With your help it will play a vital role for another 200 years—and more.

Without tobacco, the Jamestown colony would not have taken root on American soil.

Without tobacco, the Chesapeake colonies would not have flourished and attracted colonists to our shores.

Without tobacco, the Continental Congress would not have had funds to equip General Washington's army, and the Revolutionary War would have been lost.

To put it very simply, without tobacco there would have been no American history, no Bicentennial to celebrate.

Now let me ask you to think about the role that anti-tobacco zealots played in American history.

In 1621, King James came close to destroying Jamestown with a proposal to ban the tobacco trade.

In 1671, King Charles drove the price of tobacco down to half a cent a pound and almost wiped out the thriving colonies of Maryland and Virginia.

To put it very plainly, the ruinous tobacco policy of these anti-tobacco monarchs converted loyal English colonists into American revolutionaries.

Two hundreds years later, we can truly say, the more things change the more they stay the same.

In the early days, tobacco smoking was taken up by the people so fast that potentates feared and persecuted it. Today tobacco still provides pleasure to millions upon millions of people and still harassed by government bureaucrats who do not like what they cannot control.

Now, as in the past, tobacco is valued by the multitude and vilified by the elite.

The situation is unlikely to change in the near future. If anything, the attacks on tobacco will worsen. In an age dominated by science, the alleged threat to health is a powerful fuel tossed on the fires of controversy.

No longer condemned solely on moral or religious grounds, tobacco is now indicted as a menace to the health of smokers and nonsmokers.

The antismoker no longer holds himself to be only the keeper of his brother's soul, but also of his body. The right to protect a smoker from himself has always been questionable. The right to protect the nonsmokers from the smoker is a phony issue.

It is the equivalent of legislating against the mote in one fellow's eye and ignoring the beam in another's. The argument, as preposterous as it is, has nevertheless attracted headlines and support in Federal and state legislatures. Several states have restricted smoking in public places on the theory that a smoker in one corner of a room is going to affect the health of a nonsmoker in the other corner.

On this flimsy basis, many states have regulated smoking or segregated smokers in restaurants, sports arenas, supermarkets and all sorts of public places. Do not misunderstand, I do not advocate an absolute right to smoke wherever and whenever you choose. I do not advocate an absolute right to light up and puff away in total disregard of anyone else. I do, however, object to and oppose legislation that overregulates personal behavior which has always been handled by the exercise of common sense and common courtesy. And I most vigorously oppose the sacrifice of our personal freedom before the False God of Prohibition, masquerading as "public health."

As public health measures, not one of these nonsmoker bills meets the minimum standard of common sense. Not one calls for measuring the air quality in a public room before or after smoking is banned or smokers are segregated. Not one seeks to determine if the air has actually been cleared.

Not one of these bills takes any interest in the air people are forced to breathe outside of public rooms or public places. Not one is concerned about any other odors, fumes, dust, exhausts or emissions that assault the lungs, nasal passages and eyes in public places.

Why? The reason is obvious. They are not public health proposals. They are just the latest manifestation of anti-tobacco prejudice that is as old as tobacco itself. These measures are simply the latest tactic in the long crusade against the leaf. They are just the latest harassment of smoking and smokers designed to reduce millions of tobacco consumers to second-class citizens, to make them social outcasts, to get them to quit smoking. They are prohibition bills masquerading as public health bills.

These attacks will fail ... if—and only if—tobacco workers and manufacturers and growers unite in a common struggle to resist them.

Fortunately, 1976 is a Bicentennial year, it is also an election year, presidential, senatorial, congressional, and local. In a democracy, the best time to send a message to officials is when they need our votes. This is the year to get our message across to every candidate in every election.

This is the year to tell the politicians a few facts of life.

Tell them that nearly 70,000 production workers—including the 33,000 members of the TWIU—don't intend to lose their jobs because of overregulation by bureaucrats.

Tell them that 600,000 farm families who grow almost 3 billion pounds of tobacco don't intend to be driven off the land into big city welfare traps because of overregulation by bureaucrats.

Tell them manufacturers don't intend to close down plants that produce over 600 billion cigarettes because of overregulation by bureaucrats.

Tell them that the entire tobacco community is fed up with the constant attempts to shift the blame for industrial and environmental pollution on to the backs of tobacco workers, growers, and smokers.

Tell them that people who live in heavily industrialized parts of town have higher rates of lung cancer than people living in the affluent suburbs–and that can't be blamed on tobacco.

Tell them we are sick and tired of having tobacco made the scapegoat for unsolved health problems. Tell them we are sick and tired of seeing tobacco used as a red herring for other suspected health hazards.

Let me tell you a true story.

Seventy-five years ago the Journal of the American Medical Association published a doctor's report. He said that every tuberculosis patient he had seen for several years was a cigarette smoker. He jumped to the familiar conclusion– eliminate cigarettes and thus eliminate tuberculosis.

As you know. Cigarettes were not eliminated. They became increasingly popular. Yet TB has virtually disappeared due to the discovery and use of antibacterial drugs. What if cigarettes had been banned, factories closed, jobs eliminated, farms abandoned?

But what if the good doctor's advice had been taken instead? Do you supposed he would have come around to apologize for his terrible mistake? Would he have said "I'm sorry. I was wrong" to the hundreds of thousands of workers and growers his policy would have driven off their jobs and their land? Would he have apologized to the thousands of TB patients who would have died because the medical profession had chased the wrong rabbit ... had eliminated cigarettes instead of TB bacteria?

Our tobacco industry still runs the same risk of having anti-smoking zealots shooting first and maybe asking questions afterward.

For as one noted medical scientists put it recently: "Most diseases, if the truth be told, cannot be prevented because we do not comprehend their mechanism."

This admission of ignorance as to what causes disease and how is rare. It is extremely rare with respect to tobacco. Nevertheless the plain truth is that after 25 years of research, the question of smoking and health is still a question. In the effort to get at the facts this industry spends—and has spent—more funds on scientific research than all of the over-zealous private health organizations combined.

Until our nation comes up with objective scientific answers, our industry and its workers and farmers will continue to be victimized by those who only want an easy answer that serves their special interests.

The gap in our knowledge about smoking and health creates a vacuum of fact which our opponents will eagerly fill with emotional charges. This intolerable state of affairs means that—

Many who are permissive about marijuana will be repressive about tobacco.

Many who are silent about environmental and industrial pollution will shout about the greater threat of tobacco smoke as so-called personal pollution.

Many who support civil rights will callously disregard smokers' rights.

It is a national scandal to see how easily some politicians are stampeded by these pressure groups.

And it is time that we as a united industry—labor, management and agriculture—unfurl that old Revolutionary War standard that bore the words "Don't Tread on Me." Let's rally around it. Let's march out behind it. In unity.

If I have succeeded in bringing our kettle of indignation to a boil. I don't have to tell you where to pour the hot water.

Document 3: The Tobacco Master Settlement Act of 1998, November 23, 1998.

On November 23, 1998, the attorneys general and other representatives of 46 states, Puerto Rico, the U.S. Virgin Islands, American Samoa, the Northern Mariana Islands, Guam, and the District of Columbia signed the Tobacco Master Settlement Agreement Act (MSA) with the five largest tobacco manufacturers (Brown & Williamson Tobacco Corporation, Lorillard Tobacco Company, Philip Morris Incorporated, R. J. Reynolds Tobacco Company, Commonwealth Tobacco, and Liggett & Myers).

The MSA, the largest civil settlement in U.S. history, provides for restrictions on practices by tobacco companies as well as their payment of $206 billion to forty-six states, the District of Columbia, and five U.S. territories to compensate them for Medicaid costs associated with smoking-related diseases. In exchange, the states settled existing litigation on these matters, and the companies were protected from most forms of future litigation regarding harm caused by tobacco use. The agreement ended a four-year legal battle between the states and the industry that began in 1994 when Mississippi became the first state to file suit. Four states (Florida, Minnesota, Mississippi and Texas) had previously settled with tobacco manufacturers for $40 billion. Federal legislation was not required to implement the MSA.

The MSA restricted tobacco companies from targeting youth through advertising, marketing and promotions; required the industry to make a commitment to reducing youth access and consumption; disbanded tobacco trade associations; restricted industry lobbying; opened industry records and research to the public, and created a national, independent public health foundation (the Washington D.C.-based American Legacy Foundation).

Section 1, "Recitals," supplies key background information about the parties to the settlement. Section 3, "Permanent Relief," outlines the restrictions placed on the tobacco companies by the settlement. Appendix E provides total payments to each state through 2025.

This Master Settlement Agreement is made by the undersigned Settling State officials (on behalf of their respective Settling States) and the undersigned Participating Manufacturers to settle and resolve with finality all Released Claims against the Participating Manufacturers and related entities as set forth herein.

This Agreement constitutes the documentation effecting this settlement with respect to each Settling State, and is intended to and shall be binding upon each Settling State and each Participating Manufacturer in accordance with the terms hereof.

I. RECITALS

WHEREAS, more than 40 States have commenced litigation asserting various claims for monetary, equitable and injunctive relief against certain tobacco product manufacturers and others as defendants, and the States that have not filed suit can potentially assert similar claims;

WHEREAS, the Settling States that have commenced litigation have sought to obtain equitable relief and damages under state laws, including consumer protection and/or antitrust laws, in order to further the Settling States' policies regarding public health, including policies adopted to achieve a significant reduction in smoking by Youth;

WHEREAS, defendants have denied each and every one of the Settling States' allegations of unlawful conduct or wrongdoing and have asserted a number of defenses to the Settling States' claims, which defenses have been contested by the Settling States;

WHEREAS, the Settling States and the Participating Manufacturers are committed to reducing underage tobacco use by discouraging such use and by preventing Youth access to Tobacco Products;

WHEREAS, the Participating Manufacturers recognize the concern of the tobacco grower community that it may be adversely affected by the potential reduction in tobacco consumption resulting from this settlement, reaffirm their commitment to work cooperatively to address concerns about the potential adverse economic impact on such community, and will, within 30 days after the MSA Execution Date, meet with the political leadership of States with grower communities to address these economic concerns;

WHEREAS, the undersigned Settling State officials believe that entry into this Agreement and uniform consent decrees with the tobacco industry is necessary in order to further the Settling States' policies designed to reduce Youth smoking, to promote the public health and to secure monetary payments to the Settling States; and

WHEREAS, the Settling States and the Participating Manufacturers wish to avoid the further expense, delay, inconvenience, burden and uncertainty of continued litigation (including appeals from any verdicts), and, therefore, have agreed to settle their respective lawsuits and potential claims pursuant to terms which will achieve for the Settling States and their citizens significant funding for the advancement of public health, the implementation of important tobacco-related public health measures, including the enforcement of the mandates and restrictions related to such measures, as well as funding for a national Foundation dedicated to significantly reducing the use of Tobacco Products by Youth;

NOW, THEREFORE, BE IT KNOWN THAT, in consideration of the implementation of tobacco-related health measures and the payments to be made by the Participating Manufacturers, the release and discharge of all claims by the Settling States, and such other consideration as described herein, the sufficiency of which is hereby acknowledged, the Settling States and the Participating Manufacturers, acting by and through their authorized agents, memorialize and agree as follows:

III. PERMANENT RELIEF

(a) Prohibition on Youth Targeting. No Participating Manufacturer may take any action, directly or indirectly, to target Youth within any Settling State in the advertising, promotion or marketing of Tobacco Products, or take any action the primary purpose of which is to initiate, maintain or increase the incidence of Youth smoking within any Settling State.

(b) Ban on Use of Cartoons. Beginning 180 days after the MSA Execution Date, no Participating Manufacturer may use or cause to be used any Cartoon in the advertising, promoting, packaging or labeling of Tobacco Products.

(c) Limitation of Tobacco Brand Name Sponsorships.

   (1) Prohibited Sponsorships. After the MSA Execution Date, no Participating Manufacturer may engage in any Brand Name Sponsorship in any State consisting of:

      (A) concerts; or

      (B) events in which the intended audience is comprised of a significant percentage of Youth; or

      (C) events in which any paid participants or contestants are Youth; or

      (D) any athletic event between opposing teams in any football, basketball, baseball, soccer or hockey league.

   (2) Limited Sponsorships.

      (A) No Participating Manufacturer may engage in more than one Brand Name Sponsorship in the States in any twelve-month period (such period measured from the date of the initial sponsored event).

      (B) Provided, however, that

         (i) nothing contained in subsection (2)(A) above shall require a Participating Manufacturer to breach or terminate any sponsorship contract in existence as of August 1, 1998 (until the earlier of (x) the current term of any existing contract, without regard to any renewal or option that may be exercised by such Participating Manufacturer or (y) three years after the MSA Execution Date); and

         (ii) notwithstanding subsection (1)(A) above, Brown & Williamson Tobacco Corporation may sponsor either the GPC country music festival or the Kool jazz festival as its one annual Brand Name Sponsorship permitted pursuant to subsection (2)(A) as well as one Brand Name Sponsorship permitted pursuant to subsection (2)(B)(i).

(3) Related Sponsorship Restrictions. With respect to any Brand Name Sponsorship permitted under this subsection (c):

(A) advertising of the Brand Name Sponsorship event shall not advertise any Tobacco Product (other than by using the Brand Name to identify such Brand Name Sponsorship event);

(B) no Participating Manufacturer may refer to a Brand Name Sponsorship event or to a celebrity or other person in such an event in its advertising of a Tobacco Product;

(C) nothing contained in the provisions of subsection III(e) of this Agreement shall apply to actions taken by any Participating Manufacturer in connection with a Brand Name Sponsorship permitted pursuant to the provisions of subsections (2)(A) and (2)(B)(i); the Brand Name Sponsorship permitted by subsection (2)(B)(ii) shall be subject to the restrictions of subsection III(e) except that such restrictions shall not prohibit use of the Brand Name to identify the Brand Name Sponsorship;

(D) nothing contained in the provisions of subsections III(f) and III(i) shall apply to apparel or other merchandise: (i) marketed, distributed, offered, sold, or licensed at the site of a Brand Name Sponsorship permitted pursuant to subsections (2)(A) or (2)(B)(i) by the person to which the relevant Participating Manufacturer has provided payment in exchange for the use of the relevant Brand Name in the Brand Name Sponsorship or a third-party that does not receive payment from the relevant Participating Manufacturer (or any Affiliate of such Participating Manufacturer) in connection with the marketing, distribution, offer, sale or license of such apparel or other merchandise; or (ii) used at the site of a Brand Name Sponsorship permitted pursuant to subsection (2)(A) or (2)(B)(i) (during such event) that are not distributed (by sale or otherwise) to any member of the general public; and

(E) nothing contained in the provisions of subsection III(d) shall: (i) apply to the use of a Brand Name on a vehicle used in a Brand Name Sponsorship; or (ii) apply to Outdoor Advertising advertising the Brand Name Sponsorship, to the extent that such Outdoor Advertising is placed at the site of a Brand Name Sponsorship no more than 90 days before the start of the initial sponsored event, is removed within 10 days after the end of the last sponsored event, and is not prohibited by subsection (3)(A) above.

(4) Corporate Name Sponsorships. Nothing in this subsection (c) shall prevent a Participating Manufacturer from sponsoring or causing to be sponsored any athletic, musical, artistic, or other social or cultural event, or any entrant, participant or team in such event (or series of events) in the name of the corporation which manufactures Tobacco Products, provided that the corporate name does not include any Brand Name of domestic Tobacco Products.

(5) Naming Rights Prohibition. No Participating Manufacturer may enter into any agreement for the naming rights of any stadium or arena located within a Settling State using a Brand Name, and shall not otherwise cause a stadium or arena located within a Settling State to be named with a Brand Name.

(6) Prohibition on Sponsoring Teams and Leagues. No Participating Manufacturer may enter into any agreement pursuant to which payment is made (or other consideration is provided) by such Participating Manufacturer to any football, basketball, baseball, soccer or hockey league (or any team involved in any such league) in exchange for use of a Brand Name.

(d) Elimination of Outdoor Advertising and Transit Advertisements. Each Participating Manufacturer shall discontinue Outdoor Advertising and Transit Advertisements advertising Tobacco Products within the Settling States as set forth herein.

(1) Removal. Except as otherwise provided in this section, each Participating Manufacturer shall remove from within the Settling States within 150 days after the MSA Execution Date all of its (A) billboards (to the extent that such billboards constitute Outdoor Advertising) advertising Tobacco Products; (B) signs and placards (to the extent that such signs and placards constitute Outdoor Advertising) advertising Tobacco Products in arenas, stadiums, shopping malls and Video Game Arcades; and (C) Transit Advertisements advertising Tobacco Products.

(2) Prohibition on New Outdoor Advertising and Transit Advertisements. No Participating Manufacturer may, after the MSA Execution Date, place or cause to be placed any new Outdoor Advertising advertising Tobacco Products or new Transit Advertisements advertising Tobacco Products within any Settling State.

(3) Alternative Advertising. With respect to those billboards required to be removed under subsection (1) that are leased (as opposed to owned) by any Participating Manufacturer, the Participating Manufacturer will allow the Attorney General of the Settling State within which such billboards are located to substitute, at the Settling State's option, alternative advertising intended to discourage the use of Tobacco Products by Youth and their exposure to second-hand smoke for the remaining term of the applicable contract (without regard to any

renewal or option term that may be exercised by such Participating Manufacturer). The Participating Manufacturer will bear the cost of the lease through the end of such remaining term. Any other costs associated with such alternative advertising will be borne by the Settling State.

(4) Ban on Agreements Inhibiting Anti-Tobacco Advertising. Each Participating Manufacturer agrees that it will not enter into any agreement that prohibits a third party from selling, purchasing or displaying advertising discouraging the use of Tobacco Products or exposure to second-hand smoke. In the event and to the extent that any Participating Manufacturer has entered into an agreement containing any such prohibition, such Participating Manufacturer agrees to waive such prohibition in such agreement.

(5) Designation of Contact Person. Each Participating Manufacturer that has Outdoor Advertising or Transit Advertisements advertising Tobacco Products within a Settling State shall, within 10 days after the MSA Execution Date, provide the Attorney General of such Settling State with the name of a contact person to whom the Settling State may direct inquiries during the time such Outdoor Advertising and Transit Advertisements are being eliminated, and from whom the Settling State may obtain periodic reports as to the progress of their elimination.

(6) Adult-Only Facilities. To the extent that any advertisement advertising Tobacco Products located within an Adult-Only Facility constitutes Outdoor Advertising or a Transit Advertisement, this subsection (d) shall not apply to such advertisement, provided such advertisement is not visible to persons outside such Adult-Only Facility.

(e) Prohibition on Payments Related to Tobacco Products and Media. No Participating Manufacturer may, beginning 30 days after the MSA Execution Date, make, or cause to be made, any payment or other consideration to any other person or entity to use, display, make reference to or use as a prop any Tobacco Product, Tobacco Product package, advertisement for a Tobacco Product, or any other item bearing a Brand Name in any motion picture, television show, theatrical production or other live performance, live or recorded performance of music, commercial film or video, or video game ("Media"); provided, however, that the foregoing prohibition shall not apply to (1) Media where the audience or viewers are within an Adult-Only Facility (provided such Media are not visible to persons outside such Adult-Only Facility); (2) Media not intended for distribution or display to the public; or (3) instructional Media concerning non-conventional cigarettes viewed only by or provided only to smokers who are Adults.

(f) Ban on Tobacco Brand Name Merchandise. Beginning July 1, 1999, no Participating Manufacturer may, within any Settling State, market, distribute, offer, sell, license or cause to be marketed, distributed, offered, sold or licensed (including, without limitation, by catalogue or direct mail), any apparel or other merchandise (other than Tobacco Products, items the sole function of which is to advertise Tobacco Products, or written or electronic publications) which bears a Brand Name. Provided, however, that nothing in this subsection shall (1) require any Participating Manufacturer to breach or terminate any licensing agreement or other contract in existence as of June 20, 1997 (this exception shall not apply beyond the current term of any existing contract, without regard to any renewal or option term that may be exercised by such Participating Manufacturer); (2) prohibit the distribution to any Participating Manufacturer's employee who is not Underage of any item described above that is intended for the personal use of such an employee; (3) require any Participating Manufacturer to retrieve, collect or otherwise recover any item that prior to the MSA Execution Date was marketed, distributed, offered, sold, licensed, or caused to be marketed, distributed, offered, sold or licensed by such Participating Manufacturer; (4) apply to coupons or other items used by Adults solely in connection with the purchase of Tobacco Products; or (5) apply to apparel or other merchandise used within an Adult-Only Facility that is not distributed (by sale or otherwise) to any member of the general public.

(g) Ban on Youth Access to Free Samples. After the MSA Execution Date, no Participating Manufacturer may, within any Settling State, distribute or cause to be distributed any free samples of Tobacco Products except in an Adult-Only Facility. For purposes of this Agreement, a "free sample" does not include a Tobacco Product that is provided to an Adult in connection with (1) the purchase, exchange or redemption for proof of purchase of any Tobacco Products (including, but not limited to, a free offer in connection with the purchase of Tobacco Products, such as a "two-for-one" offer), or (2) the conducting of consumer testing or evaluation of Tobacco Products with persons who certify that they are Adults.

(h) Ban on Gifts to Underage Persons Based on Proofs of Purchase. Beginning one year after the MSA Execution Date, no Participating Manufacturer may provide or cause to be provided to any person without sufficient proof that such person is an Adult any item in exchange for the purchase of Tobacco Products, or the furnishing of credits, proofs-of-purchase, or coupons with respect to such a purchase. For purposes of the preceding sentence only, (1) a driver's license or other government-issued identification (or legible photocopy thereof), the validity of which is certified by the person to whom the item is provided, shall by itself be deemed to be a sufficient form of proof of age; and (2) in the case of items provided (or to be redeemed) at retail establishments, a Participating Manufacturer shall be entitled to rely on verification of proof of age by the retailer, where such retailer is required to obtain verification under applicable federal, state or local law.

(i) Limitation on Third-Party Use of Brand Names. After the MSA Execution Date, no Participating Manufacturer may license or otherwise expressly authorize any third party to use or advertise within any Settling State any Brand Name in a manner prohibited by this Agreement if done by such Participating Manufacturer itself. Each Participating Manufacturer shall, within 10 days after the MSA Execution Date, designate a person (and provide written notice to NAAG of such designation) to whom the Attorney General of any Settling State may provide written notice of any such third-party activity that would be prohibited by this Agreement if done by such Participating Manufacturer itself. Following such written notice, the Participating Manufacturer will promptly take commercially reasonable steps against any such non-de minimis third-party activity. Provided, however, that nothing in this subsection shall require any Participating Manufacturer to (1) breach or terminate any licensing agreement or other contract in existence as of July 1, 1998 (this exception shall not apply beyond the current term of any existing contract, without regard to any renewal or option term that may be exercised by such Participating Manufacturer); or (2) retrieve, collect or otherwise recover any item that prior to the MSA Execution Date was marketed, distributed, offered, sold, licensed or caused to be marketed, distributed, offered, sold or licensed by such Participating Manufacturer.

(j) Ban on Non-Tobacco Brand Names. No Participating Manufacturer may, pursuant to any agreement requiring the payment of money or other valuable consideration, use or cause to be used as a brand name of any Tobacco Product any nationally recognized or nationally established brand name or trade name of any non-tobacco item or service or any nationally recognized or nationally established sports team, entertainment group or individual celebrity. Provided, however, that the preceding sentence shall not apply to any Tobacco Product brand name in existence as of July 1, 1998. For the purposes of this subsection, the term "other valuable consideration" shall not include an agreement between two entities who enter into such agreement for the sole purpose of avoiding infringement claims.

(k) Minimum Pack Size of Twenty Cigarettes. No Participating Manufacturer may, beginning 60 days after the MSA Execution Date and through and including December 31, 2001, manufacture or cause to be manufactured for sale in any Settling State any pack or other container of Cigarettes containing fewer than 20 Cigarettes (or, in the case of roll-your-own tobacco, any package of roll-your-own tobacco containing less than 0.60 ounces of tobacco). No Participating Manufacturer may, beginning 150 days after the MSA Execution Date and through and including December 31, 2001, sell or distribute in any Settling State any pack or other container of Cigarettes containing fewer than 20 Cigarettes (or, in the case of roll-your-own tobacco, any package of roll-your-own tobacco containing less than 0.60 ounces of tobacco). Each Participating Manufacturer further agrees that following the

MSA Execution Date it shall not oppose, or cause to be opposed (including through any third party or Affiliate), the passage by any Settling State of any legislative proposal or administrative rule applicable to all Tobacco Product Manufacturers and all retailers of Tobacco Products prohibiting the manufacture and sale of any pack or other container of Cigarettes containing fewer than 20 Cigarettes (or, in the case of roll-your-own tobacco, any package of roll-your-own tobacco containing less than 0.60 ounces of tobacco).

(l) Corporate Culture Commitments Related to Youth Access and Consumption. Beginning 180 days after the MSA Execution Date each Participating Manufacturer shall:

1. promulgate or reaffirm corporate principles that express and explain its commitment to comply with the provisions of this Agreement and the reduction of use of Tobacco Products by Youth, and clearly and regularly communicate to its employees and customers its commitment to assist in the reduction of Youth use of Tobacco Products;

2. designate an executive level manager (and provide written notice to NAAG of such designation) to identify methods to reduce Youth access to, and the incidence of Youth consumption of, Tobacco Products; and

3. encourage its employees to identify additional methods to reduce Youth access to, and the incidence of Youth consumption of, Tobacco Products.

(m) Limitations on Lobbying. Following State-Specific Finality in a Settling State:

1. No Participating Manufacturer may oppose, or cause to be opposed (including through any third party or Affiliate), the passage by such Settling State (or any political subdivision thereof) of those state or local legislative proposals or administrative rules described in Exhibit F hereto intended by their terms to reduce Youth access to, and the incidence of Youth consumption of, Tobacco Products. Provided, however, that the foregoing does not prohibit any Participating Manufacturer from (A) challenging enforcement of, or suing for declaratory or injunctive relief with respect to, any such legislation or rule on any grounds; (B) continuing, after State-Specific Finality in such Settling State, to oppose or cause to be opposed, the passage during the legislative session in which State-Specific Finality in such Settling State occurs of any specific state or local legislative proposals or administrative rules introduced prior to the time of State-Specific Finality in such Settling State; (C) opposing, or causing to be opposed, any excise tax or income tax provision or user fee or other payments relating to Tobacco Products or Tobacco Product Manufacturers; or (D) opposing, or causing to be opposed, any state or local legislative proposal or administrative rule that also includes measures other than those described in Exhibit F.

2. Each Participating Manufacturer shall require all of its officers and employees engaged in lobbying activities in such Settling State after State-Specific Finality, contract lobbyists engaged in lobbying activities in such Settling State after State-Specific Finality, and any other third parties who engage in lobbying activities in such Settling State after State-Specific Finality on behalf of such Participating Manufacturer ("lobbyist" and "lobbying activities" having the meaning such terms have under the law of the Settling State in question) to certify in writing to the Participating Manufacturer that they:

(A) will not support or oppose any state, local or federal legislation, or seek or oppose any governmental action, on behalf of the Participating Manufacturer without the Participating Manufacturer's express authorization (except where such advance express authorization is not reasonably practicable);

(B) are aware of and will fully comply with this Agreement and all laws and regulations applicable to their lobbying activities, including, without limitation, those related to disclosure of financial contributions. Provided, however, that if the Settling State in question has in existence no laws or regulations relating to disclosure of financial contributions regarding lobbying activities, then each Participating Manufacturer shall, upon request of the Attorney General of such Settling State, disclose to such Attorney General any payment to a lobbyist that the Participating Manufacturer knows or has reason to know will be used to influence legislative or administrative actions of the state or local government relating to Tobacco Products or their use. Disclosures made pursuant to the preceding sentence shall be filed in writing with the Office of the Attorney General on the first day of February and the first day of August of each year for any and all payments made during the six month period ending on the last day of the preceding December and June, respectively, with the following information: (1) the name, address, telephone number and e-mail address (if any) of the recipient; (2) the amount of each payment; and (3) the aggregate amount of all payments described in this subsection (2)(B) to the recipient in the calendar year; and

(C) have reviewed and will fully abide by the Participating Manufacturer's corporate principles promulgated pursuant to this Agreement when acting on behalf of the Participating Manufacturer.

2. No Participating Manufacturer may support or cause to be supported (including through any third party or Affiliate) in Congress or any other forum legislation or rules that would preempt, override, abrogate or diminish such Settling State's rights or recoveries under this

Agreement. Except as specifically provided in this Agreement, nothing herein shall be deemed to restrain any Settling State or Participating Manufacturer from advocating terms of any national settlement or taking any other positions on issues relating to tobacco.

(n) Restriction on Advocacy Concerning Settlement Proceeds. After the MSA Execution Date, no Participating Manufacturer may support or cause to be supported (including through any third party or Affiliate) the diversion of any proceeds of this settlement to any program or use that is neither tobacco-related nor health-related in connection with the approval of this Agreement or in any subsequent legislative appropriation of settlement proceeds.

(o) Dissolution of The Tobacco Institute, Inc., the Council for Tobacco Research-U.S.A., Inc. and the Center for Indoor Air Research, Inc.

   (1) The Council for Tobacco Research-U.S.A., Inc. ("CTR") (a not-for-profit corporation formed under the laws of the State of New York) shall, pursuant to the plan of dissolution previously negotiated and agreed to between the Attorney General of the State of New York and CTR, cease all operations and be dissolved in accordance with the laws of the State of New York (and with the preservation of all applicable privileges held by any member company of CTR).

   (2) The Tobacco Institute, Inc. ("TI") (a not-for-profit corporation formed under the laws of the State of New York) shall, pursuant to a plan of dissolution to be negotiated by the Attorney General of the State of New York and the Original Participating Manufacturers in accordance with Exhibit G hereto, cease all operations and be dissolved in accordance with the laws of the State of New York and under the authority of the Attorney General of the State of New York (and with the preservation of all applicable privileges held by any member company of TI).

   (3) Within 45 days after Final Approval, the Center for Indoor Air Research, Inc. ("CIAR") shall cease all operations and be dissolved in a manner consistent with applicable law and with the preservation of all applicable privileges (including, without limitation, privileges held by any member company of CIAR).

   (4) The Participating Manufacturers shall direct the Tobacco-Related Organizations to preserve all records that relate in any way to issues raised in smoking-related health litigation.

   (5) The Participating Manufacturers may not reconstitute CTR or its function in any form.

   (6) The Participating Manufacturers represent that they have the authority to and will effectuate subsections (1) through (5) hereof.

(p) Regulation and Oversight of New Tobacco-Related Trade Associations.

   (1) A Participating Manufacturer may form or participate in new tobacco-related trade associations (subject to all applicable laws),

provided such associations agree in writing not to act in any manner contrary to any provision of this Agreement. Each Participating Manufacturer agrees that if any new tobacco-related trade association fails to so agree, such Participating Manufacturer will not participate in or support such association.

(2) Any tobacco-related trade association that is formed or controlled by one or more of the Participating Manufacturers after the MSA Execution Date shall adopt by-laws governing the association's procedures and the activities of its members, board, employees, agents and other representatives with respect to the tobacco-related trade association. Such by-laws shall include, among other things, provisions that:

(A) each officer of the association shall be appointed by the board of the association, shall be an employee of such association, and during such officer's term shall not be a director of or employed by any member of the association or by an Affiliate of any member of the association;

(B) legal counsel for the association shall be independent, and neither counsel nor any member or employee of counsel's law firm shall serve as legal counsel to any member of the association or to a manufacturer of Tobacco Products that is an Affiliate of any member of the association during the time that it is serving as legal counsel to the association; and

(C) minutes describing the substance of the meetings of the board of directors of the association shall be prepared and shall be maintained by the association for a period of at least five years following their preparation.

(3) Without limitation on whatever other rights to access they may be permitted by law, for a period of seven years from the date any new tobacco-related trade association is formed by any of the Participating Manufacturers after the MSA Execution Date the antitrust authorities of any Settling State may, for the purpose of enforcing this Agreement, upon reasonable cause to believe that a violation of this Agreement has occurred, and upon reasonable prior written notice (but in no event less than 10 Business Days):

(A) have access during regular office hours to inspect and copy all relevant non-privileged, non-work-product books, records, meeting agenda and minutes, and other documents (whether in hard copy form or stored electronically) of such association insofar as they pertain to such believed violation; and

(B) interview the association's directors, officers and employees (who shall be entitled to have counsel present) with respect to relevant, non-privileged, non-work-product matters pertaining to such believed violation.

Documents and information provided to Settling State antitrust authorities shall be kept confidential by and among such authorities, and shall be utilized only by the Settling States and only for the purpose of enforcing this Agreement or the criminal law. The inspection and discovery rights provided to the Settling States pursuant to this subsection shall be coordinated so as to avoid repetitive and excessive inspection and discovery.

(q) Prohibition on Agreements to Suppress Research. No Participating Manufacturer may enter into any contract, combination or conspiracy with any other Tobacco Product Manufacturer that has the purpose or effect of: (1) limiting competition in the production or distribution of information about health hazards or other consequences of the use of their products; (2) limiting or suppressing research into smoking and health; or (3) limiting or suppressing research into the marketing or development of new products. Provided, however, that nothing in this subsection shall be deemed to (1) require any Participating Manufacturer to produce, distribute or otherwise disclose any information that is subject to any privilege or protection; (2) preclude any Participating Manufacturer from entering into any joint defense or joint legal interest agreement or arrangement (whether or not in writing), or from asserting any privilege pursuant thereto; or (3) impose any affirmative obligation on any Participating Manufacturer to conduct any research.

(r) Prohibition on Material Misrepresentations. No Participating Manufacturer may make any material misrepresentation of fact regarding the health consequences of using any Tobacco Product, including any tobacco additives, filters, paper or other ingredients. Nothing in this subsection shall limit the exercise of any First Amendment right or the assertion of any defense or position in any judicial, legislative or regulatory forum.

APPENDIX E—TOTAL PAYMENTS TO EACH STATE THROUGH 2025

Alabama	$3,166,302,118.81
Alaska	$668,903,056.50
Arizona	$2,887,614,909.02
Arkansas	$1,622,336,125.69
California	$25,006,972,510.74
Colorado	$2,685,773,548.89
Connecticut	$3,637,303,381.55
Delaware	$774,798,676.89
D.C.	$1,189,458,105.56
Florida	$0.00
Georgia	$4,808,740,668.60

Hawaii	$1,179,165,923.07
Idaho	$711,700,479.23
Illinois	$9,118,539,559.10
Indiana	$3,996,355,551.01
Iowa	$1,703,839,985.56
Kansas	$1,633,317,646.19
Kentucky	$3,450,438,586.10
Louisiana	$4,418,657,915.22
Maine	$1,507,301,275.81
Maryland	$4,428,657,383.58
Mass.	$7,913,114,212.77
Michigan	$8,526,278,033.60
Minnesota	$0.00
Mississippi	$0.00
Missouri	$4,456,368,286.30
Montana	$832,182,430.63
Nebraska	$1,165,683,457.48
Nevada	$1,194,976,854.76
New Hampshire	$1,304,689,150.27
New Jersey	$7,576,167,918.47
New Mexico	$1,168,438,809.05
New York	$25,003,202,243.12
North Carolina	$4,569,381,898.24
North Dakota	$717,089,369.09
Ohio	$9,869,422,448.51
Oklahoma	$2,029,985,862.29
Oregon	$2,248,476,833.11
Penn.	$11,259,169,603.46
Rhode Island	$1,408,469,747.28
South Carolina	$2,304,693,119.82
South Dakota	$683,650,008.54
Tennessee	$4,782,168,127.09
Texas	$0.00
Utah	$871,616,513.42
Vermont	$805,588,329.25
Virginia	$4,006,037,550.26
Washington	$4,022,716,266.79
West Virginia	$1,736,741,427.33
Wisconsin	$4,059,511,421.32
Wyoming	$486,553,976.10
American Samoa	$29,812,995.31
N. Mariana Islands	$16,530,900.80
Guam	$42,978,803.27
US Virgin Island	$34,010,102.11
Puerto Rico	$2,196,791,813.07

Document 4: *United States v. Philip Morris.* Executive Summary, from Final Proposed Findings of Fact, August 17, 2006.

The U.S. Department of Justice civil lawsuit against the major tobacco companies, under the Racketeer Influenced and Corrupt Organizations (RICO) statute, held the tobacco companies legally accountable for decades of illegal and harmful practices. U.S. District Judge Gladys Kessler for the District of Columbia delivered the final order, finding that the tobacco defendants (except Liggett) were racketeers that "engaged and executed—and continue to engage in and execute—a massive 50-year scheme to defraud the public."

Despite the overwhelming wrongdoing she found, Judge Kessler could not impose remedies on the tobacco industry because of a controversial appeals court ruling that restricted financial remedies under the civil RICO law. Judge Kessler's Final Judgment and Remedies Order prohibited tobacco companies from committing acts of racketeering in the future or making false, misleading, or deceptive statements concerning cigarettes and their health risks; banned terms including low tar, light, ultralight, mild, and natural *that have misled consumers about the health risks of smoking; and prohibited the tobacco companies from conveying any health messages for any cigarette brand. The order required tobacco companies to make corrective statements concerning the health risks of smoking and secondhand smoke through newspaper and television advertising, their Web sites, and cigarette packaging. The order required that the tobacco companies make public their internal documents produced in litigation.*

The Final Proposed Findings of Fact submitted by the United States establish the facts that support the allegations set forth in Counts 3 and 4 of the United States Amended Complaint. Both counts are brought under the Racketeer Influenced and Corrupt Organizations Act ("RICO"), 18 U.S.C. § 1961–1968. These facts establish entitlement to equitable relief, including the disgorgement of Defendants' ill-gotten gains and non-monetary injunctive measures. As set forth in these Final Proposed Findings of Fact, substantial evidence establishes that Defendants have engaged in and executed—and continue to engage in and execute—a massive 50-year scheme to defraud the public, including consumers of cigarettes, in violation of RICO. Moreover, Defendants' past and ongoing conduct indicates a reasonable likelihood of future violations.

CIGARETTE SMOKING, DISEASE AND DEATH

Cigarette smoking and exposure to secondhand smoke kills nearly 440,000 Americans every year. The annual number of deaths due to cigarette smoking is substantially greater than the annual number of deaths due to illegal drug use, alcohol consumption, automobile accidents, fires, homicides, suicides, and AIDS combined. Approximately one out of every five deaths that occurs in the United States is caused by cigarette smoking. Smoking causes lung cancer, atherosclerosis, bladder cancer, cerebrovascular disease, chronic obstructive pulmonary disease, cardiovascular disease, including myocardial infarction and coronary heart disease, esophageal cancer, kidney cancer, laryngeal cancer, oral cancer, peptic ulcer disease, and respiratory morbidity. Smoking also causes cancers of the stomach, uterine cervix, pancreas, and kidney; acute myeloid leukemia, pneumonia; abdominal aortic aneurysm; cataract; and periodontitis. On May 27, 2004, the U.S. Surgeon General announced causal conclusions in connection with a substantial number of additional diseases and further acknowledges that smoking generally diminishes the health of smokers.

By the middle of the twentieth century, physicians and public health officials in the United States had widely noted an alarming increase in numbers of cases of lung cancer. Virtually unknown as a cause of death in 1900, by 1935 there were an estimated 4,000 deaths annually. A decade later, the annual death toll from lung cancer had nearly tripled. The meteoric rise in lung cancers followed the dramatic increase in cigarette consumption that had begun early in the twentieth century. Annual per capita consumption of cigarettes in 1900 stood at approximately forty-nine cigarettes; by 1930, annual per capita consumption was over 1,300; by 1950, it was over 3,000. Population studies showed that the increases in lung cancer cases and deaths, though they lagged in time behind this increase in cigarette use, closely tracked the spike in cigarette smoking. This apparent association led to considerable speculation about the relationship between cigarette smoking and ill health. The initial speculation was confirmed by scientific study.

By late 1953, there had been at least five published epidemiologic investigations, as well as others identifying and examining carcinogenic components in tobacco smoke and their effects. The researchers conducting these studies had come to a categorical understanding of the link between smoking and lung cancer. This understanding was both broader and deeper than that obtained from the case studies and preliminary statistical findings earlier in the century. While some of the epidemiological methods were innovative, the scientists using them were careful to approach them in a thorough manner; these methods were completely consistent with established scientific procedures and process. Epidemiology was not just based on statistics, but also was an interdisciplinary, applied field. The studies substantially transformed the scientific knowledge base concerning the harms of cigarette use. Unlike earlier anecdotal and clinical assessments, these studies offered new and pathbreaking approaches to investigating and resolving causal relationships.

THE FORMATION OF THE ENTERPRISE

In response to this growing body of evidence that smoking caused lung cancer, Defendants and their agents joined together and launched their coordinated scheme in the early 1950s. Defendants developed and implemented a unified strategy that sought to reassure the public that there was no evidence that smoking causes disease. At the end of 1953, the chief executives of the five major cigarette manufacturers in the United States at the time—Philip Morris, R. J. Reynolds, Brown & Williamson, Lorillard, and American—met at the Plaza Hotel in New York City with representatives of the public relations firm Hill & Knowlton and agreed to jointly conduct a long term public relations campaign to counter the growing evidence linking smoking as a cause of serious diseases. The meeting spawned an association—in fact enterprise ("Enterprise") to execute a fraudulent scheme in furtherance of their overriding common objective—to preserve and enhance the tobacco industry's profits by maximizing the numbers of smokers and number of cigarettes smoked and to avoid adverse liability judgments and adverse publicity. The fraudulent scheme would continue for the next five decades.

As a result of the Plaza Hotel meetings, the companies launched their long term public relations campaign by issuing the "Frank Statement to Cigarette Smokers," a full page announcement published in 448 newspapers across the United States. The Frank Statement included two representations that would lie at the heart of Defendants' fraudulent scheme—first, that there was insufficient scientific and medical evidence that smoking was a cause of any disease; and second, that the industry would jointly sponsor and disclose the results of "independent" research designed to uncover the health effects of smoking through the new industry-funded Tobacco Industry Research Committee ("TIRC"), later renamed the Council for Tobacco Research ("CTR"). At the same time that Defendants announced in their 1954 "Frank Statement to Cigarette Smokers" that "we accept an interest in people's health as a basic responsibility, paramount to every other consideration in our business," they established a sophisticated public relations apparatus in the form of TIRC—based on the "cover" of conducting research—to deny the harms of smoking and to reassure the public. Once they had organized and set in motion the essential strategy of generating "controversy" surrounding the scientific findings linking smoking to disease, Defendants stick to this approach, without wavering, for the next half-century.

Over time, other entities joined and actively participated in the affairs of the ongoing Enterprise and conspiracy, including Defendants Liggett and BATCo, Brown & Williamson's affiliate. In 1958, the members of TIRC formed Defendant The Tobacco Institute, Inc., to assume many of TIRC's public relations functions. In 1958, Philip Morris Companies joined the Enterprise, becoming a direct parent to Philip Morris as well as Philip Morris International, which had previously been a division of Philip Morris.[1] The Enterprise operated through both formal structures, including jointly funded and directed entities such as TIRC/CTR and the Tobacco Institute, and other less formal means, including scientific and legal committees, to communicate, advance, and maintain a united front, and to ensure lockstep adherence to achieve their shared aims. Defendants developed and used this extensive and interlocking web because they recognized that any departure from the industry-wide approach to the content of public statements made anywhere in the world, or the nature of research would have severe adverse consequences for the entire industry. To coordinate and further their fraudulent scheme, Defendants made and caused to be made and received innumerable mail and electronic transmissions from the 1950s through present.

THE ROLE OF TIRC/CTR AND THE TOBACCO INSTITUTE IN DEFENDANTS' DECADES-LONG CAMPAIGN TO DENY AND DISTORT THE HEALTH EFFECTS OF SMOKING

From the outset, the dual cf TIRC/CTR, public relations and scientific research, were intertwined. Rather than carefully and critically assessing the emerging scientific data concerning the harms of smoking, TIRC/CTR focused its energies and resources in two areas. First, in its public relations capacity, it repeatedly attacked scientific studies that demonstrated the harms of cigarette smoke and worked to assure smokers about cigarettes. Second, it developed and funded a research program that concentrated on basic processes of disease and that was distant from, if not completely irrelevant to, evaluating the immediate and fundamental questions of the risks and harms associated with smoking.

Similarly, the Tobacco Institute actively designed and wrote issue statements, advertisements, pamphlets, and testimony that advanced Defendants' jointly formulated positions on smoking and health issues, including denying that smoking cigarettes was addictive and caused diseases, and supporting the false claim that the link between smoking cigarettes (and exposure to secondhand smoke) and adverse health effects remained a legitimate "open question." In this way, the functions (public relations and research) of these two entities were integrally related; both were fully committed to Defendants' goals of denying and discrediting the substantial scientific evidence of smoking's harms and convincing the public (especially smokers and potential smokers) that smoking was not harmful to health.

Defendants repeatedly represented to the public that they sponsored independent research aimed at discovering the health effects of smoking. Indeed, defendants claimed that they created TIRC/CTR to administer this effort. These statements were misleading and deceptive half-truths, because the Cigarette Company Defendants[2] used TIRC/CTR to serve as a "front" organization to advance their public relations and litigation defense objectives. Through CTR, the Cigarette Company Defendants funded "Special Projects–research projects conceived and directed by committees of industry representatives, including lawyers, to support scientists who had shown a willingness and ability to generate information and provide testimony that could bolster the industry's litigation defenses before courts and government bodies and cast doubt on the scientific evidence that smoking caused cancer and other diseases. Similarly, Defendants also sponsored jointly funded research throughout lawyer-administered "Special Accounts"—to recruit and support industry-friendly researchers to serve as expert witnesses in litigation and to represent the industry's scientific position in legislative and regulatory proceedings.

Within the individual Cigarette Company Defendants, high-ranking corporate employees and lawyers, as well as outside lawyers representing the companies, acknowledged that if they conducted research internally that confirmed that cigarettes cause disease and are addictive, such research, if disclosed, would jeopardize their unified public relations and legal positions, would threaten industry profits, and would expose not just individual companies, but the entire industry, to legal liability and product regulation. Of course, the Cigarette Company Defendants did, in fact, acknowledge internally that cigarettes caused lung cancer and other diseases; they recognized the legitimacy of the scientific consensus, and the limited amount of internal research that their scientists did perform was wholly consistent with the results of mainstream scientific study.

The public statements issued through organizations like TIRC/CTR, the Tobacco Institute and by Cigarette Company Defendants themselves, were flatly inconsistent with Defendants' actual understanding of the causal link between smoking and disease. At the same time that Defendants assured the public through their "Frank Statement" that "there is no proof that cigarette smoking is one of the causes [of cancer]," internally they documented a large number of known human carcinogens in their products and replicated mainstream scientific research showing the health effects of smoking. Defendants' internal documents acknowledge that their public denial that smoking cigarettes causes disease both was contrary to the overwhelming medical and scientific consensus—established through extensive epidemiological and other scientific investigation by the early 1950s—and was intended to convince smokers and potential smokers that there remained genuine scientific "controversy" about whether smoking caused disease.

The Agreement Not to Compete on Health Claims or to Perform Certain Biological Research

Defendants' joint commitment to publicly denying that cigarettes were a proven cause of disease had profound effects on all aspects of their business, including their marketing and research activities. For example, extensive documentary evidence proves that defendants recognized that there was a substantial market for a cigarette that could be marketed as potentially less hazardous, but that they collectively agreed not to do anything in the marketing and development of cigarettes that would jeopardize the public relations at the core of the scheme to defraud: the denial that any commercially sold cigarettes were a proven cause of disease.

Defendants made public statements proclaiming their commitment—and ability—to develop potentially less hazardous cigarettes, but indicated that such actions were unnecessary unless and until cigarettes were proven to cause disease:

> In March 1954, George Weissman, a Philip Morris Vice President, publicly reaffirmed the industry's commitment to protect the health of its customers, claiming that the cigarette industry would "stop business tomorrow" if it "had any thought or knowledge that in any way we were selling a product harmful to consumers."

In 1964, Bowman Gray, Chairman of the Board of R. J. Reynolds, stated publicly on behalf of R. J. Reynolds, Philip Morris, Brown & Williamson, Lorillard, Liggett, and American, that "[i]f it is proven that cigarettes are harmful, we want to do something about it regardless of what somebody else tells us to do. And we would do our level best. This is just being human."

In 1971, Philip Morris chief executive officer Joseph Cullman III explained in a "Face the Nation" TV interview that "this industry can face the future with confidence because when, and if any ingredient in cigarette smoke is identified as being injurious to human health, we are confident that we can eliminate that ingredient."

In the January 24, 1972 issue of the Wall Street Journal, Philip Morris Senior Vice President James Bowling declared that "[i]f our product is harmful ... we'll stop making it. We now know enough that we can take anything out of our product, but we don't know what ingredients to take out." Bowling further stated that "[w]e don't know if anything is harmful to health, and we think somebody ought to find out."

Moreover, Defendants repeatedly recognized the potential economic boon to selling a cigarette that could be truthfully marketed as potentially less hazardous. For example, in a June 1966 report, a key Philip Morris research told research executives that "If we could develop a ... 'healthy' cigarette that tasted exactly like a Marlboro, delivered the nicotine of a Marlboro, and was called Marlboro, it would probably become the best selling brand." However, Defendants agreed not to compete on smoking and health issues in the marketing of cigarettes. Accordingly, when a Defendant designed a cigarette—or developed a cigarette component—intended to potentially reduce the delivery of harmful smoke constituents to the smoker, the Defendant limited the types of information that it provided to consumers in marketing such products.

Evidence shows that Defendants failed to provide information—even if they believed it to be truthful scientific information—that certain brands of types of cigarettes were likely to be less harmful than others, because such information carried the obvious implication that cigarettes were harmful. In one of the most notable of such instances, after Defendant Liggett spent twelve years and $15 million developing a cigarette—the XA—that its research showed to be significantly less carcinogenic than its conventional cigarettes, it killed the entire project before marketing the cigarette to consumers after defendant Brown & Williamson threatened Liggett's "very existence" if it marketed the cigarette. Brown & Williamson also threatened to freeze Liggett out of joint defense agreements and exclude Liggett from the Tobacco Institute. Delivered through Brown & Williamson's representative on the Tobacco Institute's Committee of Counsel, the threat was based on Brown & Williamson's fear that selling XA would be an admission against the interest of all Cigarette Company Defendants. Later, in the late 1980s, R. J. Reynolds told the FDA that it would not make health-related marketing claims about its Premier cigarette because the tobacco industry maintained that "conventional cigarettes are not unsafe, and that it would never reverse this position." Promoting one cigarette as "safer" than others "would be an indictment of the tobacco industry and its long standing position that conventional cigarettes are not unsafe."

Similarly, documents show that Defendants limited the types of research they conducted, because they did not want to generate internal evidence to suggest that the companies believed there was any need to examine whether a causative link existed between smoking and disease, let alone create scientific information that demonstrated such a link. Accordingly, Defendants jointly agreed not to perform certain types of biological tests using commercially sold cigarette brands in their domestic research facilities. Further, there is substantial evidence that during the past five decades Defendants have decided not to incorporate design features of processes that Defendants' own research concluded were likely to reduce the hazards of smoking, were technically feasible, and were acceptable to smokers. In short, Defendants' conduct in this area is powerful evidence of defendants' well documented agreement not to compete on smoking and health issues.

Environmental Tobacco Smoke

In their efforts to prevent restrictions on where and when people could smoke, in the face of growing evidence since the 1970s of the adverse health effects of secondhand smoke, Defendants engaged in similar conduct and misleading public statements concerning the health effects of secondhand smoke. Environmental tobacco smoke ("ETS") also called secondhand smoke, is a mixture of mostly sidestream smoke given off by the smoldering cigarette and some exhaled mainstream smoke, which is the smoke an active smoker exhales. Conclusions about the causal relationship between ETS exposure and health outcomes are based not only on epidemiological evidence, abut also on the extensive evidence derived from epidemiological and toxicological investigation of active smoking. Additionally, studies using biomarkers of exposure and dose, including the nicotine metabolite cotinine and white cell adducts, document the absorption of ETS by exposed nonsmokers, adding confirmatory evidence to the observed association of ETS with adverse effects.

In adults, ETS exposure causes lung cancer and ischemic heart disease. In 1986, the Surgeon General and the National Research Council of the National Academy of Sciences concluded that passive smoking causally increases the risk of lung cancer in nonsmokers, accounting for two to three percent of all lung cancer cases. ETS exposure of infants and children has adverse effects on respiratory health, including increased risk for severe lower respiratory infections, middle ear disease (otitis media), chronic respiratory symptoms and asthma, as well as a reduction in the rate of lung function growth during childhood, and is associated with sudden infant death syndrome and cognitive and behavioral disorders.

Defendants approached the issue of the health effects of exposure to secondhand smoke with a sense of urgency, based on their concern as expressed in internal documents, that in the United States, the ETS issue would have a devastating effect on sales. Defendants specifically saw concerns about the health effects of ETS as a threat to the "number of smokers & number of cigarettes they smoke." Publicly, Defendants promised to "seek answers," assuring the public that they would fund and support "independent" and "arms length" research into the health effects of exposure to secondhand smoke. These public promises, however, were false and fraudulent and were intended to deceive the public. Defendants' true goal with respect to passive smoking was not to support independent and valid research in order to answer questions about the link between ETS and disease, but rather the goal was simply "to keep the controversy alive," just as they had done with active smoking. Defendants designed a sophisticated public relations and research strategy to attempt to "alter public perception that ETS is damaging," but did so despite their specific, internal acknowledgment that there was "[l]ack of objective science" to support their public relations campaign. This lack of objective science did not stand in Defendants' way. They asked: "Is $100 million campaign worth an x increase in sales?" The answer: "Yes."

Pursuant to Defendants' carefully designed and coordinated strategy, the Center for Indoor Air Research (CIAR) was officially created in 1988 to take over the research responsibilities of the committee that had previously operated under the direction of Defendants' law firms Shook, Hardy & Bacon and Covington & Burling—that is, to act as a coordinating organization for Defendants' efforts to fraudulently mislead the American public about the health effects of ETS exposure. CIAR was created by Philip Morris, Lorillard, and R. J. Reynolds. Brown & Williamson joined CIAR as a voting board member in 1995. While Liggett was never officially a member of CIAR, it attended meetings of the organization and participated in ETS seminars and meetings organized by Covington & Burling and was fully cognizant of, and in fact assented to, the activities of the organization. BATCo, while not a member of CIAR, provided funding to CIAR to hide BATCo and Philip Morris's involvement in at least one CIAR "sponsored" study.

CIAR's stated mission was to serve as a hub that would sponsor and foster quality, objective research in indoor air issues with emphasis on ETS and effectively communicate pertinent research findings to the broad scientific community. But while Philip Morris, Lorillard, and R. J. Reynolds publicly represented that CIAR was independent, its by-laws revealed otherwise. The by-laws required that charter members be tobacco companies; dictated that only charter members have the power to choose CIAR's officers; and significantly, gave charter members the exclusive power to decide what research the organization would fund. CIAR was intended to allow Defendants to perpetuate a "scientific controversy" surrounding the health effects of ETS exposure. As Covington & Burley attorney John Rupp explained in March 1993: "In sum, while one might wish it otherwise, the value of CIAR depends on the industry's playing an active role (1) in identifying research projects likely to be of value and (2) working to make sure that the findings of funded research are brought to the attention of decision makers in an appropriate and timely manner." According to a former CIAR board member, "ETS was a litigation issue and a PR issue."

Defendants engaged in a global effort to fraudulently deny and distort the harms associated with exposure to secondhand smoke. The international ETS Consultancy program was an extension and amplification of multifaceted domestic initiatives by industry counsel to counter ever-mounting evidence of implicating secondhand smoke as a cause of disease and other health problems; however, Defendants acted on a global scale. Through this program, Defendants worked to identify, "educate," and financially reward scientists in every world market to generate research results, present papers, pen letters to scientific journals, plan and attend conferences, and publicly speak on behalf of the cigarette companies. The overarching goal was to "keep the controversy alive" and forestall legislation and any restrictions on public or workplace smoking. Defendants issued numerous false and deceptive statements denying and distorting the health risks of involuntary exposure in connection with this massive, coordinated effort to maintain cigarette sales efforts in the fact of what they recognized internally as legitimate scientific evidence of the dangers associated with secondhand smoke.

Addiction and the Manipulation of Nicotine Levels in Cigarettes

Cigarette smoking is an addictive behavior, a dependency characterized by drug craving, compulsive use, tolerance, withdrawal symptoms, and relapse after withdrawal. Underlying the smoking behavior and its remarkable intractability to cessation is the drug nicotine. Nicotine is the primary component of cigarettes that creates and sustains addiction to cigarettes.

Defendants have studied nicotine and its effects since the 1950s, and the documents describing their examination and knowledge of nicotine's pharmacological effects on smokers—whether they characterized that effect as "addictive," "dependence" producing or "habituating,"—demonstrate unequivocally that defendants understood the central role nicotine plays in keeping smokers smoking, and thus its critical importance to the success of their industry. Additional internal records demonstrate that Defendants knew that cigarette smoking was the vehicle for delivering nicotine, which was the critical component in maintaining the addiction necessary to sustain and enhance their profits. Indeed, Defendants purposefully designed and sold products that delivered a pharmacologically effective dose of nicotine in order to create and sustain nicotine addiction in smokers. Indeed, an internal document drafted by Philip Morris scientist Helmut Wakeham in 1969, for example, recognized:

We share the conviction with others that it is the pharmacological effect of inhaled smoke which mediates the smoking habit ... We have then as our first premise, that the primary motivation for smoking is to obtain the pharmacological effect of nicotine. In the past we at R & D have said that we're not in the cigarette business, we're in the smoke business. It might be more pointed to observe that the cigarette is the vehicle of smoke, smoke is the vehicle of nicotine, and nicotine is the agent of a pleasurable body response. The primary incentive to smoking gets obscured by the overlay secondary incentives, which have been superimposed upon the habit. Psychoanalysts have speculated about the importance of the sucking behavior, describing it as oral regression. Psychologists have proposed that the smoker is projecting an ego-image with puffing and his halo of smoke. One frequently hears "I have to have something to do with my hands" as a reason. All are perhaps operative motives, but we hold that none are adequate to sustain the habit in the absence of nicotine. We are not suggesting that the effect of nicotine is responsible for the initiation of the habit. To the contrary. The first cigarette is a noxious experience to the novitiate. To account for the fact that the beginning smoker will tolerate the unpleasantness, we must invoke a psychosocial motive. Smoking for the beginner is a symbolic act. The smoker is telling the world: "This is the kind of person I am ..." As the force from the psychosocial symbolism subsides, the pharmacological effect takes over to sustain the habit ...

Similarly, R. J. Reynolds researcher Claude Teague acknowledged in an internal 1972 report, "Thus a tobacco product is, in essence, a vehicle for the delivery of nicotine, designed to deliver the nicotine in a generally acceptable and attractive form. Our industry is then based upon design, manufacture and sale of attractive dosage forms of nicotine."

Nevertheless, just as Defendants long denied, contrary to fact, that smoking causes disease, Defendants consistently and publicly denied that smoking is addictive. Defendants intentionally maintained and coordinated their fraudulent position on addiction and nicotine as an important part of their overall efforts to influence public opinion and persuade people that smoking is not dangerous. In this way, defendants' have kept more smokers smoking, recruited more new smokers, and maintained or increased profits. Additionally, defendants have sought to discredit proof of addiction in order to preserve their "Smoking is a free choice" arguments in smoking and health litigation. As with Defendants' statements designed to undermine the scientific evidence of smoking's harms, the statements denying addiction were knowingly false and misleading when made, and intended to avoid product regulation, to bolster the industry's defenses in smoking and health litigation, and to minimize consumers' concerns about smoking.

Defendants' awareness of the critical importance of nicotine to the cigarette smokers, and thus to the continued profits of the industry, was such that the Defendants dedicated extraordinary resources to the study of nicotine and its effects on the smoker. The evidence shows that Defendants have long had the ability to modify and manipulate the amount of nicotine that their products deliver, and have studied extensively how every characteristic of every component of cigarettes—including the tobacco blend, the paper, the filter, and the manufacturing process—impacts nicotine delivery. Indeed, defendants' internal documents indicate that, in light of Defendants' recognition that "no one has ever become a cigarette smoker by smoking cigarettes without nicotine," Cigarette Company Defendants have designed their cigarettes with a central overriding objective—to ensure that smoker can obtain enough nicotine to create and sustain addiction. Notwithstanding the substantial evidence that Defendants designed their products to deliver doses of nicotine sufficient to create and sustain addiction, Defendants have publicly and fraudulently denied that they manipulate nicotine. Defendants have sought to mislead the public about their manipulation of nicotine by publicly and fraudulently maintaining that the level of nicotine in a cigarette is inextricably linked to the cigarette's tar level and that nicotine delivery levels follow tar delivery levels in cigarette smoke. Through these and other false statements, Defendants have furthered their common efforts to deceive the public regarding their use and manipulation of nicotine.

Light and Low Tar Cigarettes

The understanding of nicotine's primary role in keeping people smoking and Cigarette Company Defendants' desire to capitalize on smokers' growing desire for a less hazardous cigarette in the face of growing evidence of the health effects of smoking, underlie another central component of the scheme to defraud–the design and marketing of the so-called "low tar/low nicotine" cigarettes. As awareness and concern about the adverse health risks associated with smoking began to grow in the early 1950s, Defendants began developing cigarettes they internally referred to as "health reassurance" brands in an effort to keep smokers in the market. Initially, Defendants explicitly marketed and promoted these brands as safer as the result of an added filter which purportedly protected smokers from the harmful tar in cigarette smoke. Having established the link in the minds of consumers between low tar/filtration and reduced harm through use of explicit health claims, Defendants' later advertisements contained implied health claims that built on their earlier advertisements in an effort to avoid suggesting to consumers that any cigarettes were harmful. For several decades, Defendants have marketed and promoted their so-called "low tar/nicotine" cigarettes using brand descriptors like "Light," "Ultralight," "Mild," and "Medium" and claims of "low tar and nicotine" to suggest to consumers that these products are safer than regular, full flavor cigarettes.

Defendants made, and continue to make, health benefit claims regarding filtered and low tar cigarettes when they either lacked evidence to substantiate the claims or knew that they were false. Internal industry research documents show that defendants never had adequate support for their claims of reduced health risk from low tar cigarettes, but rather confirm Defendants' awareness by the late 1960s— early 1970s that low tar cigarettes were unlikely to provide any health benefits to smokers compared to full flavor cigarettes. In fact, the public health and scientific communities now recognize what defendants have long known internally: there is no meaningful reduction in disease risk in smoking low tar cigarettes as opposed to smoking regular cigarettes.

In addition, Defendants have known for decades that their low tar cigarettes, as designed, do not actually deliver the low reported and advertised levels of tar and nicotine—which are derived from a standardized machine test originally developed by Defendants and adopted by the Federal Trade Commission in 1967 ("FTC Method")—to human smokers. Defendants have long known that to obtain an amount of nicotine sufficient to satisfy their addiction, smokers of low tar cigarettes modify their smoking behavior, or "compensate," for the reduced yields by inhaling smoke more deeply, holding smoke in their lungs longer, covering cigarette ventilation holes with fingers or lips, and/or smoking more cigarettes. As a result of this nicotine-driven smoker behavior, smokers of light cigarettes concurrently boost their intake of tar, thus negating what Defendants have long promoted as a primary health-related benefit of light cigarettes: lower tar intake.

For decades. Defendants have affirmatively exploited their understanding of compensation by deliberately designing low tar cigarettes that register low tar yields on the standardized FTC Method., but that also facilitate a smoker's ability to compensate to ensure adequate delivery of nicotine to create and sustain addiction. Even as they designed low tar cigarettes to facilitate compensation, and despite having evidence that low tar cigarettes provide no health benefits and may in fact deter people from quitting, Defendants have withheld and suppressed such evidence from public dissemination. Extensive evidence shows that defendants used terms such as "Light" and "Low Tar" intentionally to convey their false "health reassurance" message rather than just a "taste" message, because their research showed that people smoked low tar products despite, not because of, the taste. Accordingly Defendants' marketing themes repeatedly tried to convince smokers that their brands could provide the main claimed benefit of light cigarettes—increased safety—without sacrificing "taste." Further, defendants used both verbal and non-verbal communications to convey their health reassurance message, employing colors and imagery that their research indicated people associated with healthier products.

Defendants' campaign of deception has impacted Americans' decision to smoke. The availability of low yield cigarettes and the messages conveyed by Defendants' advertising, marketing, and public statements regarding low taw cigarettes, has caused many smokers to perceive them as an acceptable alternative to quitting smoking. As a result of Defendants' conduct, health concerned smokers have switched from regular cigarettes to those with lower reported tar yields rather than quitting smoking altogether. Smokers of "light" and "ultra light" cigarettes are less likely to quit smoking than are smokers of regular cigarettes. Additionally, as a result of Defendants' fraudulent marketing and deceptive design of "light" and "ultra light" cigarettes, many smokers of these cigarettes consume more cigarettes than do smokers of regular cigarettes. Defendants' conduct relating to low tar cigarettes furthers the aims of the Enterprise and the scheme to defraud by providing a false sense of reassurance to smokers that weakens their resolve to quit smoking, and serves to draw ex-smokers back into the market. In short, Defendants' concerted campaign of deception regarding low tar cigarettes has been a calculated—and extremely successful—scheme to increase their profits at the expense of the health of the American public.

Youth Marketing

Cigarette smoking, particularly that begun by young people, continues to be the leading cause of preventable disease and premature mortality in the United States. Of Children and adolescents who are regular smokers, one out of three will die of smoking-related disease. As part of the scheme to defraud, Defendants have intentionally marketed cigarettes to youth under the legal smoking age while falsely denying that they have done and continue to do so. As is evident from defendants' own documents, Defendants have long recognized that the continued profitability of the industry depends upon new smokers entering the "franchise" as current smokers die from smoking-related diseases or quit. Defendants have similarly known that an overwhelming majority of regular smokers begin smoking before age eighteen. In 1966, Defendants, in the face of threatened federal advertising restrictions, adopted a voluntary advertising code in which they pledged to refrain from marketing activity likely to attract youth. Thereafter, defendants continued unabated their efforts to capture as much of the youth market as possible, effectively ignoring the voluntary advertising code and designing advertising themes, marketing campaigns, and promotional activities known to resonate with adolescents.

Defendants' internal documents indicate their awareness that the majority of smokers began smoking as youths and develop brand loyalties as youths, that youths were highly susceptible to advertising, and that persons who began smoking when they were teenagers were very likely to remain lifetime smokers. For example:

A March 31, 1981 report conducted by the Philip Morris Research Center entitled "Young Smokers Prevalence, Trends, Implications, and related Demographic Trends," stated that "Today's teenager is tomorrow's potential regular customer, and the over-whelming majority of smokers first begin to smoke while still in their teens ... it is during the teenage years that the initial brand choice is made."

A September 22, 1989 report prepared for Philip Morris by its main advertising agency, Leo Burnett U.S.A., described Philip Morris's marketing's target audience as a "moving target in transition from adolescence to young adulthood."

An August 30, 1978 Lorillard memorandum stated: "The success of NEWPORT has been fantastic during the past few years ... [T]he base of our business is the high school student. Newport in the 1970s is turning into the Marlboro of the 1960s and 1970s."

A July 9, 1984 report circulated to the heads of B & W's Marketing and Research Development departments stated: "[o]ur future business depends on the size of [the] starter population.

In a November 26, 1974 memorandum entitled "R. J. Reynolds Tobacco Company Domestic Operating Goals," R. J. Reynolds stated its [p]rimary goal in 1975 and ensuing years is to reestablish R. J. Reynolds's share of growth in the domestic cigarette industry," by targeting the "14–24 age group" who, "[a]s they mature, will account for key share of cigarette volume for next 25 years. Winston has 14% of this franchise, while Marlboro has 33%. -SALEM has 9%–Kool has 17%. The memorandum indicated that R. J. Reynolds "will direct advertising appeal to this young adult group without alienating the brand's current franchise."

A September 27, 1982 memorandum written by Diane Burrows, R. J. Reynolds Market Research Department, and circulated to L.W. Hall, Vice President of R. J. Reynolds Marketing Department, stated: "The loss of younger adult males and teenagers is more important to the long term, drying up the supply of new smokers to replace the old. This is not a fixed loss to the industry: its importance increases with time. In ten years, increased rate per day would have been expected to raise this group's consumption by more than 50%."

Defendants targeted young people with their marketing efforts, their selection of which marketing activities to pursue and to shape the themes and images of those activities, and allocated substantial resources researching the habits and preferences of the youth market, including these research efforts. For instance:

An October 7, 1953 letter from George Weissman, Vice President of Philip Morris, discussed an August 1953 Elmo Report on a study of young smokers commissioned by Philip Morris, stating that "industry figures indicate that 47% of the population, 15 years and older, smokes cigarettes" and that "we have our greatest strength in the 15–24 age group."

The "1969 Survey of Cigarette Smoking Behavior and Attitudes" performed by Eastman Chemical Products for Philip Morris contained detailed analysis of beginning smokers, including interviews with 12–14 year olds.

A 1976 Brown & Williamson document containing information drawn from a study of smokers stated that [t]he 16–25 age group has consistently accounted for the highest level of starters."

In 1958 and 1959, R. J. Reynolds commissioned a series of studies of high school and college students, interviewing in sum almost 20,000 students as young as high school freshmen regarding their smoking habits and brand preferences.

In 1980, the R. J. Reynolds Marketing Development Department issued a series of internal reports entitled "Teenage Smokers (14–17) and New Adult

Smokers and Quitters" which surveyed the smoking habits of fourteen to seventeen year olds.

Knowing that advertising and promotion stimulated the demand for cigarettes, the Cigarette Company Defendants used their knowledge of young people's vulnerabilities gained in this research in order to create marketing campaigns (including advertising, promotion, and couponing) that would and did appeal to youth, in order to foster youth smoking initiation and ensure that young smokers would choose their brands. These campaigns have intentionally exploited adolescents' vulnerability to imagery utilizing themes that are, to this day, the same as they have been for decades: independence, liberation, attractiveness, adventurousness, sophistication, glamour, athleticism, social inclusion, sexual attractiveness, thinness, popularity, rebelliousness and being "cool."

The Cigarette Company Defendants continue to advertise in youth-oriented publications: employ imagery and messages that they know are appealing to teenagers; increasingly concentrate their marketing in places where they know youths will frequent such as convenience stores; engage in strategic pricing to attract youths; increase their marketing at point-of-sale locations with promotions, self-service displays, and other materials; sponsor sporting and entertainment events, many of which are televised or otherwise broadcast and draw large youth audiences; and engage in a host of other activities which are designed to attract youths to begin and continue smoking. And yet, to this day, in the face of evidence of their explicit recognition of the importance of the youth market, research into the best ways to obtain the youth market, and development of advertising campaigns, designed to capture it that have remained largely unchanged for more than thirty years, the Defendants publicly deny their efforts to appeal to he youth.

Independent scientific studies published in reputable scientific journals and in official government reports, have confirmed Defendant's knowledge, as set out in their internal documents, that their marketing contributes to the primary demand for and continuing use of cigarettes. Over the past ten years, there have been a number of comprehensive reviews of the scientific evidence concerning the efforts of cigarette marketing, including advertising and promotion, on smoking decisions by young people. From these reviews it is clear that the weight of all available evidence, including survey data, scientific studies and experiments, behavioral studies and econometric studies, supports the conclusion that cigarette marketing is a substantial contributing factor in the smoking behavior of young people, including the decision to begin smoking and the decision to continue smoking.

CONCEALMENT AND SUPPRESSION OF INFORMATION

From at least 1954 to the present, Defendants engaged in parallel efforts to destroy and conceal documents and information in furtherance of the Enterprise's goals of (1) preventing the public from learning the truth about smoking's adverse impact on health; (2) preventing the public from learning the truth about the addictiveness of nicotine; (3) avoiding or, at a minimum, limiting liability for smoking and health related claims in litigation; and (4) avoiding statutory and regulatory limitations on the cigarette industry, including limitations on advertising. These activities occurred despite the promises of the Defendants that (a) they did not conceal, suppress, or destroy evidence, and that (b) they shared with the American people all pertinent information regarding the true health effects of smoking, including research findings related to smoking and health. Indeed, as recently as 1996, Martin Broughton, Chief Executive of BAT Industries, the then ultimate parent company of BATCo and Brown & Williamson, made a statement to the *Wall Street Journal* denying that BAT Industries and its subsidiaries had concealed research linking smoking and disease. Broughton stated: "We haven't concealed, we do not conceal, and we will never conceal. We have no internal research which proves that smoking causes lung cancer or other diseases or, indeed, that smoking is addictive."

*****

In short, Defendants' scheme to defraud permeated and influenced all facets of Defendants' conduct—research, product development, advertising, marketing, legal, public relations, and communications—in a manner that has resulted in extraordinary profits for the past half-century, but has had devastating consequences for the public's health. The purpose of Defendants' overarching scheme was to defraud consumers of the purchase price of cigarettes to sustain and expand the market for cigarettes and to maximize their individual profits. Defendants executed this scheme in different but interrelated ways, including by enticing consumers to begin and to continue smoking, falsely denying the addictiveness and adverse health effects of smoking, and misrepresenting that such matters were "an open question." Thus, Defendants undertook activities specifically intended to obfuscate the public's understanding of the actual dangers posed by smoking at the same time that they were engaging in marketing efforts designed to attract them, all with the intention to sell more cigarettes and make more money.

As the Final Proposed Findings of Fact demonstrate, the United States is entitled to the equitable relief sought under RICO, including disgorgement of proceeds at least in the amount of $280 billion. The United States has produced substantial evidence that the Defendants' scheme to defraud had damaging and wide-ranging implications, including influence on initiation and continued smoking for people of all ages. All of Defendants' sales of cigarettes to all consumers from 1954 to 2001 were inextricably intertwined with this massive scheme to defraud the public. As a result, the United States would be justified in seeking disgorgement of the proceeds from all sales to people of all ages from 1954 into the future. The United States has, however, limited its request for disgorgement to proceeds from the sale of cigarettes only to the Youth Addicted Population (those youth who smoked daily when under the age of 21 and those adults who were smoking more than five cigarettes a day when they turned 21 years old), and only from the date of passage of the RICO statute in 1971.

Document 5: Centers for Disease Control and Prevention, Smoking and Tobacco Use, "Federal Policy and Legislation: Selected Actions of the U.S. Government Regarding the Regulation of Tobacco Sales, Marketing, and Use (excluding laws pertaining to agriculture or excise tax)" February 28, 2007, http://www.cdc.gov/tobacco/data_ statistics/by_topic/policy/legislation.htm.

The Centers for Disease Control and Prevention is the go-to supersite for information about tobacco products, data, and statistics from national and state surveys and Morbidity and Mortality Weekly Reports, *tobacco industry marketing, surgeons general reports, consumption data, tobacco-related costs and expenditures in the United States, and the following information on federal regulation of tobacco.*

LEGISLATION

Food and Drugs Act of 1906
- First federal food and drug law
- No express reference to tobacco products
- Definition of a drug includes medicines and preparations listed in *U.S. Pharmacoepia* or *National Formulary.*
- 1914 interpretation advised that tobacco be included only when used to cure, mitigate, or prevent disease.

Federal Food, Drug, and Cosmetic Act (FFDCA) of 1938
- Superseded 1906 Act
- Definition of a "drug" includes "articles intended for use in the diagnosis, cure, mitigation, treatment, or prevention of disease in man or other animals" and "articles (other than food) intended to affect the structure or any function of the body of man or other animals"
- FDA has asserted jurisdiction in cases where the manufacturer or vendor has made medical claims.
  - 1953—Fairfax cigarettes (manufacturer claimed these prevented respiratory and other diseases)
  - 1959—Trim Reducing-Aid Cigarettes (contained the additive tartaric acid, which was claimed to aid in weight reduction)
- FDA has asserted jurisdiction over alternative nicotine-delivery products
  - 1984—Nicotine Polacrilex gum

- 1985—Favor Smokeless Cigarette (nicotine-delivery device; ruled a "new drug," intended to treat nicotine dependence and to affect the structure and function of the body; removed from market)
- 1989—Masterpiece Tobacs tobacco chewing gum; ruled an adulterated food and removed from the market)
- 1991—Nicotine patches

Federal Trade Commission (FTC) Act of 1914 (amended in 1938)

- Empowers the FTC to "prevent persons, partnerships, or corporations ... from using unfair or deceptive acts or practices in commerce"
- Between 1945 and 1960, FTC completed seven formal cease-and-desist order proceedings for medical or health claims (e.g., a 1942 complaint countering claims that Kool cigarettes provide extra protection against or cure colds)
- In January 1964, FTC proposed a rule to strictly regulate the imagery and copy of cigarette ads to prohibit explicit or implicit health claims
- 1983—FTC determines that its testing procedures may have "significantly underestimated the level of tar, nicotine, and carbon monoxide that smokers received from smoking" certain low-tar cigarettes. Prohibits Brown and Williamson Tobacco Company from using the tar rating for Barclay cigarettes in advertising, packaging or promotions because of problems with the testing methodology and consumers' possible reliance on that information. FTC authorized revised labeling in 1986.
- 1985—FTC acts to remove the RJ Reynolds advertisements, "Of Cigarettes and Science," in which the multiple risk factor intervention trail (MRFIT) results were misinterpreted
- 1999—FTC requires RJ Reynolds to add a label to packages and ads explaining that "no additives" does not make Winston cigarettes safer.

Federal Hazardous Substances Labeling Act (FHSA) of 1960

- Authorized FDA to regulate substances that are hazardous (either toxic, corrosive, irritant, strong sensitizers, flammable, or pressure-generating). Such substances may cause substantial personal injury or illness during or as a result of customary use.
- 1963—FDA expressed its interpretation that tobacco did not fit the "hazardous" criteria stated previously and withheld recommendations pending the release of the report of the Surgeon General's Advisory Committee on Smoking and Health.

Federal Cigarette Labeling and Advertising Act of 1965

- Required package warning label—"Caution: Cigarette Smoking May Be Hazardous to Your Health" (other health warnings prohibited)
- Required no labels on cigarette advertisements (in fact, implemented a three-year prohibition of any such labels)

- Required FTC to report to Congress annually on the effectiveness of ciga-rette labeling, current cigarette advertising and promotion practices, and to make recommendations for legislation
- Required Department of Health, Education, and Welfare (DHEW) to report annually to Congress on the health consequences of smoking
- More on the Federal Cigarette Labeling and Advertising Act of 1965

Public Health Cigarette Smoking Act of 1969

- Required package warning label—Warning: The Surgeon General Has Determined that Cigarette Smoking Is Dangerous to Your Health" (other health warnings prohibited)
- Temporarily preempted FTC requirement of health labels on advertise-ments
- Prohibited cigarette advertising on television and radio (authority to Department of Justice [DOJ])
- Prevents states or localities from regulating or prohibiting cigarette advertis-ing or promotion for health-related reasons

Controlled Substances Act of 1970

- To prevent the abuse of drugs, narcotics, and other addictive substances
- Specifically excludes tobacco from the definition of a "controlled sub-stance"

Consumer Product Safety Act of 1972

- Transferred authority from the FDA to regulate hazardous substances as des-ignated by the Federal Hazardous Substances Labeling Act (FHSA) to the Consumer Product Safety Commission (CPSC)
- The term "consumer product" does not include tobacco and tobacco prod-ucts

Little Cigar Act of 1973

- Bans little cigar advertisements from television and radio (authority to DOJ)

1976 Amendment to the Federal Hazardous Substances Labeling Act of 1960

- The term "hazardous substance" shall not apply to tobacco and tobacco products (passed when the American Public Health Association petitioned CPSC to set a maximum level of 21 mg of tar in cigarettes)

Toxic Substances Control Act of 1976

- To "regulate chemical substances and mixtures which present an unreason-able risk of injury to health or the environment"
- The term "chemical substance" does not include tobacco or any tobacco products

Comprehensive Smoking Education Act of 1984
- Requires four rotating health warning labels (all listed as Surgeon General's Warnings) on cigarette packages and advertisements (smoking causes lung cancer, heart disease and may complicate pregnancy; quitting smoking now greatly reduces serious risks to your health; smoking by pregnant women may result in fetal injury, premature birth, and low birth weight; cigarette smoke contains carbon monoxide) (preempted other package warnings)
- Requires Department of Health and Human Services (DHHS) to publish a biennial status report to Congress on smoking and health
- Creates a Federal Interagency Committee on Smoking and Health
- Requires cigarette industry to provide a confidential list of ingredients added to cigarettes manufactured in or imported into the United States (brand-specific ingredients and quantities not required)

Cigarette Safety Act of 1984
- To determine the technical and commercial feasibility of developing cigarettes and little cigars that would be less likely to ignite upholstered furniture and mattresses

Comprehensive Smokeless Tobacco Health Education Act of 1986
- Institutes three rotating health warning labels on smokeless tobacco packages and advertisements (this product may cause mouth cancer; this product may cause gum disease and tooth loss; this product is not a safe alternative to cigarettes) (preempts other health warnings on packages or advertisements [except billboards])
- Prohibits smokeless tobacco advertising on television and radio
- Requires DHHS to publish a biennial status report to Congress on smokeless tobacco
- Requires FTC to report to Congress on smokeless tobacco sales, advertising, and marketing
- Requires smokeless tobacco companies to provide a confidential list of additives and a specification of nicotine content in smokeless tobacco products
- Requires DHHS to conduct public information campaign on the health hazards of smokeless tobacco

Public Law 100-202 (1987)
- Banned smoking on domestic airline flights scheduled for two hours or less Public Law 101-164 (1989)
- Bans smoking on domestic airline flights scheduled for six hours or less
- Synar Amendment to the Alcohol, Drug Abuse, and Mental Health Administration (ADAMHA) Reorganization Act of 1992
- Requires all states to adopt and enforce restrictions on tobacco sales and distribution to minors

Pro-Children Act of 1994

- Requires all federally funded children's services to become smoke-free. Expands upon 1993 law that banned smoking in Women, Infants, and Children (WIC) clinics

NOTES

CHAPTER 1

1. U.S. Department of Health and Human Services, *Reducing the Health Consequences of Smoking: 25 Years of Progress. A Report of the Surgeon General* (Atlanta, Ga.: U.S. Department of Health and Human Services, Public Health Service, Centers for Disease Control and Prevention, Office on Smoking and Health, 1989), p. 270.
2. Centers for Disease Control and Prevention, Office on Smoking and Health, "Smoking & Tobacco Use Fact Sheet: Adult Cigarette Smoking in the United States: Current Estimates" (updated November 2007), http://www.cdc.gov/tobacco/data_statistics/fact_sheets/adult_data/adult_cig_smoking.htm.
3. CDC, "Smoking & Tobacco Use Fact Sheet" (updated November 2007).
4. U.S. Department of Health and Human Services, *Reducing the Health Consequences of Smoking,* pp. 319–20.
5. Centers for Disease Control and Prevention, "Smoking & Tobacco Use Fact Sheet: Smokeless Tobacco" (updated April 2007), http://www.cdc.gov/tobacco/data_statistics/fact_sheets/smokeless/smokeless_tobacco.htm.
6. Centers for Disease Control and Prevention, "Youth Risk Behavioral Surveillance-United States, 2007," *MMWR Surveillance Summaries* 57, SS-4 (June 6, 2008): 1–131.
7. CDC, "Youth Risk Behavioral Surveillance-United States, 2007."
8. American Cancer Society, "Cigar Smoking," last revised on October 1, 2009, http://www.cancer.org/docroot/PED/content/PED_10_2X_Cigar_Smoking.asp.
9. Robert N. Proctor, "Not a Cough in a Carload," exhibit at New York Public Library, October 7 to December 26, 2008.

10. U.S. Department of Health and Human Services, *Reducing the Health Consequences of Smoking,* p. 270; CDC, "Smoking & Tobacco Use Fact Sheet" (updated November 2007).

11. U.S. Public Health Service, *Smoking and Health, Report of the Advisory Committee to the Surgeon General of the Public Health Service* (U.S. Department of Health, Education, and Welfare, Public Health Service, Centers for Disease Control and Prevention, 1964), p. 363.

12. "Smokeless Tobacco Use in the Southeast," *Southern Medical Journal* 93, no. 5 (2000): 456–62, http://www.medscape.com/viewarticle/410540_3; *Focus Groups of Y-K Delta Alaska Natives toward Tobacco Use and Tobacco Dependence Interventions,* http://www.ncbi.nlm.nih.gov/pubmed/15020175? dopt=Abstract.

13. *The NSDUH Report,* "Cigarette Use among Pregnant Women and Recent Mothers," February 9, 2007, http://oas.samhsa.gov/2k7/pregCigs/pregCigs.pdf.

14. Centers for Disease Control and Prevention, National Center for Health Statistics, *National Vital Statistics Reports. Births: Final Data for 2005.* December 5, 2007, 56 (10).

15. *The NSDUH Report,* pp. 2–3.

16. U.S. Department of Health and Human Services. *Tobacco Use among U.S. Racial/Minority Groups—African Americans, American Indians and Alaska Natives, Asian American and Pacific Islanders, and Hispanics: A Report of the Surgeon General.* (Atlanta, Ga.: Centers for Disease Control and Prevention, 1998).

17. U.S. Department of Health and Human Services, *Tobacco Use among U.S. Racial/Ethnic Minority Groups.*

18. CDC, "Smoking & Tobacco Use Fact Sheet" (updated November 2007).

19. U.S. Department of Health and Human Services, Substance Abuse and Mental Health Services Administration, Office of Applied Studies, *Results from the 2007 National Survey on Drug Use and Health: National Findings,* http://oas.samhsa.gov/nsduh/2k7nsduh/2k7Results.pdf.

20. U.S. Department of Health and Human Services, *Results from the 2007 National Survey on Drug Use and Health.*

21. Centers for Disease Control and Prevention, "Cigarette Use among High School Students—United States, 1991–2007," *MMWR Weekly* 57, no. 25 (June 27, 2008): 689–91, www.cdc.gov/mmwr/preview/mmwrhtml/mm5725a3.htm.

22. "Monitoring the Future Press Release," December 11, 2008, http://www. monitoringthefuture.org/pressreleases/08cigpr_complete.pdf.

23. American Cancer Society, "Cigar Smoking," October 28, 2008, p. 3, http:// www.cancer.org/docroot/PED/content/PED_10_2X_Cigar_Smoking.asp.

24. U.S. Department of Health and Human Services, *Reducing the Health Consequences of Smoking,* p. 271.

25. Centers for Disease Control and Prevention, "Cigarette Smoking Adults-United States, 2007," *MMWR Weekly* 57, no. 45 (November 14, 2008): 1221–26, http://www.cdc.gov/mmwr/preview/mmwrhtml/mm5745a2.htm.

26. U.S. Department of Health and Human Services, *Results from the 2007 National Survey on Drug Use and Health.*
27. U.S. Public Health Service, *Smoking and Health,* p. 363.
28. U.S. Department of Health and Human Services, *Reducing the Health Consequences of Smoking,* pp. 272–73.
29. U.S. Department of Health and Human Services, *Results from the 2007 National Survey on Drug Use and Health.*
30. CDC, "Cigarette Smoking Adults-United States, 2007," pp. 1221–26.
31. Centers for Disease Control and Prevention, Table 1 in "State-Specific Prevalence of Cigarette Smoking among Adults and Quitting among Persons Aged 18–35 Years-United States, 2006," *MMWR Weekly* 56, no. 38 (2007): 993–96, http://www.medscape.com/viewarticle/563892_Tables.
32. U.S. Department of Health and Human Services, *Reducing the Health Consequences of Smoking,* p. 279.
33. U.S. Department of Health and Human Services, *Results from the 2007 National Survey on Drug Use and Health.*
34. U.S. Department of Health and Human Services, *Reducing the Health Consequences of Smoking,* pp. 276–77.
35. "Smoking and Soldiers," University of Wisconsin Carbone Comprehensive Cancer Center, October 1, 2008, http://www.cancer.wisc.edu/uwccc/article_soldiersandsmoking.asp.
36. Saul Spigel, "Smoking Among Veterans," OLR Research Report, September 7, 2007, http://www.cga.ct.gov/2007/rpt/2007-R-0534.htm.
37. Spigel, "Smoking Among Veterans."
38. R. P. Sanchez and R. M. Bray, "Cigar and Pipe Smoking in the U.S. Military: Prevalence, Trends, and Correlates," *Military Medicine* 166 (2001): 903–8.
39. Michael A. Wilson, "Prevalence of Tobacco Abuse in a United States Marine Corps Infantry Battalion Forward Deployed in the Haditha Triad of Operation, et al., Abar, Iraq." *Chest* (2008): s53001.

CHAPTER 2

1. Allan M. Brandt, *The Cigarette Century: The Rise, Fall, and Deadly Persistence of the Product That Defined America* (New York: Basic Books, 2007), p. 11.
2. Gene Borio, "Tobacco Timeline: The Seventeenth Century—The Great Age of the Pipe," 2003. http://www.tobacco.org/resources/history/Tobacco_History 17.html.
3. Ibid.
4. Gene Borio, "Tobacco Timeline: Notes," 2003. http://www.tobacco.org/resources/history/Tobacco_Historynotes.html#aa4.
5. Count Egon Caesar Corti, *A History of Smoking* (New York: Harcourt, Brace, 1932), p. 115–16.
6. Joel Chew, M.D., *Tobacco: Its History, Nature, and Effects on the Body and Mind* (Stoke, England: G. Turner, 1849), p. 22.

7. Charles E. Slocum, *About Tobacco and Its Deleterious Effects: A Book for Everybody, Both Users and Non-Users* (Toledo, Ohio: The Slocum Publishing Co., 1909), p. 24.

8. John Harvey Kellogg, "The Decay of American Manhood," *Association Men* 43, no. 2 (October 1917): 115.

9. John Harvey Kellogg, *Tobaccoism, or, How Tobacco Kills* (Battle Creek, Mich.: The Modern Medicine Publishing Co., 1922), p. 7.

10. Brown & Williamson Company, "Tobacco Risk Awareness Timeline," http://www.cigarette.com/images/timeline.pdf.

11. Brandt, *The Cigarette Century*, p. 108.

12. Ibid., p. 109.

13. Ibid., p. 112.

14. Bertha Van Hoosen, "Should Women Smoke?" *Medical Women's Journal* 34 (1927): 227.

15. "Infant Mortality in Relation to Smoking by Mothers," *Hygeia* (June 1934): 564.

16. C. A. Werner, "Triumph of the Cigarette," *American Mercury* 6 (1925): 419–20.

17. John Parascandola, "The Surgeons General and Smoking," *Public Health Reports* 112 (September/October 1997): p. 441, http://www.ncbi.nlm.nih.gov/pmc/articles/PMC1381953/pdf/pubhealthrep00038-0086.pdf.

18. Brandt, *The Cigarette Century*, p. 117.

19. Raymond Pearl, "Tobacco Smoking and Longevity," *Science* 87, no. 2253 (1938): 216–17.

20. Brown & Williamson Company, "Tobacco Risk Awareness Timeline."

21. Alton Ochser and Michael DeBakey, "Symposium on Cancer: Primary Pulmonary Malignancy, Treatment by Total Pneumonectomy: Analysis of 79 Collected Cases and Presentation of Personal Cases," *Surgery, Gynecology, and Obstetrics* 68 (1939): 435–51.

22. Brandt, *The Cigarette Century*, pp. 121–22.

23. Parascandola, "The Surgeons General and Smoking," p. 442.

24. Richard Kluger, *Ashes to Ashes: America's Hundred-Year War, the Public Health, and the Unabashed Triumph of Philip Morris* (New York: Alfred A. Knopf, 1996), 132.

25. Richard Doll and Austin Bradford Hill, "Smoking and Carcinoma of the Lung: Preliminary Report," *British Medical Journal* 224 (1950): 747.

26. LeRoy E. Burney, "Smoking and Lung Cancer: A Statement of the Public Health Service," *JAMA* 71, no. 13 (1959): 1835–36.

27. Brandt, *The Cigarette Century*, p. 216–17.

28. U.S. Public Health Service, *Smoking and Health, Report of the Advisory Committee to the Surgeon General of the Public Health Service*.

29. U.S. Department of Health and Human Services, *The Health Consequences of Smoking Tobacco: A Report of the Surgeon General* (Washington, DC: GPO, 1972).

30. U.S. Department of Health and Human Services, *The Health Consequences of Involuntary Smoking: A Report of the Surgeon General* (Washington, DC: GPO, 1986).

31. John Hill, *Cautions against the immoderate use of snuff.* (London: Printed for R. Baldwin, 1761).

32. U.S. Department of Health and Human Services, *The Health Consequences of Using Smokeless Tobacco: A Report of the Advisory Committee to the Surgeon General* (Bethesda, Md.: U.S. Department of Health and Human Services, Public Health Service, National Institutes of Health, 1986), p. xix.

33. U.S. Department of Health, Education, and Welfare, *Smoking and Health: A Report of the Surgeon General.* (Washington, DC: GPO, 1979).

34. Richard Craver, "Smokeless Tobacco Becomes a Target," *Winston-Salem Journal,* November 10, 2008, http://www2.journalnow.com/content/2008/nov/10/smokeless-tobacco-becomes-a-target.

35. Ibid.,

36. Ibid.

37. Michael C. Fiore, Carlos Roberto Jaén, Timothy B. Baker, William C. Bailey, Neal L. Benowitz, Susan J. Curry, Sally Faith Dorfman, et al. *Treating Tobacco Use and Dependency: 2008 Update* (Rockville, Md.: U.S. Department of Health and Human Services, May 2008), p. 1. http://www.surgeongeneral.gov/tobacco/treating_tobacco_use08.pdf.

38. Ibid.

CHAPTER 3

1. *Anti-Tobacco Journal,* November 1859, p. 5.

2. Richard Kluger, *Ashes to Ashes: America's Hundred-Year Cigarette War, the Public Health, and the Unabashed Triumph of Philip Morris* (New York: Alfred A. Knopf, 1996), p. 16.

3. Ibid., pp. 38–39.

4. Ibid., p. 15.

5. Ibid., p. 69.

6. Ibid., p. 133.

7. Ernst L. Wynder and Evarts A. Graham, "Tobacco Smoking as a Possible Etiological Factor in Bronchiogenic Carcinoma: A Study of 684 Proved Cases," *JAMA* 143, no. 4 (1950): 329–36.

8. Ernst L. Wynder, "Tobacco as a Cause of Lung Cancer: Some Reflections," *American Journal of Epidemiology* 146, no. 9 (November 1, 1997): 690.

9. Ibid., p. 687.

10. Ibid.

11. Ibid., p. 689.

12. American Cancer Society History, http://www.cancer.org/docroot/AA/content/AA_1_4_ACS_History.asp.

13. E. Cuyler Hammond and Daniel Horn, "Smoking and Death Rates-Report on 44 Months of Follow-up of 187,783 Men: II. Death Rates by Cause," *JAMA* 166, no. 10 (1958): 1294.

14. Ibid, 1307.

15. E. Cuyler Hammond and Daniel Horn, "Smoking and Death Rates-Report on 44 Months of Follow-up of 187,783 Men: I. Total Mortality," *JAMA* 166, no. 10 (1958): 1159–72; Hammond and Horn, "Smoking and Death Rates-Report on 44 Months of Follow-up of 187,783 Men: II. Death Rates by Cause," 1294–308.

16. Richard Doll, M.D., and Bradford Hill, CBE, "The Mortality of Doctors in Relation to Their Smoking Habits: A Preliminary Report," *British Medical Journal* 228 (1954): 1451–55.

17. "Tobacco as a Cause of Lung Cancer," p. 690.

18. Allan Brandt, *The Cigarette Century: The Rise, Fall and Deadly Persistence of the Product That Defined America* (New York: Basic Books, 2007), p. 211.

19. Ibid, p. 212.

20. Ibid., pp. 212, 215.

21. Frank M. Strong et al., "Smoking and Health: Joint Report of the Study Group on Smoking and Health," *Science* 125, no. 3258 (1957): 1129–33.

22. Brandt, *The Cigarette Century,* p. 213.

23. L. E. Burney, M.D., "Policy over Politics: The First Statement on Smoking and Health by the Surgeon General of the United States Public Health Service," *New York State Journal of Medicine* 83, no. 13 (December 1983): 1252.

24. Ibid., p. 1253.

25. LeRoy Burney, "Smoking and Lung Cancer: A Statement of the Public Health Service," *JAMA* 171, no. 15 (1959): 1835–36.

26. John Talbott, Editorial response, *JAMA,* 171, no. 15 (1959): 2104.

27. Kluger, *Ashes to Ashes,* p. 204.

28. American Cancer Society Milestones, http://www.cancer.org/docroot/AA/content/AA_1_3_Milestones.asp?sitearea=&level=.

29. U.S. Public Health Service, *Smoking and Health: A Report of the Surgeon General* (Washington, D.C.: GPO, 1964), pp. 29, 32.

30. Brandt, *The Cigarette Century,* p. 211.

31. Ibid., p. 237.

32. Ibid.

33. Office of the Surgeon General, *Luther Leonidas Terry (1961–1965),* http://www.surgeongeneral.gov/about/previous/bioterry.htm.

34. Legacy Tobacco Documents Library, University of California San Francisco, "1965 Cigarette Advertising Code," http://legacy.library.ucsf.edu/action/document/page?tid=dld91f00.

35. Luther Terry, M.D., Daniel Horn, Ph.D., with Madelyn Ferrigan, M.S., *To Smoke or Not to Smoke* (New York: Lothrop, Lee & Shepard Co., 1969), p. 31.

36. American Lung Association (ALA), http://www.lungusa.org/site/pp.asp?
c=dvLUK9OOE&b=23686. In 1975 the ALA established nonsmoker's
rights as a major program priority. According the ALA Web site (http://
www.lungusa.org/about-us/our-history/our-history), the organization "was
among the first to tackle smoking as the nation's greatest preventable
health risk, and to make the connection between air pollution and lung
disease. Landmark victories included The Clean Air Act, banning smoking on airplanes, and passage of the bill which gave the U.S. Food and
Drug Administration authority over the marketing, sale and manufacturing of tobacco products to stop tobacco companies from preying on children and deceiving the American public."

37. ALA, http://www.lungusa.org/site/pp.asp?c+dvLUK90OE&b=23686.

38. Kluger, *Ashes to Ashes,* pp. 325–26.

39. Arlene Hirschfelder, *Encyclopedia of Smoking and Tobacco* (Phoenix, Ariz.:
Oryx Press, 1999), p. 16.

40. Ronald Bayer and James Colgrove, "Science, Politics, and Ideology in the
Campaign against Environmental Tobacco Smoke," *American Journal of
Public Health* 92, no. 6 (June 2002): 949–54.

41. Ibid., p. 950.

42. U.S. Department of Health and Human Services, *The Health Consequences
of Smoking Tobacco: Cancer. A Report of the Surgeon General* (Washington,
DC: Public Health Service, Office on Smoking and Health, 1982). p. 251.

43. American Lung Association, "Gallup Organization Survey of Attitudes toward Smoking," news release, September 20, 1983.

44. Bayer and Colgrove, "Science, Politics, and Ideology in the Campaign against
Environmental Tobacco Smoke," p. 951.

45. Americans for Nonsmokers Rights, *http://no-smoke.org/pdf/mediaordlist.pdf.*

46. Bayer and Colgrove, "Science, Politics, and Ideology in the Campaign against
Environmental Tobacco Smoke," p. 953.

47. Ibid.

48. Food and Drug Administration, http://www.globalink.org/tobacco/docs/
na-docs/fda6.txt.

49. Kluger, *Ashes to Ashes,* p. 701.

50. Ibid., pp. 704–5.

51. Massachusetts Tobacco Control Program, http://www.mass.gov/Eeohhs2/
docs/dph/tobacco_control/program_overview.pdf.

52. Florida Pilot Program on Tobacco Control: Ursula E. Bauer, Tammie M.
Johnson, Richard S. Hopkins, and Robert G. Brooks, "Changes in Youth
Cigarette Use and Intentions Following Implementation of a Tobacco Control
Program," *JAMA* 284, no. 6 (August 9, 2000): 724.

53. Ibid.

54. Kluger, *Ashes to Ashes,* p. 569.

55. Karen K. Kerlach and Michelle A. Larkin, "The SmokeLess States Program,"
in *The Robert Wood Johnson Foundation Anthology,* vol. 8, *To Improve Health*

and Health Care, ed. Stephen L. Isaacs and James R. Knickman (Princeton, N.J.: Robert Wood Johnson Foundation, 2005), p. 11.

56. Brandt, *The Cigarette Century,* p. 422.
57. Campaign for Tobacco-Free Kids. *Special Reports: State Tobacco Settlement.* January 31, 2001. http://tobaccofreekids.org/reports/settlements.
58. Michigan Nonprofit Association and Council of Michigan Foundations, "Tobacco Settlement," *Michigan in Brief 2002–2003,* http://www.michigan inbrief.org/edition07/Chapter5/TobaccoSet.htm.
59. Campaign for Tobacco-Free Kids, http://tobaccofreekids.org/campaign/kbd 2008_report/KBD2008_Report.pdf.
60. Matthew C. Farrelly, Cheryl G. Healton, Kevin C. Davis, Peter Messeri, James C. Hersey, M. Lyndon Haviland, et al., "Getting to the Truth: Evaluating National Tobacco Countermarketing Campaigns," *American Journal of Public Health* 92, no. 6 (June 2002): 906.
61. American Legacy Foundation, http://www.americanlegacy.org/whoweare. aspx.
62. M. C. Farrelly, J. Nonnemaker, K. C. David, and A. Hussin. "The Influence of the National Truth Campaign on Smoking Initiation." *American Journal of Preventive Medicine,* 36, no. 5 (May 2009): 379–84; D. R. Holtgrave, K. A. Wnderink, D. M. Vallone, and C. E. Healton. "Cost-Utility Analysis of the National Truth Campaign to Prevent Youth Smoking." *American Journal of Preventive Medicine,* 36, no. 5 (May 2009): 385–88.
63. James D. Sargent, "Exposure to Movie Smoking: Its Relation to Smoking Initiation among U.S. Adolescents," *Pediatrics* 116, no. 5 (November 2005): 1183–91.
64. U.S. Public Health Service, *Smoking and Health*, pp. 29, 32.

Chapter 4

1. National Library of Medicine, "Profiles in Science: The Report of the Surgeon General,"http://profiles.nlm.nih.gov/NN/Views/Exhibit/narrative/system. html.
2. Ibid.
3. Office of the Public Health Historian, "The Surgeons General and Smoking," http://lhncbc.nlm.nih.gov/apdb/phsHistory/resources/smoking/smoking. html.
4. Richard Kluger, *Ashes to Ashes: America's Hundred-Year Cigarette War, the Public Health, and the Unabashed Triumph of Philip Morris* (New York: Alfred A. Knopf, 1996), p. 200.
5. Ibid, p. 201.
6. Mark Parascandola, "Cigarettes and the US Public Health Service in the 1950s," *American Journal of Public Health* 91, no. 2 (February 2001): 201.
7. Kluger, *Ashes to Ashes,* p. 202.
8. Ibid, p. 222.

9. Ibid, p. 243.
10. Luther Terry, M.D., "The Surgeon General's First Report on Smoking and Health: A Challenge to the Medical Profession," *New York State Journal of Medicine* 83, no. 13 (December 1983): 1255.
11. Parascandola, "Cigarettes and the US Public Health Service in the 1950s," p. 202.
12. National Library of Medicine, "Profiles in Science: The Report of the Surgeon General," http://profiles.nlm.nih.gov/NN/Views/Exhibit/narrative/system.html.
13. U.S. Public Health Service, *Smoking and Health: Report of the Advisory Committee to the Surgeon General of the Public Health Service* (Washington, D.C.: DHEW, PHS, CDC, 1964), p. 31–32. http://profiles.nlm.nih.gov/NN/B/B/M/Q/_/nnbbmq.pdf.
14. U.S. Public Health Service, *The Health Consequences of Smoking: A Public Health Service Review* (Washington, D.C.: DHEW, PHS, CDC, 1967), p. 26, 87. http://profiles.nlm.nih.gov/NN/B/B/K/P/_/nnbbkp.pdf.
15. U.S. Public Health Service, *The Health Consequences of Smoking: 1968 Supplement to the 1967 Public Health Service Review* (Washington, D.C.: DHEW, PHS, 1968). http://profiles.nlm.nih.gov/NN/B/B/K/Y/_/nnbbky.pdf.
16. U.S. Public Health Service, *The Health Consequences of Smoking: 1969 Supplement to the 1967 Public Health Service Review* (Washington, D.C.: DHEW, PHS, 1969). http://profiles.nlm.nih.gov/NN/B/B/L/H/_/nnbblh.pdf.
17. U.S. Department of Health, Education, and Welfare, *The Health Consequences of Smoking: A Report of the Surgeon General* (Washington, D.C.: DHEW, PHS, Health Services and Mental Health Administration, 1971), p. 13. http://profiles.nlm.nih.gov/NN/B/B/N/M/_/nnbbnm.pdf.
18. U.S. Department of Health, Education, and Welfare, *The Health Consequences of Smoking: A Report of the Surgeon General* (Washington, D.C.: DHEW, PHS, Health Services and Mental Health Administration, 1972), p. 1. http://profiles.nlm.nih.gov/NN/B/B/P/M/.
19. U.S. Department of Health, Education, and Welfare, *The Health Consequences of Smoking: A Report of the Surgeon General* (Washington, D.C.: DHEW, PHS, Health Services and Mental Health Administration, 1973). http://profiles.nlm.nih.gov/NN/B/B/P/X/.
20. U.S. Department of Health, Education, and Welfare, *The Health Consequences of Smoking* (Washington, D.C.: DHEW, PHS, Health Services and Mental Health Administration, 1974). http://profiles.nlm.nih.gov/NN/B/B/Q/N/.
21. U.S. Department of Health, Education, and Welfare, *The Health Consequences of Smoking* (Washington, D.C.: DHEW, PHS, Health Services and Mental Health Administration, 1975). http://profiles.nlm.nih.gov/NN/B/B/Q/X/.
22. U.S. Department of Health, Education, and Welfare, *The Health Consequences of Smoking* (Washington, D.C.: DHEW, PHS, Health Services and Mental Health Administration, 1976). http://profiles.nlm.nih.gov/NN/B/C/H/W/.

23. U.S. Department of Health, Education, and Welfare, *The Health Consequences of Smoking, 1977–1978* (Washington, D.C.: DHEW, PHS, Health Services and Mental Health Administration, 1978). http://profiles.nlm.nih.gov/NN/B/B/R/P/.

24. U.S. Department of Health, Education, and Welfare, *The Health Consequences of Smoking: A Report of the Surgeon General* (Washington, D.C.: DHEW, PHS, Health Services and Mental Health Administration, 1979). http://profiles.nlm.nih.gov/NN/B/C/M/D/.

25. U.S. Department of Health and Human Services, *The Health Consequences of Smoking for Women: A Report of the Surgeon General* (Washington, D.C.: DHEW, PHS, Health Services and Mental Health Administration, 1980). http://profiles.nlm.nih.gov/NN/B/B/R/T/.

26. U.S. Department of Health and Human Services, *The Health Consequences of Smoking—The Changing Cigarette: A Report of the Surgeon General* (Washington, D.C.: DHHS, PHS, Office on Smoking and Health, 1981). http://profiles.nlm.nih.gov/NN/B/B/S/N/.

27. U.S. Department of Health and Human Services, *The Health Consequences of Smoking—Cancer: A Report of the Surgeon General* (Washington, D.C.: DHHS, PHS, Office on Smoking and Health, 1982), p. 9. http://profiles.nlm.nih.gov/NN/B/C/D/W/.

28. U.S. Department of Health and Human Services, *The Health Consequences of Smoking—Cardiovascular Disease: A Report of the Surgeon General* (Washington, D.C.: DHHS, PHS, Office on Smoking and Health, 1983), p. iv. http://profiles.nlm.nih.gov/NN/B/B/T/D/.

29. U.S. Department of Health and Human Services, *The Health Consequences of Smoking—Chronic Obstructive Lung Disease: A Report of the Surgeon General* (Washington, D.C.: DHHS, PHS, Office on Smoking and Health, 1984). http://profiles.nlm.nih.gov/NN/B/C/C/S/.

30. U.S. Department of Health and Human Services, *The Health Consequences of Smoking—Cancer and Chronic Lung Disease in the Workplace: A Report of the Surgeon General* (Washington, D.C.: DHHS, PHS, Office on Smoking and Health, 1985). http://profiles.nlm.nih.gov/NN/B/C/B/N/.

31. U.S. Department of Health and Human Services, *The Health Consequences of Involuntary Smoking: A Report of the Surgeon General* (Atlanta, Ga.: DHHS, PHS, CDC, Office on Smoking and Health, 1986), p. vii. http://profiles.nlm.nih.gov/NN/B/C/P/M/.

32. U.S. Department of Health and Human Services, *The Health Consequences of Smoking—Nicotine Addiction: A Report of the Surgeon General* (Atlanta, Ga.: DHHS, PHS, CDC, Office on Smoking and Health, 1988). http://profiles.nlm.nih.gov/NN/B/B/Z/D/.

33. U.S. Department of Health and Human Services, *Reducing the Health Consequences of Smoking—25 Years of Progress: A Report of the Surgeon General* (Atlanta, Ga.: DHHS, PHS, CDC, Office on Smoking and Health, 1989). http://profiles.nlm.nih.gov/NN/B/B/X/S/.

34. U.S. Department of Health and Human Services, *The Health Benefits of Smoking Cessation: A Report of the Surgeon General* (Atlanta, Ga.: DHHS, PHS, CDC, Office on Smoking and Health, 1990). http://profiles.nlm.nih.gov/NN/B/B/C/T/.

35. U.S. Department of Health and Human Services, *Smoking in the Americas: A Report of the Surgeon General* (Atlanta, Ga.: DHHS, PHS, CDC, Office on Smoking and Health, 1992). http://profiles.nlm.nih.gov/NN/B/B/J/.

36. U.S. Department of Health and Human Services, *Preventing Tobacco Use among Young People: A Report of the Surgeon General* (Atlanta, Ga.: DHHS, PHS, CDC, Office on Smoking and Health, 1994). http://www.cdc.gov/tobacco/data_statistics/sgr/1994/index.htm.

37. U.S. Department of Health and Human Services. *Tobacco Use among U.S. Racial/Minority Groups—African Americans, American Indians and Alaska Natives, Asian American and Pacific Islanders, and Hispanics: A Report of the Surgeon General.* (Atlanta, Ga.: Centers for Disease Control and Prevention, 1998), p. 6.

38. Ibid.

39. U.S. Department of Health and Human Services, *Reducing Tobacco Use: A Report of the Surgeon General* (Atlanta, Ga.: DHHS, PHS, CDC, Office on Smoking and Health, National Center for Chronic Disease Prevention and Health Promotion, 2000). http://www.cdc.gov/tobacco/data_statistics/sgr/2000/index.htm.

40. U.S. Department of Health and Human Services, *Women and Smoking: A Report of the Surgeon General* (Rockville, Md.: DHHS, PHS, Office of the Surgeon General, 2001). http://www.cdc.gov/tobacco/data_statistics/sgr/2001/index.htm.

41. U.S. Department of Health and Human Services, *The Health Consequences of Smoking: A Report of the Surgeon General* (Atlanta, Ga.: DHHS, CDC, National Center for Chronic Disease Prevention and Health Promotion, Office on Smoking and Health, 2004). http://www.cdc.gov/tobacco/data_statistics/sgr/2004/index.htm.

42. U.S. Department of Health and Human Services, *The Health Consequences of Involuntary Exposure to Tobacco Smoke: A Report of the Surgeon General* (Atlanta, Ga.: DHHS, CDC, Coordinating Center for Health Promotion, National Center for Chronic Disease Prevention and Health Promotion, Office on Smoking and Health, 2006). http://www.cdc.gov/tobacco/data_statistics/sgr/2006/index.htm.

CHAPTER 5

1. Arlene Hirschfelder, *Kick Butts! A Kid's Action Guide to a Tobacco-Free America* (Parsippany, N.J.: Julian Messner, 1998), p. 21.

2. Arlene Hirschfelder, *Encyclopedia of Smoking and Tobacco* (Phoenix, Ariz.: Oryx Press, 1999), p. 3.

3. Hirschfelder, *Encyclopedia of Smoking and Tobacco,* p. 3.
4. *Wheeler–Lea Act* (1938): ch. 49 § 3, 52 Stat. 111.
5. Susan Wagner, *Cigarette Country: Tobacco in American History and Politics* (New York: Praeger Publishers, 1971), p. 89.
6. Ibid.
7. *Federal Cigarette Labeling and Advertising Act,* P.L. 89–92, 29 Stat. 282, section 9.
8. Hirschfelder, *Encyclopedia of Smoking and Tobacco,* p. 4.
9. American Cancer Society, Cancer Action Network, American Heart Association, American Lung Association, Robert Wood Johnson Foundation, and Campaign for Tobacco-Free Kids, *Deadly in Pink: Big Tobacco Steps Up Its Targeting of Women and Girls,* February 18, 2009, http://tobaccofreekids. org/reports/women_new/index.html.
10. Even as the Justice Department took action in the summer of 1995 against Philip Morris for its billboards in sports stadiums that were strategically placed to receive airtime during televised games, the company insisted it had not violated the TV ad ban.
11. Hirschfelder, *Encyclopedia of Smoking and Tobacco,* p. 124.
12. U.S. Department of Health and Human Services, *Reducing the Health Consequences of Smoking—25 Years of Progress,* p. 492.
13. Hirschfelder, *Encyclopedia of Smoking and Tobacco,* p. 4.
14. Hirschfelder, *Encyclopedia of Smoking and Tobacco,* p. 124.
15. *Coyne Beahm, Inc., vs. United States, #2:* 95CV00591, 1997 U.S. Dist. LEXIS 5453 (M.D.N.C., April 25, 1997).
16. Campaign for Tobacco-Free Kids, *A Decade of Broken Promises: The 1998 State Tobacco Settlement 10 Years Later,* http://www.tobaccofreekids.org/ reports/settlements.
17. Federal Trade Commission, *Smokeless Tobacco Report for the Years 2002–2005* (Washington, D.C.: Federal Trade Commission, 2007), http://www.ftc. gov/reports/tobacco/02-05smokeless0623105.pdf.
18. Substance Abuse and Mental Health Services Administration, *2007 National Survey on Drug Use and Health.* Office of Applied Studies, NSDUH Series H-27, DHHS Publication No. SMA 05–4061, Rockville, Md.
19. Centers for Disease Control and Prevention, *2006 National Youth Tobacco Survey and Key Prevalence Indicators,* http://www.cdc.gov/tobacco/data_ statistics/surveys/NYTS/index.htm.
20. Centers for Disease Control and Prevention, "Youth Risk Behavior Surveillance-United States, 2007," *Morbidity and Mortality Weekly Report* 55, no. 4 (2008): 1–13.
21. Centers for Disease Control and Prevention, "Changes in Cigarette Brand Preferences of Adolescent Smokers—United States, 1989–1993," *Morbidity and Mortality Weekly Report* 43, no. 32 (1994): 577–81, http://www.cdc.gov/ mmwr/preview/mmwrhtml/00032326.htm.

22. Centers for Disease Control and Prevention, "Tobacco Free Sports Initiatives," http://www.cdc.gov/tobacco/youth/educational_materials/sports/index.htm.

23. Campaign for Tobacco-Free Kids, "Justice Department Documents in Tobacco Lawsuit Show Tobacco Industry Continues to Market to Kids and Deceive Public," March 18, 2003, http://tobaccofreekids.org/Script/DisplayPressRelease.php3?Display=615.

24. Campaign for Tobacco-Free Kids, *Thirteen Years of Kicking Butts: Reducing the Appeal and Availability of Tobacco to Kids,* April 2, 2008, http://tobacco freekids.org/campaign/kbd2008_report/KBD2008_Report.pdf.

25. Sandy J. Slater, Frank J. Chaloupka, Melanie Wakefield, Lloyd D. Johnston, and Patrick O'Malley, "The Impact of Retail Cigarette Marketing Practices on Youth Smoking Update," *Archives of Pediatrics and Adolescent Medicine* 161 (May 2007): 440–45.

26. American Cancer Society et al., *Deadly in Pink.*

27. Ibid.

28. U.S. Department of Health and Human Services, *Tobacco Use among U.S. Racial/Ethnic Minority Groups—African Americans, American Indians and Alaska Natives, Asian Americans and Pacific Islanders, and Hispanics: A Report of the Surgeon General* (Atlanta, Ga.: U.S. Department of Health and Human Services, Centers for Disease Control and Prevention, 1998), http://www.cdc.gov/tobacco/sgr/sgr_1998/sgr-min-sgr.htm.

29. John Slade, "Marketing and Promotion of Cigars," *Cigars: Health Effects and Trends [Smoking and Tobacco Control, Monograph #9]* (Bethesda, Md.: National Cancer Institute, 1998), pp. 195–219. http://cancercontrol.cancer.gov/tcrb/monographs/9/m9_7.PDF.

30. Ibid.

31. American Cancer Society, "Cigar Smoking," http://www.cancer.org/docroot/PED/content/PED_10_2X_Cigar_smoking.asp.

32. Nancy A. Rigotti, Jae Eun Lee, and Henry Wechler, "U.S. College Students' Use of Tobacco Products: Results of a National Survey," *JAMA* 284, no. 6 (2000): 699–705.

33. *United States v. Philip Morris,* http://www.library.ucsf.edu/tobacco/litigation/uspm.

CHAPTER 6

1. Institute of Medicine, *Growing Up Tobacco Free* (Washington, D.C.: National Academy Press, 1984).

2. "Federal and State Cigarette Excise Taxes: United States, 1995–2009," *MMWR Weekly* 59, no. 29 (May 22, 2009): 524–27. http://www.cdc.gov/mmwr/preview/mmwrhtml/mm5819a2.htm.

3. Gerald Prante, "What Is Proper Tax Policy for Smokeless Tobacco Products?" *Tax Foundation Fiscal Fact,* no. 120 (March 26, 2008). http://www.taxfoundation.org/news/show/1858.html1.

4. Annals of Congress, 3rd Congress, 1st Session, May 2, 1794.
5. Larry Sandler, "Milwaukee Alderman Wants City Cigarette Tax," *Journal Interactive Milwaukee,* December 7, 2009, http://www.jsonline.com/news/milwaukee/35663099.html.
6. Institute of Medicine, *Growing Up Tobacco Free.*
7. Senator Frank Moss, "Harnessing Tax Rates for Public Policy Objectives," *Congressional Record: Senate,* March 12, 1973, p. 7297. *Congressional Record-Senate,* March 12, 1973, p. 7297.
8. Wendy Koch, "Biggest U.S. Tax Hike on Tobacco Takes Effect," *USA Today,* April 2, 2009, http://www.usatoday.com/money/perfi/taxes/2009-03-31-cigarettetax_N.htm.
9. National Cancer Institute Expert Panel, *The Impact of Cigarette Excise Taxes on Smoking among Children and Adults: Summary Report* (Washington, D.C.: National Cancer Institute Cancer Control Science Program, 1993), p. 7.
10. Institute of Medicine, *Growing Up Tobacco Free: Preventing Nicotine Addiction in Children and Youths* (Washington, D.C.: Institute of Medicine, 1994), p. 192.
11. Campaign for Tobacco-Free Kids, "Federal Tobacco Tax Increases Will Benefit Lower Income Households," October 25, 2007, p. 2, http://www.tobaccofreekids.org/research/factsheets/pdf/0022.pdf.
12. Ibid.
13. Campaign for Tobacco-Free Kids, "Responses to Misleading and Inaccurate Cigarette Company Arguments against State Cigarette Tax Increases," June 30, 2008, p. 4, http://www.uulmca.org/documents/cig_tax_argument_2-9-05.pdf.
14. Campaign for Tobacco-Free Kids, "Federal Tobacco Tax Increases Will Benefit Lower Income Households," p. 6.
15. Ibid.
16. Ibid, p. 2.
17. Kenneth E. Warner, "Smoking and Health Implications of a Change in the Federal Cigarette Excise Tax," in *Tobacco Control Policy,* ed. Kenneth E. Warner (San Francisco: Jossey-Bass, 2006), p. 124.
18. U.S. Department of Health and Human Services, *Reducing Tobacco Use: A Report of the U.S. Surgeon General* (Atlanta, Ga.: U.S. Department of Health and Human Services, Centers for Disease Control and Prevention, National Center for Chronic Disease Prevention and Health Promotion, Office on Smoking and Health, 2000), p. 337.
19. The Tobacco Institute, *Excise Issues: The Fairness Issue* (Washington, D.C.: The Tobacco Institute, 1985), p. 3.
20. R. B. Campbell and E. D. Balbach, "Mobilizing Public Opinion for the Tobacco Industry: The Consumer Tax Alliance and Excise Taxes," *Tobacco Control* 17, no. 5 (August 7, 2008): 351–56.
21. National Center for Policy Analysis, *Taxing the Poor: A Report on Tobacco, Alcohol, Gambling, and Other Taxes and Fees That Disproportionately*

Burden Lower Income Families, June 2007, p. 1, http://www.ncpa.org/pdfs/ st300.pdf.

22. Frank J. Chaloupka, "Tobacco Taxation, Tobacco Control Policy, and Tobacco Use," n.d., p. 8, http://www.impacteen.org/generalarea_PDFs/KY_10_04_01. pdf.

23. Campaign for Tobacco-Free Kids, "Responses to Misleading and Inaccurate Cigarette Company Arguments against State Cigarette Tax Increases."

24. Michelle C. Bucci and William W. Beach, "22 Million New Smokers Needed: Funding SCHIP Expansion with a Tobacco Tax," *Heritage Foundation,* WebMemo #1548, July 11, 2007. http:///www.heritage.org/Research/ HealthCare/wm1548.cfm.

25. Ibid., p. 1.

26. Eric Lindblom, "Public Health Benefits and Healthcare Cost Savings from the Federal Cigarette Tax Increase," Campaign for Tobacco-Free Kids, February 4, 2009, http://www.tobaccofreekids.org/research/factsheets/pdf/0314.pdf.

27. Institute of Medicine, "Ending the Tobacco Problem: A Blueprint for the Nation," report brief, 2007, p. 3, http://www.iom.edu/Object.File/Master/43/183/ Tobacco%20report%20brief%20general.pdf.

28. Lindblom, "Public Health Benefits and Healthcare Cost Savings from the Federal Cigarette Tax Increase."

29. Robert A. Levey, March 20, 2009, http://www.cato.org.

30. "Tobacco Smuggling," Tobacco Fact Sheet, 11th World Conference on Tobacco OR Health, August 6–11, 2000.

31. Campaign for Tobacco-Free Kids, "Responses to Misleading and Inaccurate Cigarette Company Arguments against State Cigarette Tax Increases," p. 3.

32. Campaign for Tobacco-Free Kids, "Raising State Cigarette Taxes Always Increases State Revenues (and Always Reduces Smoking)," August 5, 2008, p. 2, http://dls.state.va.us/groups/taxcode/073002/RaisingIncreasesReven ues.PDF.

33. Campaign for Tobacco-Free Kids, "Raising State Cigarette Taxes Always Increases State Revenues (and Always Reduces Smoking)," p. 2.

34. Campaign for Tobacco-Free Kids, "Responses to Misleading and Inaccurate Cigarette Company Arguments against State Cigarette Tax Increases," p. 3.

35. Campaign for Tobacco-Free Kids, "State Options to Prevent and Reduce Cigarette Smuggling and Block Other Illegal State Tobacco Tax Evasion," August 18, 2008, p. 1. http: www.tobaccofreekids.org/research/factsheets/ pdf/0274.pdf.

36. Campaign for Tobacco-Free Kids, State Options to Prevent and Reduce Cigarette Smuggling and Black Other Illegal State Tobacco Tax Evasion," pp. 1–3.

37. Michael D. LaFaive, Patrick Fleenor, and Todd Nesbit, *Cigarette Taxes and Smuggling: A Statistical Analysis and Historical Review* (Midland, Mich.: Mackinac Center for Public Policy, 2007).

38. LaFaive, Fleenor, and Nesbit, "Executive Summary."

39. Richard McGowan, *Business, Politics and Cigarettes: Multiple Levels, Multiple Agendas* (Santa Barbara, Calif.: Quorum Press, 1995), pp. 104–7.

40. David B. Caruso, "Higher Cigarette Taxes Could Promote Smuggling," *USA Today,* April 10, 2008.

41. Gale Courney Toensing, "Seneca Educates Lawmakers on Treaty Rights, Tobacco Economy," *Indian Country Today,* 29, no. 22 (November 4, 2009): 3.

42. "Washington state cancels cigarette deal with Yakama Tribe." *News from Indian Country,* July 21, 2008, p. 9.

43. Ibid.

44. Ibid.

45. Kurt M. Ribisi, Annice E. Kim, and Rebecca S. Williams, "Sales and Marketing of Cigarettes on the Internet: Emerging Threats to Tobacco Control and Promising Policy Solutions," in *Reducing Tobacco Use: Strategies, Barriers, and Consequences* (Washington, D.C.: National Academy Press, 2007).

46. Ibid.

47. Ibid.

48. *The 1949 Jenkins Act,* 15 U.S.C.,§375–78.

49. Robert Rubin, Chris Charron, and Moira Dorse, "Online Tobacco Sales Grow, States Lose," April 27, 2001, http://www.forrester.com/ER/Research/Brief/Excerpt/0,1317,12253,00.html.

50. Campaign for Tobacco-Free Kids, "State Options to Prevent and Reduce Cigarette Smuggling and Block Other Illegal State Tobacco Tax Evasion," pp. 3–4.

51. Ibid., p. 4.

CHAPTER 7

1. Debra Jones Ringold and John E. Calfee, "Content of Cigarette Ads: 1926–1986," *Journal of Public Policy and Marketing* 8 (1999): 3.

2. *United States v. Philip Morris,* Executive Summary, from Final Proposed Findings of Fact, August 17, 2006, p. 18. htttp://www.justice.gov/civil/cases/tobacco2/U.S.%Final%20ODF%20Exsc%Summary.pdf.

3. Arlene Hirschfelder, *Encyclopedia of Smoking and Health* (Phoenix, Ariz.: Oryx Press, 1999), p. 175. Between 1952 and 1956, people who smoked Kent cigarettes with micronite filters were also smoking asbestos. Throughout this period, Lorillard never advised or warned consumers that its Kent cigarette filters contained crocidolite asbestos, the most potent carcinogen of the various asbestos fiber types. Despite independent testing conducted at the request of Lorillard in 1954, which demonstrated fiber release from Kent cigarette filters, the company continued to manufacture and sell its product, without recall, for another two years. Between 1952 and 1956, when a new filter media was substituted, Lorillard sold thirteen billion Kent Micronite asbestos-filtered

cigarettes. Law Offices of Brayton Purcell LLP, "Jury Awards $1,048,100.00 in Kent Micronite Asbestos Cigarette Filter Case," May 8, 2000, http://www.braytonlaw.com/news/verdicts/2000traverso.htm.

4. Hirschfelder, *Encyclopedia of Smoking and Health,* p. 126.

5. Federal Trade Commission Report for 2004 and 2005. Issued 2007; p. 11. http://www.ftc.gov/reports/tobacco/2007cigarette2004–2005.pdf.

6. Ringold and Calfee, "Content of Cigarette Ads," p. 4.

7. John E. Calfee, "The Ghost of Cigarette Advertising Past," *Regulation* 10, no. 2 (1986), reprinted June 1, 1997, http://www.aei.org/publications/pubID.15245,filter.all/pub_detail.asp.

8. Richard Kluger, *Ashes to Ashes: America's Hundred-Year Cigarette War, the Public Health, and the Unabashed Triumph of Philip Morris* (New York: Alfred A. Knopf, 1996), p. 190.

9. John Slade, "Marketing and Promotion of Cigars."

10. National Cancer Institute, "The Truth About 'Light' Cigarettes: Questions and Answers," August 17, 2004, http://www.cancer.gov/cancertopics/factsheet/Tobacco/light-cigarettes.

11. National Cancer Institute, "The Truth About 'Light' Cigarettes."

12. *United States v. Philip Morris,* p. 19.

13. John L. Pauly, A. B. Mepani, J. D. Lesses, K. M. Cummings, and R. J. Streck, "Cigarettes with Defective Filters Marketed for 40 Years: What Philip Morris Never Told Smokers," *Tobacco Control* 11, Suppl. no. 1 (March 1, 2002): i51–61, http://tobaccocontrol.bmj.com/cgi/content/full/11/suppl_1/i51.

14. *United States v. Philip Morris,* p. 18.

15. Pauly et al., "Cigarettes with Defective Filters Marketed for 40 Years."

16. National Cancer Institute, *Risks Associated with Smoking Cigarettes with Low Machine-Measured Yields of Tar and Nicotine,* Smoking and Tobacco Control Monograph 13 (Washington, D.C.: U.S. Department of Health and Human Services, National Institutes of Health, National Cancer Institute, November 27, 2001), preface, p. ii.

17. Peter G. Shields, "Molecular Epidemiology of Smoking and Lung Cancer," *Oncogene* 21 (2002): 6820–76.

18. "Low Tar Cigarettes Don't Cut Lung Cancer Risk," American Cancer Society News Center, January 9, 2004, http://www.cancer.org/docroot/NWS/content/NWS_1_1x_Low_Tar_Cigarettes_Dont_Cut_Lung_Cancer_Risk.asp.

19. National Cancer Institute, "The Truth About 'Light' Cigarettes."

20. Weil and Gotshal, *Altria Group, Inc. v. Good,* http://www.weil.com/altriagroupvgood. *Altria Group, Inc., et al. v. Good et al.,* December 15, 2008, http://www.scotuswiki.com/index.php?title=Altria_Group_v._Good.

21. *Altria Group, Inc., et al. v. Good et al.,* December 15, 2008, http://www.scotuswiki.com/index.php?title=Altria_Group_v._Good.

22. Ibid.

23. Ibid.

24. Ibid.

25. Michelle Lore, "Local Smokers' Lawyers Fired Up for 'Light' CigaretteFraud Claims," *Minnesota Lawyer,* January 9, 2009, http://www.minnlawyer.com/article.cfm/2009/01/12/Local-smokers-lawyers-fired-up-for-light-cigarette-fraud-claims.

26. David Hammond, Martin Dockrell, Deborah Arnott, Alex Lee, and Ann McNeill, "Cigarette Pack Design and Perceptions of Risk among UK Adults and Youth," *The European Journal of Public Health* (2009).

27. Duff Wilson, "No More 'Light' Cigarettes, but Companies Are Betting Smokers Will Recognize the Gold Box," *New York Times,* February 10, 2010, p. B1.

28. Ibid., p. 5.

29. Ibid.

30. Hammond et al., "Cigarette Pack Design."

Chapter 8

1. United Statues at Large, *Pure Food and Drugs Act,* 59th Cong., sess. 1, 1906, chp. 3915, p. 768–72.

2. David A. Rienzo, "About-Face: How FDA Changed Its Mind, Took On the Tobacco Companies in Their Own Back Yard, and Won," *Food and Drug Law Journal* 53 (1998): 244.

3. Senator Reed Smoot, "Tobacco Regulation Speech in the U.S. Senate," *Congressional Record* 71, no. 2 (June 10, 1929): S 2589, http://medicolegal.tripod.com/smoot1929.htm.

4. Ibid.

5. Allan M. Brandt, *The Cigarette Century: The Rise, Fall, and Deadly Persistence of the Product That Defined America* (New York: Basic Books, 2007), p. 60.

6. David Kessler, *A Question of Intent: A Great American Battle with a Deadly Industry* (New York: Public Affairs, 2001), pp. 29–31.

7. Ibid., p. 336.

8. *Coyne Beahm, et al. v. FDA, et al.; United States Tobacco Company, et al. v. FDA, et al.; National Association of Convenience Stores, et al. v. Kessler, et al.; American Advertising Federation, et al. v. Kessler, et al.* April 25, 1997.

9. *Brown & Williamson Tobacco Corporation; Lorillard Tobacco Company; Philip Morris, Incorporated; R. J. Reynolds Tobacco Company, Plaintiffs-Appellants, and Coyne Beahm, Incorporated; Liggett Group, Incorporated, Plaintiffs, v. Food & Drug Administration; David A. Kessler, M.D., Commissioner of Food and Drugs.* http://lw.bna.com/lw/19980825/971604.htm.

10. Ibid.

11. Ibid.

12. *FDA v. Brown & Williamson Tobacco Corp.* (98-1152) 529 U.S. 120 (2000).

13. Ibid.

14. Ibid.

15. Ibid.
16. Ibid.
17. *FDA v. Brown & Williamson Tobacco Corp.* (98-1152) 529 U.S. 120 (2000): Dissent, http://www.law.cornell.edu/supct/pdf/98-1152P.ZD.
18. C. Stephen Redhead and Vanessa Burrows, "FDA Regulation of Tobacco Products: A Policy and Legal Analysis," *CRS Report for Congress,* updated April 20, 2007, p. 19.
19. Ibid., pp. 21–22.
20. The White House, Office of the Press Secretary, "Fact Sheet: *The Family Smoking Prevention and Tobacco Control Act of 2009,*" June 22, 2009. http://www.whitehouse.gov/the_press_office/Fact-sheet-and-expected-attendees-for-todays-Rose-Garden-bill-signing/.
21. Duff Wilson, "Veterans' Doctor to Lead F.D.A. Tobacco Division," *The New York Times,* August 20, 2009, p. B3.
22. United States District Court Western District of Kentucky Bowling Green Division. Civil Action NO. 1:09-CV-117-M. *Commonwealth Brands, Inc; Tobacco City and Lottery, Inc.; Lorillard Tobacco Company; National Tobacco Company, L.P.; and R.J. Reynolds Tobacco Company v. United States of America; United States Food and Drug Administration; Margaret Hamberg, Commissioner of the United States Food and Drug Administration, and Kathleen Sebelius, Secretary of the United States Department of Health and Human Services.* http://www.tobaccofreekids.org/pressoffice/district_court_opinion_01052010.pdf.
23. Ibid., p. 14.
24. Ibid., p. 35.
25. Ibid., p. 21.
26. Ibid., p. 24–25.

CHAPTER 9

1. Centers for Disease Control and Prevention, CDC Surveillance Summaries, "Surveillance for Selected Tobacco-Use Behaviors-United States, 1900–1994," *MMWR* 43, no. SS-3 (November 18, 1994): 35.
2. Department of Health and Human Services, *Preventing Tobacco among Young Peoples: A Report of the Surgeon General.* (Atlanta, Ga.: U.S. Department of Health and Human Services, Public Health Service, Centers for Disease Control and Prevention, Office on Smoking and Health, 1994), p. 72.
3. C. Cassandra Tate, "The American Anti-Cigarette Movement, 1880–1930" (Ph.D. diss., University of Washington, 1995), p. 133.
4. Ibid, p. 133–34.
5. Ibid., pp. 1, 502–3.
6. Arlene Hirschfelder, *Kick Butts! A Kid's Action Guide to a Tobacco-Free America* (Parsippany, N.J.: Julian Messner, 1998), p. 15.

NOTES

6NOTES

7. C. Cassandra Tate, *Cigarette Wars: The Triumph of the Little White Slaver* (New York: Oxford University Press, 1998), pp. 3, 81, 115.
8. Ibid., p. 161.
9. Gordon L. Dillow, "Thank You For Not Smoking: The Hundred-Year War Against the Cigarette," *American Heritage* (February–March 1981): 106.
10. Tate, "The American Anti-Cigarette Movement," p. 402.
11. Massachusetts Department of Public Health, *School Tobacco Policies: Applicable Laws, Sample Policies, and Penalty Options* (Boston: Author, October 2007), p. 7.
12. Nebraska State Law Code, Chapter 79, Section 79–712: Public school; health education; requirements, http://www.youthdevelopment.org/aef/nebraska.htm#law.
13. Department of Health and Human Services, Substance Abuse and Mental Health Services Administration, Office of Applied Studies, *Results from the 2005 National Survey on Drug Use and Health,* http://oas.samhsa.gov/nsduh/2k5nsduh/2k5results.pdf.
14. Department of Health and Human Services, Substance Abuse and Mental Health Administration, Office of Applied Studies, *Results of the 2007 National Survey on Drug Use and Health: National Findings,* http://oas.samhsa.gov/nsduh/2k7nsduh/2k7Results.pdf.
15. American Cancer Society, "Smokeless Tobacco and How to Quit," http://www.cancer.org/docroot/PED/content/PED_10_13X_Quitting_Smokeless_Tobacco.asp?sitearea=&level=.
16. Jacob Sullum, *For Your Own Good: The Anti-Smoking Crusade and the Tyranny of Public Health* (New York: The Free Press, 1998), p. 28.
17. Allan M. Brandt, *The Cigarette Century: The Rise, Fall, and Deadly Persistence of the Product that Defined America* (New York: Basic Books, 2007), p. 32.
18. U.S. Department of Health and Human Services, *Reducing Tobacco Use: A Report of the Surgeon General* (Atlanta, Ga.: U.S. Department of Health and Human Services, Centers for Disease Control and Prevention, Office on Smoking and Health, 2000), p. 16.
19. Hirschfelder, *Kick Butts!,* p. 58.
20. Sullum, *For Your Own Good,* p. 96.
21. U.S. Department of Health and Human Services, *Reducing Tobacco Use,* p. 177.
22. Ibid., p. 189.
23. Ibid., p. 191.
24. David A. Kessler, Ann M. Witt, Philip S. Barnett, Mitchell R. Zeller, Sharon L. Natanblut, Judith P. Wilkenfeld, Catherine C. Lorraine, Larry J. Thompson, and William B. Schultz, "The Food and Drug Administration's Regulation of Tobacco Products," *The New England Journal of Medicine* 335, no. 13 (September 26, 1996): 991.
25. Ibid., p. 188.

26. National Conference of State Legislatures, "Summary of the Attorneys General Master Tobacco Settlement Agreement," http://www.ncsl.org/state fed//tmsasumm.htm.

27. Sullum, *For Your Own Good,* p. 251.

28. Ibid., p. 105.

29. John A. Tauras, Patrick O'Malley, and Lloyd Johnston, "Effects of Price and Access Laws on Teenage Smoking Initiation: A National Longitudinal Analysis," Bridging the Gap Research, *ImpacTeen,* April 24, 2001. http://impacteen.org/imp_yes.htm.

30. Leonard A. Jason, Peter Y. Ji, Michael D. Anes, and Scott H. Birkhead, "Active Enforcement of Cigarette Control Laws in the Prevention of Cigarette Sales to Minors," in *Tobacco Control Policy,* ed. Kenneth E. Warner (San Francisco: Jossey-Bass, 2006), p. 396.

31. U.S. Department of Health and Human Services, *Reducing Tobacco Use,* pp. 209–10.

32. Ibid., p. 210.

33. American Lung Association, *State Legislated Actions on Tobacco Issues: 2007* (Washington, D.C.: American Lung Association, 2008), pp. 6–7, http://slati.lungusa.org/reports/SLATI_07.pdf.

34. Survey of 507 teens aged 12–17 interviewed between March 5 and 9, 2008, via International Communication Research's TEENEXCEL national telephone Omnibus.

35. American Lung Association, *State Legislated Actions on Tobacco Issues,* pp. 6–7.

36. Institute of Medicine, "Ending the Tobacco Problem: A Blueprint for the Nation," *Report Brief,* May 2007, http://www.iom.edu/Object.File/Master/43/183/Tobacco%20report%20brief%20general.pdf.

37. Sullum, *For Your Own Good,* p. 128.

38. Institute of Medicine, "Ending the Tobacco Problem."

39. American Legacy Foundation, Youth Media Campaign, http://www.american legacy.org/PDF/Youth_Media_Campaign.pdf.

40. Centers for Disease Control and Prevention, *Best Practices for Comprehensive Tobacco Control Programs-2007* (Atlanta, Ga.: U.S. Department of Health and Human Services, Centers for Disease Control and Prevention, National Center for Chronic Disease Prevention and Health Promotion, Office on Smoking and Health, October 2007), http://www.cdc.gov/tobacco/tobacco_control_programs/stateandcommunity/best_practices/00_pdfs/2007/BestPractices_Complete.pdf.

CHAPTER 10

1. Twyman Abbott, "The Rights of the Nonsmoker," *Outlook* (1910): 763–67, quoted in Allan M. Brandt, *The Cigarette Century: The Rise, Fall, and Deadly Persistence of the Product That Defined America* (New York: Basic Books, 2007), p. 49.

2. *New York Times,* August 21, 1913.
3. "Refuges for Non-Smokers," *Literary Digest,* November 22, 1924, p. 28.
4. United States Senate, "March 9, 1914, Smoking Ban." http://www.senate. gov/artandhistory/history/minute/Smoking_Ban.htm.
5. C. Cassandra Tate, "The American Anti-Cigarette Movement, 1880–1930" (Ph.D. diss., University of Washington, 1995), p. 161.
6. "Senate Bans Tobacco Sales in Own Shops," http://usgovinfo.about.com/ b/2007/11/19/senate-bans-tobacco-sales-in-own-shops.htm.
7. *The Boy* (new series) 2, no. 1 (first quarter, 1914): 19.
8. Tate, "The American Anti-Cigarette Movement," pp. 502–3.
9. Gordon L. Dillow, "Thank You for Not Smoking: The Hundred Year War against the Cigarette," *American Heritage Magazine* 32 (February–March 1981): 106.
10. Emil Bogen, "The Composition of Cigaretes and Cigaret [sic] Smoke," *Journal of the American Medical Association* 93, no. 15 (October 12, 1929): 1112.
11. U.S. Environmental Protection Agency, *Respiratory Health Effects of Passive Smoking: Lung Cancer and Other Disorders,* (Washington, D.C., Environmental Protection Agency, 1992), p. vi.
12. U.S. Department of Health, Education, and Welfare, Public Health Service, *The Health Consequences of Smoking* (Washington, D.C.: Public Health Service, 1972), pp. 19–20.
13. Allan M. Brandt, *The Cigarette Century: The Rise, Fall, and Deadly Persistence of the Product That Defined America* (New York: Basic Books, 2007), p. 281.
14. Brandt, *The Cigarette Century,* p. 288.
15. Richard Kluger, *Ashes to Ashes: America's Hundred-Year Cigarette War, the Public Health, and the Unabashed Triumph of Philip Morris* (New York: Alfred A. Knopf, 1996), p. 373.
16. Ibid.
17. Jacob Sullum, *For Your Own Good: The Anti-Smoking Crusade and the Tyranny of Public Health* (New York: The Free Press, 1998), p. 146.
18. Roper Organization. *A Study of Public Attitudes toward Cigarette Smoking and the Tobacco Industry in 1978, Volume 1.* (Roper Organization: May 1978).
19. Kluger, *Ashes to Ashes,* p. 375.
20. Brandt, *The Cigarette Century,* p. 285.
21. Takeshi Hirayama, "Nonsmoking Wives of Heavy Smokers Have a Higher Risk of Lung Cancer: A Study from Japan," *British Medical Journal* 28 (January 17, 1981): 183–85.
22. U.S. Department of Health and Human Services, Public Health Service, Office on Smoking and Health, *The Health Consequences of Involuntary Smoking: A Report of the Surgeon General* (Rockville, Md.: U.S. Public Health Service, Office on Smoking and Health, 1986), p. x.

23. Ronald Bayer and James Colgrove, "Science, Politics, and Ideology in the Campaign against Environmental Tobacco Smoke," *American Journal of Public Health* 92, no. 6 (June 2002): 951.

24. Kluger, *Ashes to Ashes,* p. 690.

25. Stanton A. Glantz, "Achieving a Smokefree Society," *Circulation* 76, no. 4 (October 1987): 746–52 (originally presented at the Tobacco-Free Young America by the Year 2000 conference, October 1986).

26. Bayer and Colgrove, "Science, Politics, and Ideology in the Campaign against Environmental Tobacco Smoke," p. 951.

27. Kluger, *Ashes to Ashes,* p. 679.

28. Brandt, *The Cigarette Century,* p. 284.

29. Bayer and Colgrove, "Science, Politics, and Ideology in the Campaign against Environmental Tobacco Smoke," p. 951.

30. Brandt, *The Cigarette Century,* p. 298.

31. U.S. Environmental Protection Agency, *Respiratory Health Effects of Passive Smoking,* pp. v, x.

32. Brandt, *The Cigarette Century,* p. 306.

33. "No Right to Cause Death," *New York Times,* January 10, 1993, p. 22.

34. "No Smoking," *Wall Street Journal,* June 7, 1994, A14.

35. Kluger, *Ashes to Ashes,* p. 738.

36. Sullum, *For Your Own Good,* pp. 172–74.

37. U.S. Department of Health and Human Services, *The Health Consequences of Involuntary Exposure to Tobacco Smoke: A Report of the Surgeon General* (Atlanta, Ga.: U.S. Department of Health and Human Services, Centers for Disease Control and Prevention, National Center for Chronic Disease Prevention and Health Promotion, Office on Smoking and Health, 2006).

38. Americans Nonsmokers' Rights Foundation, http://www.no-smoke.org/pdf/mediaordlist.pdf.

39. National Resource Center for Family-Centered Practice and Permanency Planning, "Smoking Policies for Foster Parents, last updated on June 5, 2008, http://www.hunter.cuny.edu/socwork/nrcfcpp/downloads/policy-issues/Smoking_Policies.pdf.

40. Bayer and Colgrove, "Science, Politics, and Ideology in the Campaign against Environmental Tobacco Smoke," p. 953.

41. Ibid.

APPENDIX **B, DOCUMENT 4:** *UNITED STATES V. PHILIP MORRIS*

1. In January 2003, Defendant Philip Morris Inc. changed its name to Philip Morris USA Inc., and Defendant Philip Morris Companies Inc. changed its name to Altria Group Inc. These Final Proposed Findings of Fact refer to Philip Morris USA as "Philip Morris" and "Philip Morris USA" interchangeably, and refer to Altria as "Philip Morris Companies" and "Altria" interchangeably.

2. As used here and throughout these Final Proposed Findings of Fact and Conclusions of Law, "Cigarette Company Defendants" refers to Defendants American Tobacco, British American Tobacco (Investments) Limited, Brown & Williamson, Liggett, Lorillard, Philip Morris, and R. J. Reynolds.

FURTHER READING

BOOKS AND JOURNALS

Allen, Steve, and Bill Adler, Jr. *The Passionate Nonsmokers' Bill of Rights.* New York: William Morrow & Co., 1989.

American Journal of Public Health: Focus: Taking on Tobacco 91, no. 2 (February 2001).

American Journal of Public Health: Substance Abuse, Including Tobacco 90, no. 3 (March 2000).

American Journal of Public Health: Tobacco and the Media 92, no. 6 (June 2002).

American Medical Association. Special issue devoted to smoking and health, *Journal of the American Medical Association* 253, May 24/31 (1985).

American Medical Women's Association. Special issue: Smoking and Women's Health, *Journal of the American Medical Women's Association* 51, nos. 1–2 (January/April 1996).

Austin, Gregory A. *Perspectives on the History of Psychoactive Substance Abuse.* NIDA Research Issues, no. 24. Washington, D.C.: U.S. Government Printing Office, 1978.

Barth, Ilene. *The Smoking Life.* Columbus, Miss.: Genesis Press, 1997.

Bernays, Edward. *Biography of an Idea: Memoirs of Public Relations Counsel Edward L. Bernays.* New York: Simon and Schuster, 1965.

Blum, Alan, ed. *The Cigarette Underworld.* Secaucus, N.J.: Lyle Stuart, 1985. (Previously published as a special edition of the *New York State Journal of Medicine,* December 1983.)

Brecher, Edward M., and the editors of Consumer Reports. *Licit and Illicit Drugs.* Boston: Little, Brown & Co., 1972.

British Medical Association. *Smoking Out the Barons: The Campaign against the Tobacco Industry. A Report of the British Medical Association Public Affairs Division.* New York: Wiley, 1986.

Brooks, Jerome. *Green Leaf and Gold Tobacco in North Carolina.* Chapel Hill, N.C.: North Carolina Archives, 1975.

Brooks, Jerome E. *The Mighty Leaf: Tobacco through the Centuries.* Boston: Little, Brown & Co., 1952.

Buckley, Christopher. *Thank You for Smoking.* New York: Random House, 1994. (A novel.)

Califano, Joseph A., Jr. *Governing America. An Insider's Report from the White House and the Cabinet.* New York: Simon and Schuster, 1981.

Casey, Karen. *If Only I Could Quit: Recovering from Nicotine Addiction.* Center City, Minn.: Hazelden, 1996.

Corina, Maurice. *Trust in Tobacco: The Anglo-American Struggle for Power.* New York: St. Martin's Press, 1975.

Corti, Egon Caesar. *A History of Smoking.* New York: Harcourt & Brace, 1932.

Cunningham, Rob. *Smoke & Mirrors: The Canadian Tobacco Wars.* IDRC Books, 1996.

Dillow, Gordon L. *The Hundred-Year War against the Cigarette.* New York: American Heritage Publishing Co., 1981.

Duke, Maurice, and Daniel P. Jordan. *Tobacco Merchant: The Story of Universal Leaf Tobacco Company.* Lexington: University Press of Kentucky, 1995.

Dunhill, Alfred H. *The Gentle Art of Smoking.* London: Max Reinhardt, 1954.

Dunhill, Alfred H. *The Pipe Book.* London: Arthur Barker, 1969.

Ehwa, Carl, Jr. *The Book of Pipes and Tobacco.* New York: Random House, 1974.

Evans Nicola, Arthur Farkas, Elizabeth Gilpin, Charles Berry, and John Pierce. "Influence of Tobacco Marketing and Exposure to Smokers on Adolescent Susceptibility to Smoking." *Journal of the American Cancer Institute* 87, no. 20, (October 18, 1995): 1538–45.

Eysenck, Hans J. *Smoking, Health, and Personality.* New York: Basic Books, 1965.

Ferrence, Roberta G. *Deadly Fashion: The Rise and Fall of Cigarette Smoking in North America.* New York: Garland, 1989.

Fitzgerald, Jim. *The Joys of Smoking Cigarettes.* New York: Holt, Rinehart and Winston, 1983.

Ford, Barry J. *Smokescreen: A Guide to the Personal Risks and Global Effects of the Cigarette Habit.* North Perth, Australia: Halcyon Press, 1994.

Fox, Maxwell. *The Lorillard Story.* New York: P. Lorillard Company, 1947.

Fritschler, A. Lee. *Smoking and Politics.* Englewood Cliffs, N.J.: Prentice Hall, 1989.

Glantz, Stanton A. *Tobacco, Biology & Politics.* Waco, Tex.: WRS Group, 1994.

Glantz, Stanton A., John Slade, Lisa A. Bero, Peter Hanauer, and Deborah E. Barnes. *The Cigarette Papers.* Berkeley: University of California Press, 1996.

Goodman, Jordan. *Tobacco in History and Culture.* 2 vols. Detroit, Mich.: Thomson Gale, 2005.

Goodman, Jordan. *Tobacco in History: The Cultures of Dependence.* New York: Routledge, 1995.

Greaves, Loraine. *Smoke Screen: Women's Smoking and Social Control.* Halifax, Canada: Fernwood Publishing, 1996.

Grossman, Michael, and Philip Price. *Tobacco Smoking and the Law in Canada.* Charlottesville, Va.: Lexis Law Library, 1992.

Heimann, Robert K. *Tobacco and Americans.* New York: McGraw-Hill Book Company, 1960.

Henningfield, Jack E. *Nicotine: An Old-Fashioned Addiction.* New York: Chelsea House, 1992.

Hilts, Philip. *Smokescreen.* Reading, Mass.: Addison-Wesley, 1996.

Hirschfelder, Arlene B. *Encyclopedia of Smoking and Tobacco.* Phoenix, Ariz.: Oryx Press, 1999.

Houston, Thomas P., ed. *Tobacco Use: An American Crisis.* Chicago: American Medical Association, 1993.

Institute of Medicine. *Growing Up Tobacco Free.* Washington, D.C.: National Academy Press, 1984.

Jacobson, Bobbie. *Beating the Ladykillers: Women and Smoking.* London: Gollancz, 1988.

Jacobson, Bobbie. *The Ladykillers: Why Smoking Is a Feminist Issue.* London: Pluto Press, 1981; New York: Continuum Publishing Co., 1982.

Jacobson, Peter D., and Jeffrey Wasserman. *Tobacco Control Laws: Implementation and Enforcement.* Santa Monica, Calif.: Rand Corporation, 1997.

Kasper, Rhona. *A Woman's Guide to Cigar Smoking: Everything You Need to Know to Be the Ultimate Cigar Aficionada.* New York: St. Martin's Press, 1988.

Kerlach, Karen K., and Michelle A. Larkin. "The SmokeLess States Program." In *The Robert Wood Johnson Foundation Anthology,* edited by Stephen L. Isaacs and James R. Knickman. Princeton, N.J.: Robert Wood Johnson Foundation, 2005.

Kessler, David. *A Question of Intent: A Great American Battle with a Deadly Industry.* New York: Public Affairs, 2001.

Keyishian, Elizabeth. *Everything You Need to Know about Smoking.* New York: Rosen Group, 1995.

Kirchner, Wendy. *Dying to Smoke: One Family's Struggle with America's Deadliest Drug.* Melbourne, Fla.: Starr Publishing, 1997.

Klein, Richard. *Cigarettes Are Sublime.* Durham, N.C.: Duke University Press, 1993.

Kluger, Richard. *Ashes to Ashes: America's Hundred-Year War, the Public Health, and the Unabashed Triumph of Philip Morris.* New York: Alfred A. Knopf, 1996.

Koop, C. Everett. *Koop: The Memoirs of America's Family Doctor.* New York: Random House, 1991.

Koven, Edward L. *Smoking: The Story Behind the Haze.* Commack, N.Y.: Nova Science Publishers, 1996.

Krantzler, Nora, and Kathleen Rae Miner. *Tobacco: Health Facts.* Santa Cruz, Calif.: ETR Associates, 1995.

Krogh, David. *Smoking, The Artificial Passion.* New York: W. H. Freeman and Co., 1991.

Kulikoff, Allan. *Tobacco and Slaves: The Development of Southern Cultures in the Chesapeake, 1680–1800.* Durham: University of North Carolina Press, 1988.

Lee, P. N. *Environmental Tobacco Smoke and Mortality: A Detailed Review of Epidemiological Evidence Relating Environmental Tobacco Smoke to the Risk of Cancer.* Farmington, Conn.: S. Karger, 1992.

Lloyd, Barbara B., and Kevin Lucas. *Smoking in Adolescence: Images and Identities.* New York: Routledge, 1998.

Marrero, Eumelio Espino. *Cuban Cigar Tobacco: Why Cuban Cigars Are the World's Best.* Neptune, N.J.: TFH Publications, 1997.

McFarland, J. Wayne, M.D., and Elman J. Folkenberg. *How to Stop Smoking in Five Days.* Englewood Cliffs, N.J.: Prentice Hall, 1962.

McGrath, Sally V., and Patricia J. McGuire, ed. *The Money Crop: Tobacco Culture in Calvert County, Maryland.* Crownsville, Md.: Division of History and Culture Programs, 1992.

McKeen, W. E. *Blue Mold of Tobacco.* Saint Paul, Minn.: American Phytopathology Society, 1989.

Miles, Robert H. *Coffin Nails and Corporate Strategies.* Englewood Cliffs, N.J.: Prentice Hall, 1982.

Mollenkamp, Carrick, Adam Levy, Joseph Menn, and Jeffrey Rothfeder. *The People vs. Big Tobacco: How the States Took On the Cigarette Giants.* Princeton, N.J.: Bloomberg Press, 1998.

Moore, James. *Very Special Agents: The Inside Story of America's Most Controversial Law Enforcement Agency—The Bureau of Alcohol, Tobacco & Firearms.* New York: Pocket Books, 1997.

Neuberger, Maurine B. *Smoke Screen: Tobacco and the Public Welfare.* Englewood Cliffs, N.J.: Prentice Hall, 1963.

Nuttall, Floyd H. *Memoirs in a Country Churchyard: A Tobaccoman's Plea-Clean Up Tobacco Row!* Lawrenceville, Va.: Brunswick Publisher, 1996.

Orey, Michael. *Assuming the Risk.* New York: Little, Brown & Co., 1999. (On tobacco litigation.)

Orleans, C. Tracy, and John Slade, ed. *Nicotine Addiction: Principles and Management.* New York, NY: Oxford University Press, 1993.

Ortiz, Fernando. *Cuban Counterpoint: Tobacco and Sugar.* Durham, N.C.: Duke University, 1995.

Pan American Health Organization. *Tobacco or Health: Status in the Americas.* Scientific Publication No. 536. Washington, D.C.: Pan American Health Organization,1992.

Pertschuk, Michael. *Smoke Gets in Their Eyes: Lessons in Movement Leadership from the Tobacco Wars.* Nashville, Tenn.: Vanderbilt University Press, 2001.

Petrone, Gerard S. *Tobacco Advertising: The Great Seduction.* Atglen, Pa.: Schiffer Publishing, 1996.

Pomerleau, Ovide F., and Cynthias S. Pomerleau, eds. *Nicotine Replacement: A Critical Evaluation.* Binghamton, N.Y.: Haworth Publisher, 1992.

Pringle, Peter. *Cornered: Big Tobacco at the Bar of Justice.* New York: Henry Holt and Company, 1998.

Rabin, Robert, and Stephen Sugarman. *Smoking Policy.* 2 vols. New York: Oxford University Press, 1993.

Raw, Martin, Patti White, and Ann McNeill. *Clearing the Air: A Guide for Action on Tobacco.* London: World Health Organization, 1990.

Read, Melvyn D. *The Politics of Tobacco: Policy Networks and the Cigarette Industry.* Brookfield, Vt.: Ashgate Publishing Co., 1996.

Robert, Joseph C., *The Story of Tobacco in America.* Chapel Hill: University of North Carolina Press, 1967.

Rogozinski, Jan. *Smokeless Tobacco in the Western World: 1550–1950.* Santa Cruz, Calif.: Devin, 1990.

Roleff, Tamar L., and Mary Williams, eds. *Tobacco & Smoking: Opposing Viewpoints.* San Diego, Calif.: Greenhaven, 1998.

Schmitz, Cecilia M., and Richard A. Gray. *Smoking: The Health Consequences of Tobacco Use: An Annotated Bibliography with Analytical Introduction.* Ann Arbor, Mich.: Pierian, 1995.

Simonich, William L. *Government Antismoking Policies.* New York: Peter Lang Publishers, 1991.

Sloan, Frank A., Jan Ostermann, Gabriel Picone, Christopher Conover, and Donald H. Taylor, Jr. *The Price of Smoking.* Cambridge, Mass.: The MIT Press, 2004.

Smith, Jane Webb. *Smoke Signals: Cigarettes, Advertising and the American Way of Life.* Richmond, Va.: Valentine Museum, 1990. (An exhibition catalog from the Valentine Museum.)

Sobel, Robert. *They Satisfy: The Cigarette in American Life.* New York: Anchor Press/Doubleday, 1978.

Sullum, Jacob. *For Your Own Good: The Anti-Smoking Crusade and the Tyranny of Public Health.* New York: Free Press, 1998.

Tate, Cassandra. *Cigarette Wars: The Triumph of the Little White Slaver.* New York: Oxford University Press, 1999.

Tate, C. Cassandra. "The American Anti-Cigarette Movement, 1880–1930." Ph.D. diss. University of Washington. Ann Arbor, Mich.: UMI Dissertation Services, 1995.

Tate, C. Cassandra. "In the 1800s, Antismoking Was a Burning Issue." *Smithsonian,* July 1989, pp. 107–17.

Taylor, C. Barr, and Joel D. Killen. *The Facts about Smoking.* Yonkers, N.Y.: Consumer Reports Books, 1991.

Taylor, Peter. *The Smoke Ring: Tobacco, Money, and Multinational Politics.* New York: Pantheon Books, 1984.

Tennant, Robert E. *The American Cigarette Industry: A Study in Economic Analysis and Public Policy.* Hamden, Conn.: Archon Books, 1971.

Thibodeau, Michael, and Jane Martin. *Smoke Gets in Your Eyes: A Fine Blend of Cigarette Packaging, Branding and Design.* New York: Abberville Press, 2000.

Tilley, Nannie Mae. *The R. J. Reynolds Tobacco Company.* Durham: University of North Carolina Press, 1985.

Troyer, Ronald J., and Gerald E. Markle. *Cigarettes: The Battle over Smoking.* New Brunswick, N.J.: Rutgers University Press, 1983.

Van Willigen, John, and Susan C. Eastwood. *Tobacco Culture: Farming Kentucky's Burley Belt.* Lexington: University of Kentucky Press, 1998.

Vicusi, W. Kip. *Smoking: Making the Risky Decision.* New York: Oxford University Press, 1991.

Vizzard, William J., *In the Cross Fire: A Political History of the Bureau of Alcohol, Tobacco and Firearms.* Boulder, Colo.: Lynne Rienner, 1997.

Voges, Ernst, ed. *Tobacco Encyclopedia.* Mainz, Germany: Tobacco Journal International, 1984.

Wagner, Susan. *Cigarette Country: Tobacco in American History and Politics.* New York: Praeger, 1971.

Wald, Nicholas, and Sir Peter Froggatt. *Nicotine, Smoking, and the Low Tar Programme.* New York: Oxford University Press, 1989.

Warner, Kenneth E. *Selling Smoke: Cigarette Advertising and Public Health.* Washington, D.C.: American Public Health Association, 1989.

Wekesser, Carol, ed. *Smoking* (Current Controversies). San Diego, Calif.: Greenhaven, 1997.

Wetherall, Charles F. *Quit for Teens/Read This Book and Stop Smoking.* Kansas City, Mo.: Andrews & McMeel, 1995.

Whelan, Elizabeth M. *Cigarettes: What the Warning Label Doesn't Tell You.* Amherst, N.Y.: Prometheus Books, 1997.

Whelan, Elizabeth M. *A Smoking Gun: How the Tobacco Industry Gets Away with Murder.* Philadelphia: George F. Stickley Co., 1984.

White, Larry. *Merchants of Death: The American Tobacco Industry.* New York: Beech Tree Books/William Morrow and Co., 1988.

Whiteside, Thomas. *Selling Death: Cigarette Advertising and Public Health.* New York: Liveright, 1971.

"World Cigarette Pandemic, Part I." Special issue, *New York State Journal of Medicine* 83, no. 12 (December 1983).

"World Cigarette Pandemic, Part II." Special issue, *New York State Journal of Medicine* 85, no. 7 (July 1985).

Zalis, Marian. *Dictionary of Tobacco Terminology.* New York: Philip Morris, 1980.

Zegart, Dan. *Civil Warriors.* New York: Delacorte, 2000. (On tobacco litigation.)

WEB SITES

Action on Smoking and Health: http://www.ash.org
American Cancer Society: http://www.cancer.org/docroot/home/index.asp
American Council on Science and Health: http://www.acsh.org/
American Health Foundation: http://www.americanhealthfoundation.com/
American Heart Association: http://www.amhrt.org/
American Journal of Public Health Collections on "Tobacco": http://www.ajph.org/collections
American Legacy Foundation: http://www.americanlegacy.org/
American Lung Association: http://www.lung.usa.org/
American Medical Association: http://www.ama-assn.org/
American Medical Women's Association: http://www.amwa-doc.org/
Americans for Nonsmokers' Rights: http://www.no-smoke.org/learnmore.php?id=480
Breed's Collection of Tobacco History Sites: http://smokingsides.com/docs/hist.html
Bureau of Alcohol, Tobacco, and Firearms, Alcohol and Tobacco Division: http://www.atf.treas.gov/
Campaign for Tobacco-Free Kids: http://www.tobaccofreekids.org/index.php
Centers for Disease Control and Prevention: http://www.cdc.gov/tobacco
Corporate Accountability International: http://stopcorporateabuse.org/
Department of Health and Human Services: http://www.hhs.gov/
Environmental Protection Agency: http://www.epa.gov/
Federal Trade Commission: http://www.ftc.gov/index.html
Food and Drug Administration: http://www.fda.gov/
FORCES (Fight Ordinances & Restrictions to Control & Eliminate Smoking): http://www.forces.com
Global Tobacco Control: Globallink: http://www.globalink.org/
Legacy Tobacco Documents Library: http://legacy.library.ucsf.edu
National Cancer Institute: http://www.cancer.gov/
National Smokers Alliance: http://www.speakup.org/
Office on Smoking and Health: http://www.cdc.gov/tobacco/osh/index.htm
Public Health Service: http://www.usphs.gov/
QUITNET: http://www.quitnet.com/qnhomepage.aspx
SourceWatch of the Center for Media and Democracy, Tobacco Portal: http://www.sourcewatch.org/index.php?title=Portal:Tobacco
Tobacco Documents Online: http://www.tobaccodocuments.org
Tobacco Institute Document Site: http://www.tobaccoinstitute.com/
Tobacco News and Information: http://www.tobacco.org/
Tobacco Products Liability Project: http://www.tobacco.neu.edu
Tobacco Technical Assistance Consortium: http://ttac.org
University of California, San Francisco Tobacco Control Archives: http://www.library.ucsf.edu/tobacco
U.S. Department of Agriculture: http://www.usda.gov/
World Health Organization: http://www.who.int/en/

INDEX

Abbe, Robert, 29
ACS. *See* American Cancer Society
Adler, Isaac, 21
Adolescence. *See* adolescents
Adolescents: advertising, 77, 78, 136–41, 178, 190, 192, 216, 217–18; cigarette prices, 94, 96, 143; harm from smoking, 22, 43, 64, 216; sales to, 45, 97, 99, 103, 121, 122, 133, 141–43, 151, 152, 162, 182, 184, 223; smoking prevention, 47, 52, 87, 94, 96, 97, 131, 134, 140–41, 144, 153, 168, 171; tobacco use, 5, 6, 10–12, 16, 29, 51, 55, 67, 77–80, 82, 93, 135, 138, 216
Advertising, 69–83, 105–16
African Americans and tobacco use, 4, 7, 10, 64, 65, 81, 132
AHA. *See* American Heart Association
Air pollution, 26, 27, 53, 54, 58
ALA. *See* American Lung Association
Alabama, 87, 90, 142
Alaska, 45, 142
Alaska Natives and tobacco use, 7, 10, 64, 65
ALF. *See* American Legacy Foundation
Altria Group, 112, 114, 115, 173. *See also* Philip Morris

AMA. *See* American Medical Association
AMA Alliance, 48
American Academy of Pediatrics, 48
American Cancer Society (ACS): findings, 25, 35, 52, 112; Great American Smokeout, 166; smokeless tobacco, 30, 37, 41, 45; women, 80
American Heart Association (AHA), 37, 39, 40, 48, 53
American Indians. *See* Native Americans and tobacco use
American Legacy Foundation (ALF), 47–48, 144, 173
American Lung Association (ALA), 16, 39, 40, 41, 48
American Medical Association (AMA), 23, 25, 26, 37, 38, 45, 48
Americans for Nonsmoker's Rights Foundation, 43
American Tobacco Company, 72, 74, 118, 131, 162, 168
Animal experimentation, 23, 25, 36, 105
Antismoking advocates, 20, 33, 40, 42, 43
Antitobacco advocacy, 42, 45
Antitobacco legislation, 45, 46
Archives of Pediatrics and Adolescent Medicine, 80
Arizona, 42, 47, 87, 90, 100, 150, 165, 202

Asian Americans and tobacco use, 4,
     7, 64, 65, 81
Asians and tobacco use, 4, 7, 10, 29,
     64–66, 81
ASSIST (American Stop Smoking
     Intervention Study for
     Cancer Prevention), 45
Assistant surgeon general, 53
ATF. *See* United States Bureau of
     Alcohol, Tobacco, Firearms,
     and Explosives
Auerbach, Oscar, 35

Baseball, 29, 30, 69, 74, 132, 161, 164
Bayne-Jones, Stanhope, 53
Behavioral Risk Factor Surveillance
     System (BRFSS), 15
Bill of Rights for the Nonsmoker, 27
Brandt, Allan M., 23, 37, 39, 149, 150
Brown & Williamson Tobacco Corpora-
     tion, 74, 123, 162, 163, 166,
     169, 170
Burdette, Walter J., 53
Burney, LeRoy, 26, 37, 38, 52, 53,
     55, 149

California, 42, 44, 83, 90, 98, 100,
     150, 166
Camel cigarettes: advertising of, 14,
     71–73, 77–79, 88, 137, 162,
     163, 168
Campaign for Tobacco-Free Kids, 30,
     47
Cancer: appropriations for, 27; death
     rates, 25, 28, 37, 60, 65,
     81, 126, 154, 205; increase
     in, 25, 35, 53; laboratory
     animals, 25, 36, 105; men,
     54, 57, 67; prevention of, 39;
     surveys, 15; 67; secondhand
     smoke, 27, 28, 42, 61, 151,
     152, 155, 167, 170, 210;
     smoking and, 25, 26, 28,
     35–40, 53, 54, 55, 57, 59,

61, 73, 76, 93, 105, 112,
     149, 163, 164, 166, 171,
     205, 207, 208, 219, 223;
     snuff and, 35; study of, 36,
     42; types of, 20, 21, 28, 29,
     38, 57, 58, 62, 65–68, 83,
     167, 179, 205, 223; women,
     54, 67, 152
Carnes, Betty, 42
CDC. *See* Centers for Disease Control
Centers for Disease Control, 4, 10, 11,
     13, 15, 17, 41, 48
Chewing tobacco, 5, 6, 10, 16, 23, 28,
     29, 76
Children: advertising, 40, 69, 74, 77,
     78, 131–32, 136–38, 140,
     171; harm from smoking,
     22, 23, 27; sales to, 77, 103,
     121, 122, 132, 168, 184;
     secondhand smoke and, 27,
     59, 60, 67, 154, 156, 210,
     216; smoking prevention, 33,
     41, 48, 131, 132, 134–35,
     138–41, 144, 171
Chronic bronchitis, 26, 28, 39, 54, 57,
     179
Cigarette Advertising Code, 40
Cigarette sales: adolescents, 44, 45, 97,
     99, 104, 121, 122, 141–43,
     162, 169, 171; decrease
     in, 106; impact of surgeon
     general report, 26–27, 40;
     increase in, 72, 77, 107, 132,
     163; Internet, 102, 103; Philip
     Morris, 127; taxes, 99, 101–2;
     Senate shops, 147
Cigarette smoking: crime, 33; decline
     in, 3–6, 10, 11, 14, 30, 45;
     drinking and, 33; educational
     attainment and, 7, 12, 65–67;
     ethnicity and, 3, 7, 11, 15,
     64–66; infant mortality and,
     23; men, 25, 26; pregnancy
     and, 23; physicians and,

33; restrictions on, 41–43; women, 6, 23, 26, 52; workers, 28
Cigar smoking, 5, 6, 81, 82, 131, 168
Civil Aeronautics Board, 41
Civil rights and clean air, 41
Class-action lawsuits and tobacco industry, 46, 112, 169, 171–72
Clinton, Bill, 120, 121, 169–71, 173
Cochran, William G., 53
Columbia University, 54
Comic books and tobacco advertising, 40
Compensatory damages, 113, 167, 172
Congress: acts of, 56, 72–74, 76; bans by, 123–24, 153; bills, 46, 122, 125; Federal Trade Commission, 27, 74–76, 109, 113, 164–65, 167, 222; health warnings, 75, 76, 83, 125, 128; nicotine, 121, 170, 171; State Children's Health Insurance Program (SCHIP), 95; Synar Amendment, 141, 142, 168; tobacco smuggling, 100
Consumer Reports Magazine, 105, 152
Consumers Union, 109
Copenhagen (tobacco), 29
Council of Michigan Foundations, 46
C-rations, 14
Cumming, Hugh, 52

De Bakey, Michael, 24
Delaware, 48, 87
De Medici, Catherine, 19
De Villemain, Jean Nicot, 19
DHHS. *See* United States Department of Health and Human Services
DOD. *See* United States Department of Defense
Doll, Richard, 25, 37

Eastern Band Cherokee, 6. *See also* Native Americans and tobacco use
Ebony Magazine, 81
Education, 12, 65, 66, 67
Elders, Jocelyn, 64, 168
Emphysema, 26, 28, 54, 57, 81
Environmental Protection Agency (EPA), 43
Environmental tobacco smoke. *See* secondhand smoke
EPA. *See* Environmental Protection Agency
Essence Magazine, 81

Family Smoking Prevention and Tobacco Control Act, 115, 128, 175
Farber, Emmanuel, 53
FCC. *See* Federal Communications Commission
FDA. *See* Food and Drug Administration
Federal Cigarette Labeling and Advertising Act of 1965, 27, 39, 109, 113, 168, 221, 222
Federal Communications Commission (FCC), 41, 47
Federal Trade Commission (FTC), 27, 74–76, 109, 113, 164–65, 167, 222
Fieser, Louis F., 54
First International Conference on Smokeless Tobacco, 29–30
Florida, 44–48, 79, 102, 107
Food and Drug Administration (FDA): children, 44; history of, 115, 118–19; regulation of cigarettes, 46, 78, 115, 115–40; tobacco companies, 78
FTC. *See* Federal Trade Commission
Furth, Jacob, 54
Gallup poll, 41, 43

Gaston, Lucy Page, 33
Global Settlement, 46
Graham, Evarts A., 24–26, 35, 36
Great American Smokeout, 166
Group Against Smokers' Pollution
        (GASP), 4

Hammond, Cuyler E., 25, 36, 40
Harvard University, 53, 54
Heart disease and tobacco: death
        rates, 65; secondhand smoke,
        68, 152, 166, 205, 210, 223;
        smoking and, 21, 23, 26, 28,
        36, 39, 40, 54, 57, 61, 132;
        women, 67, 81
Hickam, John B., 54
Hill, Austin Bradford, 25
Hill, John, 28
Hispanics and tobacco use, 4, 6, 7, 10,
        64, 66, 81
Horn, Daniel, 25, 36, 40
Hundley, James M., 53

Iditarod, 45
Indiana University, 54
Indoor clean air policies, 45
Institute of Medicine (IOM), 48
Interstate Commerce Commission, 41
Iraq, 14

JAMA. See *Journal of the American
        Medical Association*
James I (king), 20
Jet Magazine, 81
Joe Camel: advertising, 77, 78,
        137–38, 171; increasing sales
        to children and teens, 77,
        78, 137, 138, 171. *See also*
        Camel cigarettes
Johns Hopkins University, 24
Johnson, Lyndon B., 53
*Journal of the American Medical
        Association* (*JAMA*), 25, 35,
        38, 53, 148

Kellogg, John Harvey, 21
Kennedy, John F., 39, 53
Kentucky, 5, 13
Kick Butts Day, 80
Kick the Habit (campaign), 41
Kluger, Richard, 37, 44, 150, 152
Koop, C. Everett, 27–29, 42, 43, 46,
        152
K-rations, 14
Kress, Daniel H., 21

Lancet, 29, 33
LeMaistre, Charles, 54
Life Magazine, 26
Little, Clarence Cook, 26
Looseleaf (tobacco), 5
Lorillard, 74, 106, 127, 161, 163, 206,
        209
Lumbee, 6. *See also* Native Americans
        and tobacco use

Maine, 48, 112, 113, 115, 184, 203
Major league baseball, 29. *See also*
        baseball
Marketing: adolescents, 46, 47, 77–80,
        138, 140, 161, 169, 170, 175,
        177, 190, 192; ethnic groups,
        81; expenditures, 79; history
        of tobacco industry use
        of, 69, 71; light cigarettes,
        112–13, 115, 127, 214–18;
        warning labels, 128; women,
        66, 75, 80–81
Massachusetts, 44, 83, 90, 100, 134,
        184
Massachusetts Institute of Technology
        (MIT), 112
Master Settlement Agreement (MSA),
        46–48, 79, 138, 144, 172,
        173
McNally, William, 23
Medicinal uses of tobacco, 28
Memorial Center for Cancer and
        Allied Diseases, 25

Michigan Nonprofit Association
Foundation, 46
Michigan, 21, 23, 47, 48, 100,
184
Minnesota, 42, 46
Minors. *See* adolescents; children
Mississippi, 13, 46
Missouri, 48, 98
MIT. *See* Massachusetts Institute of
Technology
Monitoring the Future Survey (MTF),
10, 16
Montana, 5
Moore, Michael, 46
Morality and tobacco use, 21
*Morbidity and Mortality Weekly
Report (MMWR)*, 12, 13, 17
Motion Picture Association of America,
48
Movies, 48
Movie studios, 48
Myers, Matthew, 30

National Academy of Sciences, 27,
93, 153, 210
National Association for the Study and
Prevention of Tuberculosis,
40. *See* American Lung
Association
National Cancer Institute (NCI):
adolescents, 132; baseball
players, 29; cigarette smok-
ing, 52, 83; conferences, 30,
37–38; light cigarettes,
110–12; secondhand smoke,
154; survey, 15
National Center for Health Statistics,
5, 15
National Clearinghouse for Smoking
and Health, 40, 55. *See also*
United States Public Health
Service
National Football League, 74
National Health Interview Survey
(NHIS), 4, 6, 12, 15

National Heart Institute (NHI), 37, 52
National Institute on Drug Abuse, 16
National Institutes of Health Con-
ference, 144
National Interagency Council on
Smoking and Health, 40
National Library of Medicine, 54
National Surveys on Drug Use and
Health (NSDUH), 6
Native Americans and tobacco use, 6,
7, 28, 64, 65; adolescents,
10; marketing to, 69, 81, 132;
sale of cigarettes, 90, 97, 101
Native Hawaiians and tobacco use, 7
NCI. *See* National Cancer Institute
New Hampshire, 48, 174
New Jersey, 45, 87, 90, 100, 142, 167,
174
New York Academy of Medicine, 24
NHI. *See* National Heart Institute
NHIS. *See* National Health Interview
Survey
Nicorette, 166, 170,
Nicotine: addiction to, 62, 78, 82,
93; in cigarettes, 46, 58, 60,
67, 73, 74, 105–7, 109–14;
in smokeless tobacco, 29;
replacement products, 30
Nicotrol, 170
Nixon, Richard, 56, 137
North Carolina, 6, 78, 90, 121, 141,
155, 156
NSDUH. *See* National Surveys on
Drug Use and Health

Obama, Barack, 90, 96, 115, 128, 175
Ochsner, Alton, 24, 25
Office on Smoking and Health of the
Centers for Disease Control
and Prevention, 3. *See*
also CDC
Ohio, 30, 185
Oklahoma, 5, 13, 133, 185
Osteen William L., Sr., 78, 121–22,
171

Pacific Islanders and tobacco use, 4, 7
Passive smoking. *See* Secondhand
    smoke
Pearl, Raymond 24
Pediatrics, 48
Pennsylvania, 5
Philaretes, 19, 20
Philip Morris: advertising, 106;
        deception, 110, 112–13,
        116; FDA, 127; history of,
        161; secondhand smoke,
        153; sponsorships, 74,
        75, 164; Supreme Court,
        114–15; tobacco regulations
        supported, 128; women,
        75, 80, 165. *See also*
        Altria Group
PHS. *See* United States Public Health
    Service
Pipe smoking, 5, 6, 57
Plug (tobacco), 5
Pneumonia, 27, 59, 67, 205,
Pregnancy, 6–7, 58, 59, 62, 67, 121,
    166
President's cancer panel, 48
Pro-Children Act of 1994, 224
Pro-Children Act of 2001, 173
Proctor, Robert N., 6
Proposition 99, 44
Public health advocates, 41–43, 48
Public Health Cigarette Smoking Act
        of 1969, 39, 56, 74, 125,
        137, 165, 222
Punitive damages, 46, 113, 172–74

Readers Digest, 26, 105
Reagan, Ronald, 42, 166; adminis-
        tration, 150
Richmond, Julius, 29
Robert Wood Johnson Foundation,
        45, 80
Roosevelt, Franklin D., 118, 163
Rush Medical College, 23
Rustica plant, 19

SAMSHA. *See* Substance Abuse and
    Mental Health Services
    Administration
SCHIP. *See* State Children's Health
    Insurance Program
Schuman, Leonard, 54
Science Magazine, 24
Secondhand smoke: exposure to,
        67–68, 149–56, 167, 174,
        204, 207; health risks of,
        27–28, 42, 43, 145, 210–11,
        212; lawsuits, 170, 173;
        protection from, 44, 94
Shew, Joel, 20
Silvers, Maurice H., 54
SKOAL, 29
Slocum, Charles E., 21
Smokeless States Program, 45
Smokeless tobacco: adolescents, 10,
        122, 131, 135, 138, 143,
        171; advertising, 76, 77, 79;
        cancer, 29; Congress, 125,
        223; education about, 12;
        ethnicity and, 65; men, 5,
        14; surgeon general, 28, 30,
        60, 64, 167; taxes, 87; users
        by region, 13; types of, 5;
        women, 6; user age, 10
Smoking cessation, 30, 46, 48, 61, 62,
        166, 170
Snuff. *See* smokeless tobacco
Snus. *See* smokeless tobacco
South Carolina, 47, 90, 148
Sports, 29, 74, 76, 79, 169
Stanford University, 6
State Children's Health Insurance
        Program (SCHIP), 95
Steinfeld, Jesse, 27, 58, 149
Stroke and tobacco, 23, 62, 65,
        81, 97
Substance Abuse and Mental Health
        Services Administration
        (SAMSHA), 6, 15
Sullivan, Louis, 29, 120

Supreme Court, 112, 113, 114, 115, 123, 140
Surgeon general: adolescents, 77, 132, 137, 138, 141, 142, 168; advisory committee, 53, 221; cancer, 26, 28, 38, 39, 149, 166; cigarette smoking, 52–53, 55; ethnicity of smokers, 7; history of, 51; Global Settlement, 46; nicotine, 167; nonsmokers, 27; reports, 3, 20, 30, 37, 49, 55, 57–67, 73, 74, 76, 92, 109, 126; secondhand smoke, 41–43, 152, 153, 156, 164, 165, 210; smokeless tobacco, 29, 167; warning, 40, 56, 83, 165, 222, 223; women smokers, 6, 166, 181

Talbott, John, 38
Tappius, Jacobus, 20
Tar: cancer, 25, 36, 58, 59. 105, 163; deceptive claims and, 75, 80, 111–15, 174, 204, 214–16; filter-tip and, 106–8, 163; measurement of, 74, 109, 110, 166, 221; Philip Morris, 127; taxes on, 92; warning, 128
Teens. *See* adolescents
Tennessee, 5, 33, 48, 185
Terry Luther L., 39, 40, 53, 57, 164
Texas, 46, 54, 79, 171, 185, 190
Thun, Michael, 30
Time Magazine, 24
Tobacco health warnings: 40, 56, 75, 76, 83, 125, 128, 165, 222, 223
Tobacco industry: adolescents, 77, 171; advertising, 144; campaigns against, 47; deception and, 107, 110–12,

170; foreign countries and, 64, 165; lawsuits against, 46, 79, 115, 172–74, 206, 209–10; marketing, 66–67, 79, 80–81; Native Americans and, 101–2; opposition to scientific findings, 26,43, 152, 154–55; political power of, 36; regulation of, 40, 73–75, 78, 121, 127, 171; secondhand smoke, 150–51; smokers rights, 154, Surgeon General's Advisory Committee, 53–54; taxes, 94; women, 80
Tobacco Industry Research Committee, 26, 206
Tobacco lawsuits, 46, 79, 103, 112–15, 142, 169, 172
Tobacco plant, 19
Tobacco prevention: adolescents, 44, 45, 47, 134, 144, 169; CDC, 48; taxes and, 95, 103; World Health Organization, 55
Tobacco Research Council, 37
Tobacco settlements, 46, 79
Tobacco smuggling, 97–101
Tobacco taxation: federal, 92; history of, 88; increases in, 45, 89, 93, 94; Internet and, 103; opponents of, 97; smoking cessation and, 30; as smoking deterrent, 131, 143, 144; socioeconomic factors and, 93, 95, 96; states and, 90, 99, 100, 174; types of, 87
Towns, Charles B., 23
Trask, George, 33
Twist (tobacco), 5

United States Bureau of Alcohol, Tobacco, Firearms, and Explosives (ATF), 100

United States Department of Defense
    (DOD), 14, 168
United States Department of Health,
    Education, and Welfare, 27,
    56, 222
United States Department of Health
    and Human Services, 15, 29,
    55, 56, 153, 167, 223
United States Public Health Service
    (PHS): cigarette smoking,
    26, 38, 53, 132, 181; history
    of, 51; reports of, 57–68;
    secondhand smoke, 149;
    survey, 15
United States Tobacco Company, 29
University of Michigan, 16
Utah, 13, 87, 90, 142, 148, 166

Valentini, Michael Bernhard, 19
Van Hoosen, Bertha, 23

Washington University, 35
West Virginia, 5, 13, 47, 184
Whites and tobacco use, 4, 6, 7, 10, 82,
    132
Wilson, Michael A., 14
Wisconsin, 5, 87
Women's Field Army, 36
World Health Organization (WHO),
    48, 55
World War I, 21, 71, 162
World War II, 14, 71
Wynder, Ernst L., 25, 26, 35, 36, 37,
    151
Wyoming, 5

Youth. *See* adolescents
Youth Risk Behavior Survey, 10,
    16
Yupik, 6. *See also* Native Americans
    and tobacco use

ABOUT THE AUTHOR

Arlene Hirschfelder, historian and educator, has been writing about tobacco for almost 20 years. Her works include *Tobacco Practices, Policies, and Research among American Indians and Alaska Natives; Encyclopedia of Tobacco and Smoking;* and *Kick Butts!: A Kid's Action Guide for a Tobacco-Free America.*